The Supply-Side Revolution

The Supply-Side Revolution

An Insider's Account of Policymaking in Washington

PAUL CRAIG ROBERTS

Harvard University Press
Cambridge, Massachusetts
London, England
1984

For my wife, Linda Jane Roberts

This book is printed on acid-free paper, and its binding materials
have been chosen for strength and durability.

Library of Congress Cataloging in Publication Data

Roberts, Paul Craig, 1939–
    The supply-side revolution.

    1. United States—Economic policy—1981–
2. Supply-side economics.   I. Title.
HC106.8.R6   1984   338.973   83-18340
ISBN 0-674-85620-1

Acknowledgments

AN AUTHOR HAS MANY DEBTS. MY GREATEST IS TO LINDA, MY wife, who shared eight years of our life with supply-side economics. She listened to my complaints, advised me, encouraged this book, edited the manuscript, improved the clarity of my prose, prepared the index, and sustained the decision to write a forthright account. Peter Barlerin, my assistant, helped in many ways to put this book together, from research reports on the media's treatment of Reagonomics, which became an integral part of the story, to checking and double-checking quotes, dates, facts and figures. Aida Donald and Joyce Backman of Harvard University Press supplied a final editorial polish.

I would like to acknowledge some of the unsung heros of supply-side economics who from their positions on the congressional staff helped to create a new economic policy: Bruce Bartlett, Steve Entin, John Mueller, Jan Olson, Mark Policinski, Joe Rogers, and Bruce Thompson. This list is not exhaustive, but these seven carried heavy burdens. Later my deputy and successor as assistant secretary of the Treasury, Manuel Johnson was equally indispensable, as were the professional staff and secretaries of the Treasury's Office of Economic Policy, who gave unstintingly of their time and expert abilities in support of the new policy.

Contents

Introduction

THIS IS THE STORY OF A REVOLUTION IN ECONOMIC POLICY
from its origin in Congressman Jack Kemp's office in the summer of
1975 through the first thirty months of the Reagan Administration.
Jack Kemp was the first supply-side politician, and Ronald Reagan
was the first supply-side President. It was a revolution brought
about by the unstinting efforts of a few people. By the middle of the
1970s it was apparent that the United States economy under the policies of the time could no longer grow without inflation. Concerns
arose whether it would be possible to maintain the level of social security benefits, provide for an adequate national defense, meet other
social goals, and create enough new jobs to maintain full employment. A debate began over capital formation, but it did not lead to
any new policies until supply-side economics provided a new perspective.

By the end of 1978, supply-side economics had won its spurs in
the budget policy debates and captured the imagination of the Congress. With presidential leadership from Reagan, the result was en-
actment in 1981 of what was called "the largest tax cut in history." A
year later the same administration presided over the "largest tax increase in history." Nine months after that, President Reagan re-
emerged as a supply-side leader. The story of these events includes
the role played by personalities in the policy process and the factors
that inhibit successful leadership. Once the public policy process is
understood, people will expect less from it.

For an author a simple approach to material is appealing, and
there were two obvious choices: organize the material around the

competing economic theories and let the story unfold as a contest between them for dominance over policymaking in Washington, or organize the material around the problems in the economy and tell the story in terms of how those problems produced a need for a new economic theory and policy. Both approaches had advantages. The first would allow the contending theories to be explained systematically before the story began, thus providing a primer for the non-economist as well as establishing a framework in terms of the competition of ideas. The second would allow the story to be told in terms of the needs of the economy, which not only provides a convenient organization but also grants inevitability to the new supply-side policy.

Either approach offers an author convenience. But the price would be a misleading account, although of a sort with which the modern consciousness is comfortable. We are used to portraying change as the outcome of people swept up in a battle of ideas, or as the result of historical forces and economic needs producing their inevitabilities while people simply watch, prevented by class consciousness or vested interest from altering their destiny. Such portrayals overlook that individuals are a causative force in history—they create and they destroy. The story in this book is one of the interplay of individual personalities, ideas, the economy, political opportunities, and economic policy. As a result, the political narrative and the economic theory are intertwined.

Supply-side economics did not appear full-fledged in Washington to meet the needs of the time, and there was nothing inevitable about it. Supply-side economics developed largely as a creative response to opportunities. Had a relatively few people not decided to challenge the economic policy establishment, supply-side economics might not have happened, and the Republicans would not have had a message of hope with which to gain another chance at governing.[1]

1. After supply-side economics became a public policy issue, economists began writing genealogies of supply-side thought (see Robert E. Keleher and William P. Or-zechowski, "Supply-Side Fiscal Policy: An Historical Analysis of a Rejuvenated Idea," in Richard H. Fink, ed. *Supply-Side Economics: A Critical Appraisal,* University Publications of America, 1982). However, prior to its ascendancy in Washington, supply-side economics was not a topic of study in economics courses. Although the supply-side approach to tax policy and economic growth is well grounded in classical economics, the supply-side revolution was not the product of a classical revival.

Change is difficult to achieve, and leadership is difficult to provide. Both are restrained by the dead hand of the past, and the momentum of the status quo can be overpowering. This book owes one of its themes to William E. Simon, former secretary of the Treasury, who observed that "as soon as a President is elected, he is captured by the past." With Simon's forewarning, the efforts of a few people prevented President Reagan from being captured for one year. During that year some important changes in economic policy occurred. If they prove lasting, the outlook for America will be brighter.

Although more was achieved in principle than in practice, more change occurred than I expected. On November 9, 1980, five days after the election of Ronald Reagan, I wrote in the *New York Times* that in the wake of the Republican Party's sweeping victory, news items about the fate of Prime Minister Margaret Thatcher's policies in Britain might be a better guide to the next four years than the euphoria of conservatives or the fears of liberal Democrats. Newspapers that reported Reagan's landslide election victory also reported that tax boosts were being considered by Britain's Conservative government and that Thatcher was resigned to the fact that her effort to cut spending could not spare the defense budget. Only eighteen months earlier, the "iron lady" had swept to power intending to cut taxes and raise defense spending.

I thought that Reagan would have great difficulty avoiding similar reverses in his own policies. He, too, intended to cut taxes and increase defense spending, but he had many advisers who encouraged him to balance the federal budget first. Such advice may sound reasonable, but it sets a contentious agenda: some people have to lose before others can gain. The President would find that people would not relinquish their benefits without a fight and that the problem of managing the fight over budget shares would crowd out the real items on the agenda.

Paul McCracken, former chairman of the Council of Economic Advisers, spelled out the past result of this indirect approach to goals in the *Wall Street Journal:* "For well over a decade our strategy has been to reach a better economy by a generalized resistance to spending in order to achieve a balanced budget, thereby winning the right to tax reduction. This predictably has left us with swollen Federal outlays, deficits, and an enervated economy." In view of the past failures of the traditional Republican approach, McCracken thought it was "at least worth trying" to reverse the process and begin with tax cuts.

I knew it would be hard for President Reagan to have a tax-reduction policy if it lacked the support of his advisers. Although the President campaigned as a supply-sider, the coterie of supply-siders was too small to staff a Reagan administration. Many people who were not supply-siders were given policymaking roles, and they were unwilling to assume the risks of change for the sake of someone else's issue. Generally, people do not exhaust themselves in promoting the success of others.

The Reagan revolution was loaded down with policymakers who believe that tax cuts are a reward to be given out after the economy has been revitalized by other policies—the very approach that Paul McCracken thought had failed. They do not see tax cuts as a means to a stronger economy and agree with the approach of President Carter's treasury secretary, G. William Miller, who said: "There will be a day, we hope soon, when our economy is working better and showing progess and revitalization when we can embark upon a program of reducing taxes for Americans."[2] In the appointments process, no supply-siders penetrated the White House compound. The advisers with the readiest access to the President were mostly people who saw tax *increases* as the means to a stronger economy. Once in that situation, Reagan's managerial style made it impossible for him to keep overruling his advisers, and other personal traits undercut his policies. His conciliatory attitude is admirable, for example, but it works against change by ransoming his policies to compromise. Margaret Thatcher had also been conciliatory, and in a spirit of cooperation and unity she too appointed a team that did not share her faith in her policies.

It seemed too that the Republican takeover of the Senate would contribute more to the failure than to the success of Reagan's policies. Tax cutting had actually made more inroads in the Democratic Senate than among traditional Republicans. Democratic committee chairmen like Russell Long and Lloyd Bentsen had been more supportive of tax reduction than Howard Baker, Robert Dole, or Pete

2. G. William Miller quoted in "The Outlook," *Wall Street Journal*, September 15, 1980.

Domenici. But the problem was bigger than that. Ideas never go far without people to carry them, and Republicans had been out of power for so long that they did not have the people to staff the executive branch and Senate committees. I wrote in the *New York Times* (November 9, 1980) that "there is no telling what kind of policy will emerge from people recruited simply to fill positions." What the tax cuts had in their favor was the lack of an alternative. Still I suspected that the administration might lose its nerve in the face of the budget deficits projected by static revenue estimates. Delaying the tax cuts because of the deficit would send a signal that the administration lacked confidence in its policy, and once that signal was sent "Congress and the Fed will have the administration on the run."[3]

In part this book is the story of the unfolding of these expectations, and since more was achieved than I thought possible, it is not the tale of a disillusioned man. Reaganomics was a compromise from the beginning, a conglomerate if you will, of three points of view: supply-side economics, monetarism, and traditional Republican budget balancing. Like any administration's coalition, it could survive only so long as the representatives of the different viewpoints were willing to be mutually supportive for a common purpose—which turned out not to be for very long. Nevertheless, change did occur, and although the initial gains may be frittered away by policymakers, it will be difficult to go back on the change in principle. The new policies may be well or badly managed, but the old ideas have been displaced.

Throughout this book, unless specifically indicated otherwise by definition or context, the term "tax cut" means a reduction in the marginal rate of taxation, that is, a reduction in the rate of tax on additional or new income. Keynesian fiscal policy emphasizes average tax rates, because Keynesians believe that taxation affects the economy by changing disposable income and thereby aggregate demand. Supply-side economics stresses marginal tax rates, because supply-siders believe that taxation affects the economy by changing the incentives to work, save, invest, and take risks. This different perspective is the essence of the supply-side revolution in economic

3. "Supply-Side Economics: A Fiscal Revolution?" *Wall Street Journal*, January 22, 1981. See also "Constraints on Change," *Wall Street Journal*, October 24, 1980.

policy. From it has come a broader definition of the tax burden, which must include not only total government spending but also all production that is lost as a result of the disincentives imposed by taxation.[4]

4. Paul Craig Roberts, "Caricatures of Tax-Cutting," *Wall Street Journal,* April 24, 1980.

1

Birth of a New Policy

ON FEBRUARY 23, 1977, CONGRESSMAN JOHN ROUSSELOT, A Republican from California, rose to his feet on the floor of the House of Representatives and said in a booming voice: "Mr. Chairman, I offer an amendment as a substitute for the amendment in the nature of a substitute." It was an historic date, for that arcane legislative language marked the origin of the Kemp–Roth bill and the resurrection of the Republican Party.

The House was unusually full that day and, perhaps with disbelief on both sides of the aisle, it heard uncharacteristic words from a determined Rousselot. Many expected him to offer a balanced-budget amendment, but instead he announced that the minority was offering a substitute to the third budget resolution for fiscal year 1977, consisting of "a simple across-the-board tax reduction for every American." With this amendment Republicans were ridding themselves of the albatross of "negativism." They had finally found a way to compete with the Democrats' spending programs. The supply-side movement was underway.

It is unlikely that Rousselot and the House Budget Committee minority fully understood that they had started an economic policy revolution. Five months later Representative Jack Kemp and Senator William Roth introduced a bill to cut personal income tax rates by 30 percent over three years. By the end of 1978 supply-side economics had swept through the Congress, carrying with it Democratic majority and Republican minority alike. In the fall of that year the Senate passed the Nunn amendment to the tax bill by a margin of more than three to one. The Nunn amendment, after

Senator Sam Nunn, a Democrat from Georgia, combined personal income tax rate reduction with limits on the growth of federal spending, and was known as the "son of Kemp–Roth." Harassed all year by the comparable Holt amendment to the budget resolution, the House, where Democrats had a 115-vote margin, voted to instruct its conferees to support the Nunn amendment. This was "Reaganomics" before Ronald Reagan, passed by a Democratic congress but lobbied against and killed in conference by a Democratic administration. Stymied by President Carter, supply-side economics rebounded strongly a few months later at the beginning of 1979 when the Joint Economic Committee, under the leadership of Senator Lloyd Bentsen, a Democrat from Texas, and Representative Clarence Brown, a Republican from Ohio, endorsed a supply-side economic policy with its first unanimous annual report in twenty years.

Supply-side economics won its spurs in the congressional policy process. The story of how it prevailed on analytical and political grounds contradicts its image as an extreme and risky policy, fostered on a beguiled public and president by a few voodoo magicians. Between the summer of 1975, when I became economic adviser to Representative Kemp, and the fall of 1978, some important analytical and political battles were fought, with the supply-side case prevailing against the Congressional Budget Office and the econometric establishment. Supply-side economics succeeded against the entrenched Keynesian policy. The real snake oil turned out to be in the other side's bottle. But this came later. Meanwhile Republicans were getting their first taste of the new battle as John Rousselot offered his amendment. I was there on the House floor that day, having helped to prepare the substitute budget resolution, and I was doing what I could to help the Republicans as the surprised Democrats regrouped around their chief economist, Nancy Teeters, my Democratic counterpart.

If the Republicans lacked confidence in their new tax-cutting posture, anger filled the gaps—for mad they were. The Democrats were using the new congressional budget process to legislate large deficits. The Republicans had cooperated in passing the Budget Act of 1974 setting up the new congressional budget process, because they thought it would be used to balance the budget. Fiscal conservatives thought that their liberal colleagues could too easily legislate big deficits indirectly by voting in favor of many separate appropriations bills. Conservatives believed that if the big spenders had to vote on aggregate expenditure and revenue figures, and thereby on the size of the deficit itself, there would be lower and firmer limits to spending. To their minds, the new budget process was a way to put the big spenders on the spot.

The liberal Democrats, of course, had an entirely different view of the budget act. They believed it would justify deficits as a necessary way to add enough spending to the economy to keep employment high, thereby defusing deficits as a political issue. They were attracted by the prospect of having deficits sanctioned as a requirement of full-employment policy prior to the appropriations process.[1] By defining budget control in terms of the size of the deficit needed to keep the economy growing and employment high, deficits originated in the economic policy options set out by staff experts in the Congressional Budget Office and the budget committees. Spending was no longer out of control. In other words, the liberals defined budget control in terms of taking into account the impact on employment of deficit spending. Since orthodox economics generally saw deficits as essential to a growing economy, this meant that spending would remain out of control in the Republicans' sense of things.

True to their view of the budget act, the Democrats came back into session after the Carter victory in November 1976, calling for an unprecedented third budget resolution for fiscal year 1977 to allow for more deficit spending. Normally, there are two budget resolutions each year. The first in the spring (May) sets targets to guide the work of the appropriations and tax committees. The second in the fall (September) is supposed to be binding on the fiscal year beginning in October.

The second budget resolution for fiscal year 1977, which was

1. See David Meiselman and Paul Craig Roberts, "The Political Economy of the Congressional Budget Office," in Karl Brunner and Allan Meltzer, eds., *Three Aspects of Policy and Policymaking: Knowledge, Data and Institutions,* Carnegie-Rochester Conference Series on Public Policy, Vol. 10 (New York: North Holland, 1979), pp. 283–333. See also J.W. Ellwood and J.A. Thurber, "The Congressional Budget Process, Its Causes, Consequences, and Possible Success," in S. Welch and J. Peters, eds., *Legislative Reform and Public Policy* (New York: Praeger, 1977).

passed in September 1976 just prior to the November election, contained a $50 billion deficit, as had the first budget resolution in the spring. On April 27, 1976, during debate on the first budget resolution, House Budget Committee Chairman Brock Adams, who became secretary of transportation in the Carter Administration, justified the $50 billion deficit, at a time when the recession was already over, as "a budget that arrests the recession and puts the nation on the road to economic recovery."[2] Striking of figure and eloquent of voice, Adams evoked the image of a gentleman of yore, but he could demagogue with the best of them. He accused President Ford, who wanted a smaller deficit, of trying to get the Congress to pass "a restrictive budget that will surely lead to the strangling of the recovery and a return to the recession after the election." "The President," he said, "tried to inflict upon us the kind of economic policy that would have left us wallowing in the worst recession since 1929. He failed because we would not let him and insisted instead upon the kind of economic policy that has led us out of the recession and onto the path of recovery."

Having pushed through in September $50 billion worth of deficit spending to continue fighting recession in the second year of an economic recovery, the Democrats were back in November, decrying the $50 billion deficit as too small to fuel the economic recovery. Between November 1976 and February 1977 they built up pressure for the unprecedented third budget resolution, which they claimed was needed "to accommodate additional economic stimulus measures."[3] The additional measures consisted of a $50 tax rebate to stimulate "lagging consumer demand" and an increase in government spending programs, which together raised the 1977 deficit to $70 billion—3.7 percent of projected GNP. Previously Republicans had simply railed against the deficit, voted no, and talked about building a record for that time when the voters would wake up to the ruin being inflicted upon them by the Democrats' handouts. This time, however, they had an alternative.

"The purpose of a permanent tax reduction," Rousselot instructed the House,

2. *Congressional Record,* p. 11373.
3. *Third Concurrent Resolution on the Budget—Fiscal Year 1977,* House of Representatives, Committee on the Budget, U.S. Government Printing Office, Report No. 95–12, Washington, D.C., 1977, p. 7.

is to reduce the tax bias against work, saving and investment; that is, to increase the reward to work, save and invest. Taxes at all levels constitute more than 42 percent of our national income. The present high rate of taxation holds down production and investment, reduces employment and the incentive to work, and makes people dependent on transfer payments by denying them work. A one-year $50 rebate will not change this pattern.

Then Rousselot came up with what was, at least for him and the Republicans, the clincher: "I would like to remind my colleagues that if they vote for this substitute that the minority is offering, they will be reducing the Budget Committee add-on deficit by fourteen billion dollars" (actually, by twelve billion). There it was—the statement that the supply-side tax cut would be more effective than the Democratic spending stimulus and at less deficit cost. The second budget resolution had placed the deficit at $50 billion. In the third the Democrats were moving it to $70 billion for stimulus reasons. The Republican substitute was moving it to $57.9 billion.

Jim Mattox, a Democrat from Texas, was quick to seize on the anomaly of John Rousselot's proposing a larger deficit than the one already on the books. Rousselot was defensive, and I remember my anxiety over whether Republican resolve would hold as I listened to Rousselot's reply:

I am not supporting an add-on deficit as much as a strong fourteen billion dollar reduction in the committee deficit which is a lot better than the majority proposal for an add-on deficit of twenty billion dollars. So I could promise the gentleman from Texas, who is also a distinguished member of the Committee on the Budget, that when we get to the [first budget] resolution in April that I will be back with a balanced budget. There is no way the gentleman from Texas can imply that I support deficit financing.

Mattox sensed the Republican's uneasiness and twisted the knife: "What the gentleman from California really is saying is that he is actually increasing the deficit." Perhaps it was a case of "saved by the bell," because the next entry in the *Congressional Record* is the chairman announcing that the time of the gentleman had expired. The next speaker, Carlos Moorhead of California, rose "in strong support of the substitute amendment offered by the gentleman from California." Having survived the first counterattack, the Republicans braced as the Democrats recovered from their surprise and began to test the strength of this assault on their hegemony over fiscal policy.

In a series of briefings, I had prepared the Republicans as best I could to counter the Keynesian justification of deficit spending with the supply-side case for tax-rate reduction. The Democrats had made the third budget resolution into a matter of providing economic stimulus to maintain the recovery. Since the Democrats were proposing $70 billion in deficit spending, the $58 billion deficit contained in the Republican tax-cut proposal was conservative by comparison. However, the proposal to reduce marginal tax rates[4] across the board made Republicans nervous for other reasons as well. Since the percentage reduction was equal across all tax brackets, the progressivity of taxation was not altered. But since people with higher incomes pay higher taxes, an equal percentage reduction in tax rates means a larger dollar tax cut for "the rich." For example, a 10 percent reduction in a $50,000 tax burden is $5,000, but a 10 percent reduction in a $1,000 tax burden is $100. Democrats had made Republicans sensitive to the idea that a "fair" tax cut is one that gives the most dollars to people with the lowest income. Republicans knew they would be demagogued to death about trickle-down economics, the charge that the Republican approach is to encourage the rich to enjoy the high life in hopes that a few pennies will trickle down to the poor. They did not want to be asked why they were in favor of putting more money in the hands of the rich.

The Republicans had accepted the strategy of competing against temporary tax rebates and permanent spending programs with supply-side tax cuts but, fearful of being pilloried for favoring the rich, they had found it difficult to reach agreement to go forward with a substitute budget resolution. What they wanted was impossible—an equal marginal tax-rate reduction that would give back more money to lower-income taxpayers than to higher.

To a supply-sider like myself, it was frustrating that the whole enterprise was impeded by the amount of money handed back to the various brackets—that aspect of the tax cut was irrelevant to its purposes. The supply-side reason for reducing marginal tax rates is

4. The marginal tax rate is the rate at which additions to income are taxed—for example, a cost-of-living adjustment, raise, or bonus. In a progressive tax system, it is higher than the average tax rate.

to reduce the tax rate applied to *new earnings*. In a progressive tax system any new income, whether from overtime, a raise, or income from saving and investing, is added on top of existing income and automatically taxed at the highest bracket. Reducing the marginal tax rate lets the income earner keep a larger percentage of any additions to income, and therein lies the incentive to generate additional income or GNP.

In a pure incentive tax cut, the government would not lose any revenues, since no money would be handed back on existing earnings. The tax cut would apply only to new income. A tax cut of this kind would be a revenue raiser because it expands the tax base without lowering the average tax rate. But this is not a very visible form of tax cut, which hurts it politically.

Unless offsetting action is taken (such as reducing the personal exemption, deductions, and credits), when marginal tax rates are cut across the brackets, everyone's average tax rate also falls and people get back money on their existing earnings. It is this aspect of the tax cut—emphasizing higher spending instead of better incentives—that Washington policymakers had stressed for two decades. And it was this aspect of the tax cut that was threatening to stall the minority substitute to the $50 rebate.

A solution was hit upon. A five-percentage-point reduction in marginal tax rates provided the appearance of equality on the semantic level, but in fact provided a greater percentage tax reduction for lower-income brackets. For example, a five-percentage-point reduction, which drops the 70 percent bracket to 65, is about an 8 percent tax-rate reduction. However, at the bottom bracket, which drops from 14 percent to 9, it is a 56 percent tax-rate reduction. Even so, the personal income tax falls so heavily on upper-income taxpayers (the top ten percent pay 50 percent of the total take) that an 8 percent tax cut hands back more dollars to a rich person than a 56 percent tax cut hands back to a poor person. Nevertheless, many Republicans felt themselves better fortified against the trickle-down charge with such a disproportionate tax-rate reduction.

In trying to protect themselves against charges that they were doing too much for the rich, the Republicans were improving incentives the most in the lower tax brackets (where disincentives are least) and improving incentives the least in the higher brackets (where disincentives are greatest). A 70 percent tax bracket is a much greater disincentive than a 14 percent one. It was something of a dilemma for a supply-sider. Republicans were ready to propose a tax-rate reduction as a substitute for a rebate, but it was a rate reduction that would increase the progressivity of the income tax. The afternoon before the Republicans were to offer their substitute to the third budget resolution for fiscal year 1977, a compromise was struck. They would offer both versions of the tax cut as substitutes—an equal across-the-board reduction in tax rates and the five-percentage-point reduction—and argue in general the virtues of permanent tax-rate reductions as opposed to temporary tax rebates and permanent increases in government spending.

Just as he had feared, Rousselot was assaulted for proposing to cut taxes on the rich. Paul Simon of Illinois led the attack. Walking across to the Republican side of the aisle, where our charts displayed the tax savings by income level for the two tax cuts, he announced: "It is the old trickle-down economic theory." It did little good for Rousselot to point out that, in the case of the five-percentage-point alternative, the bulk of the tax cut went to the people earning between $7,100 and $31,000. The people who need the money, countered Simon, are the people who are out of work and paying no taxes. To create jobs the unemployed must "get some income so they can buy cars and move this country ahead." Simon did not explain how the unemployed were going to buy cars with $50 tax rebates, and moved on to a new point of attack: "What the gentleman [Rousselot] is doing here is calling for a permanent tax cut," which means "unquestionably bigger and bigger deficits in the future."

Simon was hitting the Republicans where they were most sensitive. President Ford had proposed a temporary tax rebate in 1975 in order to protect against a revenue loss that could mean larger deficits in the future. The Republicans shuddered at the specter of lost revenues, but Clair Burgener of California firmed the ranks: "If we do not use this deficit in a more constructive manner than a quick fix rebate, we are going to create unacceptable inflation. We maintain that permanent tax cuts are the only thing that would justify a large deficit at this time."

Rebuffed again and growing a little concerned over the firmness of the Republican challenge, Clifford Allen and J. J. Pickle generated some smoke while someone went to find "battling Jim" Wright, the majority leader. The Republican substitute, said both congressmen, "invades the jurisdiction of the Ways and Means Committee." This was a clever move because Barber Conable, the ranking Republican on Ways and Means, was uneasy about the use of budget resolutions to propose tax cuts. At that time many were afraid that the new Budget Committee would usurp the functions of the traditional committees. But the same concern applied to the Democrats' $50 rebate, and Conable, who was also a member of the Budget Committee, had agreed to our strategy.

Ralph Regula and Marjorie Holt had time to support the tax cut before Wright strode onto the floor. Invoking the authority of the Budget Committee's professional staff, he declared the tax cut regressive: it "would give four times the benefits as a percentage of income back to the family earning $100,000 as it would to the family earning $10,000." You have to read Wright's words closely because they are confusing. It sounds as though the rich would be getting a disproportionate tax cut. But all Wright was saying was that, since the $100,000 family already pays a much larger percentage of its income in taxes, an equal cut in tax rates would give it a larger percentage of its income back.

Having accepted the agonies of higher progressivity in order to get a proposal to reduce tax rates out of the Republicans, it angered me that the Budget Committee staff was licensing Wright's misuse of language. I crossed the aisle and reminded my Democratic counterpart, Nancy Teeters, now a member of the Federal Reserve Board, that according to all the canons of economics, an across-the-board tax-rate reduction is neutral with regard to progressivity, and a five-percentage-point reduction *increases* the progressivity of the income tax. A regressive tax cut is one that cuts the higher rates more than the lower rates. The Republicans were actually proposing higher progressivity in order to lower tax rates. After reminding her of these points, I noticed that Teeters looked surprised that I could be so naive as to think that facts mattered in these fights. On many later occasions, the other side applied the term "regressive" to any tax cut that did not hand back the most dollars to those who paid the least taxes—a redefinition that destroyed the meaning of an old and honorable term.

It was Jack Kemp who took on Wright. A forceful leader, Kemp soon had the attention of the House. He had done his homework, and in his debate with the majority leader he showed that he could wield supply-side analytics deftly and had the confidence and intellect to back up his convictions. In asking the old question "Who benefits?" Wright was suggesting that the poor lose any time the tax burden on the rich is lowered. To the contrary, Kemp said, the rich pay a larger proportion of the income tax revenues when their tax rates are lowered.

This may sound impossible but it is in fact what the evidence demonstrates. Economists James Gwartney and Richard Stroup, for example, have examined the Internal Revenue Service's *Statistics of Income* and found that, when marginal tax rates were reduced on upper-income brackets, the proportion of taxes paid by the upper brackets increased, as did the tax revenues collected from the higher brackets.[5] Wright was looking at the tax reduction only in terms of the dollars handed back. He neglected the fact that tax cuts also hand back incentives—including the incentive "to put more money into enterprises and industry and less into tax-exempt securities," as a *New York Times* editorial wrote in 1923 in support of the Mellon tax cuts. The way to soak the rich and collect more money from them, Kemp argued, is to lower their tax rates, not raise them.

Kemp was pointing out that there are more important ways to benefit from a tax cut than from the money it hands back. Better incentives mean a higher saving rate, more capital formation, greater labor productivity, greater growth in real wages, and more and better job opportunities through which people can benefit themselves. Higher economic growth means both a larger tax base and lower expenditures for income-support programs. The way to cut government spending is through the growth of jobs and private sector income, not by attacking the government's budget with a paring knife in a static or declining economy. The way to reduce the burden of government spending is to have it decline as a percentage of national income as the economy grows.

The lower tax rates would also lower labor costs or at least reduce the rate of growth in pre-tax wages. The higher the tax rates, the greater the raises employers must give in order to add to take-home

5. James Gwartney and Richard Stroup, "Tax Cuts: Who Shoulders the Burden?," *Economic Review,* Federal Reserve Bank of Atlanta, March 1982, pp. 19–27.

pay. Each successive round of large wage increases during the 1970s left American products less competitive in the markets both at home and abroad. Declining competitiveness is itself a threat to jobs, and a tax system that helps to price American labor out of markets eventually produces fewer and fewer tax revenues.

The problem with the Democrats' approach to economic policy, argued Kemp, "is that it does not recognize the destructive effects that high tax rates have had on the economy." The high inflation rates were not consistent with the Keynesian view that there was a lack of demand. Why, then, were the Democrats proposing a tax rebate? A rebate is "simply a transfer payment and simply stimulates demand. It does nothing to stimulate supply." It provides no incentives to produce new supplies.

Here Kemp made two key points of supply-side analysis. First, higher prices are not only caused by the money supply growing too rapidly. Higher prices also result from redistributive policies that tax production in order to support consumption. Since higher prices result from demand growing relative to supply, the solution is not to increase demand with a tax rebate but to increase supply with better incentives to produce. In a progressive tax system, it is wrong to see increased spending as an incentive to produce. The additional spending fuels inflation and pushes people into higher tax brackets, which is the same thing as saying that the rewards for additional production fall. Thus the higher spending does more to raise prices than it does to raise output.

Keynesians themselves believe that the upward movement of income earners in the tax brackets serves as a restraint on economic growth—but because it inhibits demand. The automatic rise in tax revenues from "bracket creep" siphons purchasing power away from consumers, resulting in a decline in the growth of demand. Walter Heller, Chairman of the Council of Economic Advisers under President Kennedy, called it "fiscal drag." The fiscal drag had to be offset, or it would choke off economic expansion.

Democrats believed that one way to offset fiscal drag was to increase government spending. Here Kemp made a second key point in his debate with Wright. Curing fiscal drag cannot cure the economy. Increased government spending can fill in for the consumer spending that is siphoned off by higher taxes, but it cannot replenish the *incentives* that are also siphoned off by higher tax rates. Supply disincentives, Kemp said, "cannot be offset by increased government spending, but only by a reduction in the tax rates." Here was the supply-side concept of the "tax brake," which results from less incentive to produce additional income.[6] The tax brake is the supply-side counterpart to fiscal drag, but it cannot be released by applying Keynesian remedies.

Kemp made many references to the similar and successful tax cut associated with President Kennedy which Republicans at the time had opposed. In recent years the argument has been made many times that tax cuts will no longer work because the economy is different today than it was in the 1960s. This argument was answered on the first day of the debate. At the time of the Kennedy tax cuts, Kemp noted, "only about three percent of all tax returns were subject to marginal tax rates of 30 percent. Today nearly a third of all tax returns are in these higher brackets." Since people are positioned higher in the tax brackets where disincentives are stronger, "the positive effects on employment, investment and production which would result from an across-the-board cut in tax rates could be expected to be much greater today."

In his debate with Wright, Kemp argued with analysis and not with rhetoric. Bested, Wright simply turned his back and walked off the floor. Kemp called after him: "Mr. Wright, I'm speaking to you!" The challenge was deleted from the *Record,* as such things generally are, but I remember it. Here was a man who believed in his cause and who was going to make the majority leader listen. Eventually Kemp would prevail, but not on the House floor that day.

The chairman of the Budget Committee, Robert Giaimo, rose in opposition to the tax cuts. First of all, he said, the tax rebate was not something the Democrats had just hatched, but "was conceived by the Ford Administration." Why were the Republicans for rebates when a Republican President proposed them and against them when a Democrat proposed them? Next he repeated the erroneous charge that the tax cuts "would reduce the progressive nature of our existing tax system, and we have enough regressive taxes in this

6. See Paul Craig Roberts, "The Tax Brake," *Wall Street Journal,* January 11, 1979.

country." Then he attacked the tax cuts from the standpoint of orthodox economic analysis.

"The Rousselot amendment," said Giaimo, "would reduce individual incomes taxes in 1977 by $19 billion," but it would also "reduce spending by almost $14 billion in fiscal year 1977, removing all the economic stimulus approved by the Committee on the Budget." He argued that the reduction in government spending would take money out of the economy, thus offsetting the tax reduction and providing no net stimulus to the economy. As a result the economy would worsen, and the "deficit would in fact be a great deal higher" than the $58 billion figure in the Republican substitute.

Republicans were still tied to Barry Goldwater's prescription from the 1964 presidential campaign of paying for tax cuts with spending cuts. The Republican tax cut measured $19 billion in static terms. The net revenue loss from the second budget resolution was $15.4 billion, indicating that the Republican substitute was relying on $3.6 billion in revenue feedbacks from a stronger economy as a result of the tax cut. If the Republicans had left spending at the level of the second budget resolution, their tax cut would have added $15 billion to the deficit, raising it to $65 billion. That was $5 billion less deficit than the Democrats' $20 billion package of rebates and spending programs. Nevertheless, not many Republicans (or conservative Democrats) were going to vote for a tax cut if it meant a $65 billion deficit. They would be more at ease voting against the Democrats' $70 billion deficit than offering a tax-cut substitute to compete against the $50 rebate. Therefore, they "paid" for part of their tax cut by dropping spending $8 billion below the level in the second budget resolution ($13.6 billion below the level in the third budget resolution). The reduction in spending together with the moderate supply-side feedbacks resulted in a package that added only $8 billion to the deficit; the Democratic demand-side stimulus added $20 billion to the deficit.

Whenever Republicans talked about cutting taxes, the Democrats would encourage their natural inclination to pay for tax cuts with spending cuts. Then the Democrats would point out how much money the Republicans were taking out of the poor's spending programs in order to give the rich a tax cut. After beating them up in this way politically, the Democrats would then argue that the Re-

publican program could have no overall effect on the economy—
the tax cuts put money in the economy but the budget cuts took
it out, and it was all a trick to benefit the rich at the expense of
the poor.

The Republicans' substitute to the third budget resolution was
put to a vote and went down with 258 nays to 148 ayes. But it was a
victory nevertheless. Republicans had accepted a new idea. They
now had a strategy and were carrying the fight to the Democrats.
They were back in political competition.

The Old Fiscal Theory and the New

The transformation of John Rousselot symbolized the transformation of the Republican Party. It was a big change. Just four months
previously Gerald Ford, the incumbent Republican, had lost the
presidency to a political unknown named Jimmy Carter from Georgia, leaving the Grand Old Party a minority both in the Senate and
in the House, where the Democrats had an overwhelming 115-vote
majority. In the aftermath of defeat the Republicans found themselves with neither an economic nor a political program, and no
forum from which to develop one.

Prior to February 23, 1977, Republican economic policy focused
on balancing the budget by raising taxes and cutting spending, an
approach that denied the party a credible economic and political
program. The Republicans were not always successful themselves at
reducing spending, but if the government was going to spend, they
at least wanted to pay for it with cash instead of borrowed money.
This put them in conflict with Keynesian economics.

Keynesian theory explained the economy's performance in terms
of the level of total spending.[7] A budget deficit adds to total spending and helps keep employment high and the economy running at
full capacity. Cutting the deficit, as the Republicans wanted to do,
would reduce spending and throw people out of work, thereby
lowering national income and raising the unemployment rate. The
lower income would produce less tax revenue, and the higher unemployment would require larger budget expenditures for unemployment compensation, food stamps, and other support programs. The

7. See John Maynard Keynes, *The General Theory of Employment, Interest and
Money* (New York: Harcourt, Brace, 1936).

budget deficit would thus reappear from a shrunken tax base and higher income-support payments. Patient (and impatient) Democrats, economists, columnists, and editorial writers had explained many times to the obdurate Republicans that cutting the deficit would simply reduce spending on goods and services, drive the economy down, and raise the unemployment rate. Keynesians argued that the way to balance the budget was to run a deficit. Deficit spending would lift the economy, and the government's tax revenues would rise, bringing the budget into balance. Since cutting the deficit was believed to be the surest way to throw people out of work, there were not many Republican economists. When Democrat Alice Rivlin was asked why there were no Republican economists on her "nonpartisan" Congressional Budget Committee staff, she was probably telling the truth when she said she could not find any.[8]

The focus on the deficit had left the Republicans without a competitive political program. They were perceived by the recipients of government benefits as the party always threatening to cut back on government programs such as social security, while the taxpaying part of the electorate saw Republicans as the party that was always threatening to raise taxes in order to pay for the benefits that others were receiving. The party that takes away with both hands competes badly with the party that gives away with both hands, and that simple fact explained the decline of the Republican Party, which had come to be known as the tax collector for Democratic spending programs.

In January 1975, alarmed by the 1974 recession, President Ford abandoned the income tax surcharge that he had proposed as an anti-inflationary measure the previous October. Declaring that "the emphasis of our economic efforts must now shift from inflation to jobs," he proposed a one-year, $16 billion "tax cut" for 1975. It consisted of a 12 percent rebate on 1974 individual income taxes and a temporary 12 percent tax credit for business investment.

In their economic policy the Republican economists were just as Keynesian as the Democrats. Both fought recession and unemployment by spending. The main difference was that, while Democrats leaned toward increasing government spending programs, Republi-

---

8. See Michael J. Malbin, *Unelected Representatives* (New York: Basic Books, 1980), p. 200.

cans preferred measures such as temporary tax rebates that would allow a "spending stimulus" without expanding government programs. Republicans saw temporary rebates (in lieu of a permanent tax reduction) as a way of holding on to future tax revenues for balancing the budget. Even so, President Ford was attacked by fellow Republicans in the Congress for proposing tax measures that would widen the deficit.

The Democratic Congress quickly turned Ford's proposals into an income-redistribution program skewed toward lower-income groups. In spite of his objections, the President signed H.R. 2166 on March 29 because "our country needs the stimulus . . . and needs it now." In those days, in keeping with the Keynesian view that spending alone drives the economy, tax cuts were seen only as a tool for manipulating the level of spending or demand by putting money into the economy (or taking it out with tax increases if inflation was the problem).

Except in a recessionary environment, Republicans did not favor tax cuts unless they paid for them with spending cuts. The competition between tax cuts and increases in government spending was politically treacherous for the Republicans. Unless the tax cut was designed to redistribute income to lower-income groups, Republicans would be asked whose benefits they proposed to cut in order to pass a tax cut for the wealthy. Did they want to take farm programs away from the farmer? Or social security benefits from the aged? Or was it the teachers and the schoolchildren they were after with cuts in aid to education and school lunches? Or national defense? With organized voting blocks defending their appropriations, there was not much tax cutting accomplished by holding down spending.

Kept on the defensive, Republicans tended to focus on the deficit. They did not think that Democrats could get away with so much vote buying if they had to raise taxes to pay for the handouts. Fearful of the charge that they represented the interests of "fat cats" and were insensitive to the poor, Republicans were uneasy about opposing income redistribution outright. Instead, they argued that deficits hurt the poor by causing inflation. It was not a particularly brilliant approach to political competition. Instead of controlling spending to protect the poor from inflation, the Congress simply indexed entitlement benefits and transfer payments so that they would automatically rise with inflation—leading to more spending.

With the 1974–75 recession behind it, the Ford Administration settled on a plan to balance the budget by restraining the growth of government spending, while allowing a moderate inflation to swell the government's coffers by pushing taxpayers into higher tax brackets. Herbert Stein, chairman of the Council of Economic Advisers in 1972–1974, was still advocating this policy in March 1980 when he advised the Senate Budget Committee that "the simplest way to do this is to keep all existing taxes in place and allow the tax burden to rise as the automatic consequence of economic growth and inflation."

It was, in other words, a plan to balance the budget by holding down the growth of real income for both the recipients of government benefits and the taxpaying public. It was certainly a courageous approach taken by sincere men. But it was not successful politics and would not have succeeded economically either, because the rising tax rates were eroding the economy's ability to perform by undermining work attitudes, the saving rate, and thereby investment, productivity, and economic growth.

The Republicans were not wrong in being concerned about persistent budget deficits. Not much can be done about deficits in a recession when they occur automatically. However, continual deficits year after year are a sign either that government spending is growing faster than the economy that supports it or that something is wrong with the economy such that the budget does not move into balance even in the best years. Where Republicans were wrong was in thinking that tax revenues could not rise unless the tax burden rose. The supply-side prescription for balancing the budget through economic growth was still an unfamiliar concept.

The Republicans were ahead of the economics profession both in seeing the deficit as a problem and in being suspicious of the argument that a nation could spend its way to prosperity—although the GOP used this argument itself when it had to fight unemployment. But these instincts were a disadvantage when so many economists saw a balanced budget and reduced government spending as a threat to full employment. It meant that the GOP did not have much professional support for trying to balance the budget with austerity measures like higher taxes and budget cutting.

The Republicans' austerity approach to the deficit gave them their image as the party that takes away. They were trying to reduce the deficit in a way that cost them both professional and public support. In addition there were practical problems. Controlling spending is hard even for Republicans, as witnessed by the fact that record government spending occurred in each of the first two years of the Reagan Administration, with expenditures rising from 23 percent of the gross national product in 1980, Carter's last year, to 23.6 percent in 1981 and to 24.6 percent in 1982.

Having failed to balance the budget while the Congress was buying votes, Republicans found themselves reduced to voting no. Perhaps because they thought they had nothing further to lose, the Republicans on the House Budget Committee listened to my arguments for a new approach; they began to shift their focus from reducing the deficit to reducing tax rates. There were three steps in this process. First, the House Republicans stopped thinking of the budget resolution as a referendum on the deficit and learned to see it instead as an economic policy forum that provided opportunities to offer voters an alternative program. Second, they realized that, with orthodox economics justifying deficits, the question was not deficit or no deficit, but its size and source. They came around to the view that smaller deficits caused by reducing tax rates were preferable to larger deficits caused by higher government spending. Third, they came to accept the political wisdom of balancing the budget through economic growth rather than by imposing austerity. Once they learned to argue that a reduction in tax rates would provide the stimulus that Keynesians claimed was needed to keep the economy moving, but with a smaller net deficit, they were ready for action.

Prior to the advent of supply-side economics, such a position was not possible. In Keynesian analysis, tax cuts affect the economy only by affecting demand. But a dollar of tax cuts results in less additional demand than a dollar of government spending. (In Keynesian terms, the tax-cut multiplier is less than the government-spending multiplier.) The reasoning is that part of a tax cut will be saved and not spent. Because of the saving "leakage" a $10 billion tax cut would not increase demand as much as a $10 billion increase in government spending. As the Congressional Budget Office put it, "a permanent income tax cut is a relatively expensive way of reducing unemployment in terms of budget dollars (net or gross costs) per additional job."[9]

That made tax cuts unattractive. To provide the same amount of demand stimulus, a larger deficit was needed if taxes were cut than if government spending were increased. Thus the Democrats could always make deficit-conscious Republicans uncomfortable if they proposed tax cuts in lieu of higher government spending. It would mean that the Republicans were proposing a larger deficit than necessary to meet GNP growth and employment goals.

Supply-side economics brought a new perspective to fiscal policy. Instead of stressing the effects on spending, supply-siders showed that tax rates directly affect the supply of goods and services. Lower tax rates mean better incentives to work, to save, to take risks, and to invest. As people respond to the higher after-tax rewards, or greater profitability, incomes rise and the tax base grows, thus feeding back some of the lost revenues to the Treasury. The saving rate also grows, providing more financing for government and private borrowing. Since Keynesian analysis left out such effects, once supply-side economics appeared on the scene the Democrats could no longer claim that government spending stimulated the economy more effectively than tax cuts. Tax cuts were now competitive, and the House Republicans began to make the most of it.

The Double Standard

The Democrats' $70 billion deficit—3.7 percent of GNP—in their third budget resolution for fiscal year 1977 exemplifies the rigid double standard that has been applied to Republican budgets. For 1982, a year of recession, President Reagan's budget projected a deficit of 3.8 percent of GNP (including "off budget" items), declining to 3.1 percent in 1983, the first year of economic recovery. Yet the entire Washington establishment, including the President's own Office of Management and Budget, Keynesian economists, the media, and Wall Street analysts took up the hue and cry that deficits measuring 3.8 percent and 3.1 percent of GNP would crowd out private investment, keep interest rates high, and *prevent* an economic recovery.

9. *Understanding Fiscal Policy* (Washington, D.C., 1978), p. 50.

But when the Democrats had control of the budget process, the logic and the clamor were exactly the opposite. The recession had ended in 1975. 1976 was the first year of recovery, with a real growth rate of 5.4 percent in spite of (the Keynesian economists claimed because of) a deficit that measured 4.5 percent of GNP. 1977 was the second year of economic recovery, with real economic growth steaming along at 5.5 percent. Yet the argument then was that the recovery would stall without higher deficit spending.

Testifying before the Senate Budget Committee in support of the Democrats' stimulus package in the third budget resolution for fiscal year 1977, Walter Heller, chairman of the Council of Economic Advisers under President Kennedy, was asked if he thought the $70 billion deficit posed a problem for the economy. He replied that the $70 billion deficit (3.7 percent of GNP) was minor, and did not raise "even a remote specter" of inflation.[10]

The argument that the deficit would mean high interest rates, less investment, and an aborted recovery was also dismissed. In the same hearings Senator Cranston asked Heller and Alice Rivlin, director of the Congressional Budget Office, if the deficit would crowd out business investment, raise interest rates, and destroy business confidence. Heller dismissed the possibility with a shake of the head. Rivlin said it was not a serious concern. She reminded the senator that people had worried about the same thing a couple of years ago but that it did not happen. She had the same answer for the House Budget Committee two weeks later on January 24. Indeed, it was the standard answer. The previous year she had assured the Senate Budget Committee that " 'crowding out' of private spending by the federal sector does not appear to have occurred. In spite of the large federal deficit and modest rates of money supply growth over the year, interest rates generally did not increase."[11]

By 1981 the Keynesians had reversed their position. They opposed the Reagan tax cuts on the grounds that they would crowd out private investment. Needless to say, the politicians and the media let the Keynesians have their double standard as long as it was used to block tax reduction. The Washington establishment labored long

10. "The Economy and the Federal Budget," Hearings before the Senate Budget Committee, 95th Congress, January 11, 1977, p. 34.
11. "Review of the President's Budget," Hearings before the Senate Budget Committee, 94th Congress, 1976, p. 88.

and hard to set up a new principle of economic policy: only tax cuts result in budget deficits that crowd out private investment.

Supply-Side Frictions

The transformation of the House Republicans between October 1976 and February 1977 was not an easy achievement. Their natural inclination was to vote against the deficit. I was new on the Budget Committee staff and had to earn the confidence of the members while encouraging the new approach. Their personal staffs were always afraid that the committee staff might gain too much influence. My chief aide was Steve Entin, who had a full-time job with the Joint Economic Committee on the other side of the Capitol. I was leaving my office on the evening of February 22 when I received a disheartening call from Jack Kemp. Arthur Laffer had convinced him not to participate the next day when the Republicans were to offer their substitute budget resolution.

Laffer, an economics professor at the University of Southern California with a fondness for parrots and cacti, was new on the congressional scene, but he had the advantage of a boost in reputation that Jude Wanniski was providing in the *Wall Street Journal*. Short in stature, Laffer is tall on enthusiasm. By creating the "Laffer curve" Wanniski's pen made him bigger than life.

Wanniski was a *Wall Street Journal* editorial writer whose black shirts and white ties were incongruous with the paper's pin-striped image. He had discovered the budding supply-side movement in the Congress and rushed in to take over as its interpreter. Soon we were submerged in the "Laffer curve," and newspapers and magazines began calling us "Lafferites."

The Laffer curve maintains that tax cuts pay for themselves by stimulating the economy so strongly that tax revenues pour into the Treasury. It was not the argument that House Republicans were making. Their argument was that tax cuts stimulate the economy in ways beyond the spending emphasis of the Keynesians. The question was not whether tax cuts paid for themselves but whether they were more effective in promoting economic growth than were increases in government spending. It is worthwhile to quote a passage from the first official expression of supply-side views, which appeared in the minority section of the House Budget Committee's report on the third budget resolution for fiscal year 1977 (published February 8, 1977).

The Budget Committee Majority has made a fundamental error in assuming that a tax rebate and a permanent tax rate reduction both impact on the economy in the same way by increasing disposable income and total spending. In support of this way of looking at things, we often hear before this committee that "the reason people produce is that people buy."

However, there are two other reasons why people produce: for income and for profit. A permanent tax rate reduction not only stimulates production indirectly like a tax rebate by stimulating spending, it also directly stimulates production by increasing the after-tax rewards to work and investment. Therefore, a permanent tax rate reduction constitutes a three-pronged attack on unemployment: (1) it increases disposable income and thereby buying; (2) it increases the incentive to work; and (3) it provides new jobs by directly stimulating investment.

In contrast, a tax rebate only increases disposable income and provides only a single-pronged attack on unemployment. And it is the weakest possible attack, because the rebate is received regardless of whether the person works any harder or invests any more—indeed, regardless of whether he works or invests at all (p. 85).

By making the Laffer curve the issue, Wanniski and Laffer covered the supply-side movement with hyperbole. It brought publicity to the movement, but criticism as well. Their exaggeration reflected their enthusiasm, which was catching. For House Republicans undertaking a strange new venture, confidence was the heart of the matter, and the Laffer curve told them that they could cut taxes and not worry about the deficit. Nevertheless, I was careful never to base any of my work on the Republican budget resolutions on the Laffer curve. It was not that the Laffer curve was devoid of merit. Indeed, many thinkers had expressed the concept over the centuries. Keynes himself had formulated it in 1933 in "The Means to Prosperity": "Nor should the argument seem strange that taxation may be so high as to defeat its object, and that, given sufficient time to gather the fruits, a reduction of taxation will run a better chance than an increase of balancing the budget."[12] The problem with the Laffer

12. "Essays in Persuasion," *Collected Works of John Maynard Keynes,* IX (New York): St. Martin's Press, 1972), p. 338.

curve was that it obscured the issue. Since the Democrats themselves were advocating deficits, it was not necessary to argue that tax cuts fully paid for themselves. The real issue was whether tax cuts improved the incentives to produce or only increased spending, as the Keynesians claimed.

Laffer may have been disappointed that the Republicans' tax-cut proposal was not going to be explicitly based on the Laffer curve. Whatever his reasons, he advised Kemp to have nothing to do with the Republican substitute since one of its two options was the 5 percentage point reduction in tax rates, which increased the progressivity of the income tax and thus was impure supply-side economics. As soon as I got Kemp's call I rushed over to his office and told him that Rousselot could stay pure too and stick with his balanced-budget amendment. So could the Budget Committee minority that controlled the forum. So could the rest of the Republicans. The point was that Republicans were about to offer reductions in marginal income tax rates as an alternative economic policy. It was an historic occasion, I argued, and besides the alternative was a $50 rebate. Kemp relented, and his star performance in the debate the next day consolidated his leadership over the issue.

It was not the last time, however, that there was friction between congressional insiders and the outsiders who were providing the publicity. Indeed, the very next morning when we were all trying to calm our nerves in anticipation of the day's debate, ominous words rolled off the editorial page of the *Wall Street Journal*. They came from Wanniski's editorial, "JFK Strikes Again," a play on the fact that Jack F. Kemp and John F. Kennedy shared the same initials. This was a mistake. You do not win a young congressman allies among his peers by comparing him to a president and making them all envious. Even worse, Wanniski assigned in advance all the credit for the day's activities to Kemp. The Budget Committee Republicans, he reported, had "signed on the Kemp idea." Wanniski went on to write only about Kemp and "his plan." The Budget Committee and party policy were simply eclipsed. The resentments sowed by this editorial dogged the supply-side movement in the years to come and left a fertile field for the machinations within the Republican Party to roll back the Reagan tax cuts.

The editorial damaged me as well. It allowed the members and staff who felt threatened at the time to tag me as "Kemp's man on the Budget Committee," the implication being that I was using the committee for the glory of Kemp, who was not a member. Afterwards, when I complained to Wanniski about his tactless editorial, he replied: "We will sacrifice you to the revolution." That response may sound callous and egotistical, but Wanniski has always reified the tax cuts. He believed they were going to bring themselves into existence strictly from the power and rightness of the idea, and that they had no need for midwives or strategically placed friends. Wanniski believes that "the global electorate " will prevail regardless of the self-interest of politicians and bureaucrats.[13] As Robert Bartley, Wanniski's former chief at the *Wall Street Journal* observed, Wanniski "sometimes seems to think a tax cut can stop an SS-18 in midflight."[14] By weakening my position, Wanniski made it possible for opponents to acquire positions on the Budget Committee minority staff. But by then it was time to carry the fight into the Senate.

Kemp-Roth and Its Antecedents

When I joined Kemp's staff in the summer of 1975, he already had a capital-formation bill that he renamed the Jobs Creation Act, a semantic change that greatly increased its salability. At final count Kemp had 136 cosponsors of his bill, with Senator McClure pushing the issue in the Senate. The Kemp-McClure bill became the alternative to the Humphrey-Hawkins bill and helped to hold at bay this socialistic approach to employment.

By 1975 a discussion had developed over whether the rate of capital formation was adequate to meet the goals of public policy and maintain growth in real wages and employment. Kemp was on top of this issue with his bill. But in the Keynesian atmosphere of the time, measures designed to increase private saving and investment faced an uphill fight. Walter Heller had called such measures "tax breaks for business," which result in "annual tax loss." To overcome the deficiency in capital formation, Heller advocated deficit spending to stimulate consumption. The additional spending would lift

13. Jude Wanniski, *The Way the World Works* (New York: Simon and Schuster, 1978).

14. Robert Bartley, "Jack Kemp's Intellectual Blitz," *Wall Street Journal,* November 29, 1979.

the economy. The result, he claimed, would be a "full employment federal budget surplus." This surplus would be a source of public saving to close the gap between capital needs and inadequate private saving.

By the end of the summer of 1975, with help from Norman Ture (who in 1981 became the first undersecretary of the Treasury for economic and tax affairs), I had provided a supply-side basis for Kemp's capital-formation bill. On September 21, 1975, in the Sunday *Washington Star* Kemp appeared for the first time as the author of an article on economic policy. The article criticized Heller and the Keynesians for fostering a tax bias against saving that shifted income away from investment and into consumption. The result was slower economic growth. After making its analytical points, the article demanded responsible debate: "Those who misrepresent the issue as the Fat Cat versus the Little Man employ an adversary rhetoric which indicates the weakness of their position."

The article was a fundamental challenge to Keynesians because it emphasized that fiscal policy works by affecting incentives rather than demand. Lower tax rates would mean a higher saving rate and a greater rate of capital formation. More capital would mean higher real wages and new jobs, which "will generate additional tax revenues that will wipe out the initial revenue loss." Among the measures the article recommended to improve incentives was "a reduction of the income tax rate graduation," that is, a reduction in marginal tax rates.

In 1976 Kemp met Wanniski and Laffer, who took an interest in the tax-cutting congressman and encouraged him. Their support was both a help and a hindrance. Kemp gained recognition, but their emphasis on the Laffer curve tended to crowd out a broader-based approach that stressed the roles of reduced government spending and a higher saving rate in mitigating any revenue loss from cutting tax rates.[15]

15. Wanniski, who has never hesitated to assume the role of spokesman for the supply-siders, has created the impression that supply-side economics began in 1976 when he and Laffer met an untutored Kemp and introduced him to the Laffer curve. Wanniski's account of supply-side history transforms Norman Ture and me into Keynesians. While helping Kemp with his book, *An American Renaissance* (New York: Harper and Row, 1979), Wanniski used the opportunity to rewrite history. He has Kemp say that he was "still thinking in Keynesian terms" until the spring of 1976 when the deficiency in his outlook "was pointed out to me by Jude Wanniski" (p. 38).

For Jack Kemp, the Republican substitute to the third budget resolution marked a new beginning. A few weeks later on April 6,
1977, Kemp introduced his first bill to cut the marginal tax rates on
personal income. H.R. 6201 called for a 30 percent reduction across
the board in one year. In July Kemp teamed up with Senator Roth,
and the 30 percent reduction was phased in over three years. There
was too much concern about the deficit to allow incentives to be improved too much at once. Republicans had progressed to the point
where they could become excited about cutting taxes, but when they
got right down to it they usually elected to back their way into a tax
cut by delaying it until the future. That is what happened to Ronald
Reagan's tax cut. Kemp, to his credit, was opposed to dawdling with
incentives.

The Republican substitute for the third budget resolution for fiscal 1977 was the culmination of twenty months of long days on the
congressional staff. After fifteen months on Kemp's staff, I left in
October 1976 to become the first chief economist on the minority
staff of the House Budget Committee. Kemp lacked a forum for developing a supply-side economic policy. He was not on the Ways
and Means Committee, which dealt with taxation, or on the Budget
Committee. Since we were not merely arguing for tax cuts but were
developing an alternative fiscal policy, the Budget Committee was
the necessary forum. Without the Congressional Budget Act of
1974, there probably would not have been a Kemp-Roth bill. Tax
bills are not a regular occurrence, and they do not provide a vehicle
for debating general economic policy. Budget resolutions, however,
appear regularly twice a year (at least) in the House and Senate,
which provides a minimum of four opportunities each year to offer
an alternative economic policy. It seemed obvious that the success of
supply-side economics depended on its becoming a party issue. A
committee responsible for the party's position on budget policy was
the place to launch a new movement.

Moving to the Budget Committee staff also provided the opportunity to shift the tax-reduction emphasis to the personal income tax.
My inclination to move in this direction was the result of my experience in mustering support for Kemp's Jobs Creation Act. Though a
good bill, it had two problems. It was business-oriented, which did
not open up any new political ground to the Republicans. And since

it was a collection of capital-formation measures, it was criticized for expanding loopholes for special interests. Cutting individual income tax rates seemed to me a more powerful vehicle for a supply-side policy.

I discussed the matter with Kemp's administrative assistant, Randall Teague, who had put together the Jobs Creation Act. He saw my points, but he had some good ones of his own. In being sensitive to the loophole charges, I was reacting in part to the opinion of my fellow economists, who are usually too academic to support anything but perfection itself, and nothing perfect was going to come out of the political process. Kemp, through long and arduous work, had built up substantial support for the Jobs Creation Act. To cast that aside for a new approach was to risk taking him from somewhere to nowhere—especially since the taxpayer had no organized lobbyists in Washington. I let the matter drop. Washington is not a place where people expect to find a sincere person. Had I persisted, I would have risked convincing Teague that I intended to undermine his influence with Kemp and to replace his bill with mine. For a new approach to become muddied in personal rivalries was a fast way to kill it. Carrying the issue to the House Budget Committee solved the problem.

2

Econometrics, Politics, and Public Policy

SUPPLY-SIDE ECONOMICS WAS A FUNDAMENTAL CHALLENGE not only to political interests but to economists as well. The U.S. government had been formulating economic policy on the basis of economic models that ignored major ways in which taxation affected the economy. For example, on January 24, 1977, John Rousselot asked the Congressional Budget Office what the economic effects would be of cutting the corporate income tax rate. In her reply (February 3, 1977) Alice Rivlin did not give CBO's own estimate, but she reported that "according to some model simulations we did not long ago," cutting corporate income taxes could cause the gross national product to decline. Accompanying her reply was a table showing that the Wharton model devised by Nobel laureate Lawrence Klein and the DRI model built by Harvard professor Otto Eckstein both forecast that reducing the tax on corporate income would result in a fall in GNP. Only the Chase model built by Michael Evans showed a positive effect from cutting corporate income taxes.

This was quite an anomaly. Here were economic models of a capitalist economy showing that a tax cut which increased the profitability of investment would result in less investment and lower income. The government did not notice the anomaly—it used the Wharton and DRI models to formulate the economic policy of the United States. The economics profession did not notice the anomaly—it gave Klein a Nobel Prize. Not even the capitalists noticed—Eckstein sold his model in 1979 for $100 million.[1]

1. See *Wall Street Journal* editorial, "Buy Low, Sell High," August 13, 1979.

Americans have become anxious about the decline of their fabled economy and the lid placed on their living standards, but there is really no puzzle. The economy's performance is not independent of the government's economic policy, and we have had years of the wrong policy. The Keynesian economic models produced results that were biased against profits and investments. Official government reports claimed that a policy of increased government purchases (more deficit spending) was the best way to increase GNP and that public employment programs were the most effective way to reduce unemployment.[2] Judging by the strong claims made for public service employment, many economists no longer had a meaningful definition of what a job is and believed that jobs can be created by redefining unemployment compensation as public service employment. It certainly hides unemployment if funds in the budget are moved from the "unemployment compensation" category to "public service jobs." But a tax-supported job that does not produce marketable goods and services is not the same as a tax-generating job that does. One reason America has been declining is that its policymakers could not tell the difference between these two kinds of jobs. Real jobs depend on incentives to save and invest, but incentives were left out of the Keynesian models, which stressed spending.

I prepared a critique of the economic models for the House Budget Committee showing that they left incentives out of the picture, and two days after the debate on the third budget resolution for fiscal year 1977 Rousselot and Del Latta, the ranking Republican on the House Budget Committee, officially brought the criticism to the attention of Alice Rivlin. For good measure Rousselot also asked Bert Lance for a response from the Office of Management and Budget. The war was on.

The fight over the models turned out to be a long and bitter one. Initially it was John Rousselot who was the point man, pressing the attack from his forum on the House Budget Committee. Later it was Senator Orrin Hatch, a Republican from Utah, who took up the issue in the Joint Economic Committee and the Senate Budget Committee. Hatch, tall and prepossessing with the civilized looks of

2. See *Understanding Fiscal Policy*, Congressional Budget Office (Washington, D.C.: U.S. Government Printing Office, 1978).

an English gentleman, was known for his sincerity. He was also, as was Rousselot, an intelligent and aggressive fighter who was not afraid to make waves. Both men were prepared to stand on principle and to establish the facts. Hatch readily took on powerful committee chairmen and entire committee staffs, Republican and Democrat. Had either man been easily intimidated by authority or willing to compromise the issue, supply-side economics would have been stonewalled by the establishment.

In her reply (March 4, 1977) Rivlin admitted that the models did leave out incentives, but these missing supply-side effects, she said, were not important.[3] In the Keynesian view, which was Rivlin's, fiscal policy works through the demand-side by changing spending. I was arguing that fiscal policy works through the supply-side by changing relative prices and, thereby, incentives to produce. Since Keynesians did not believe in any such effects, they obviously would not incorporate them in their models of how the economy behaves.

The relative-price argument is straightforward. On the supply side of the economy there are two important relative prices. One governs people's decisions about how they allocate their income between consumption and saving. The cost to the individual of allocating a unit of income to current consumption is the future income stream given up by not saving and investing that unit of income. The value of that income stream is determined by marginal tax rates. The higher the tax rate, the less the value of the income stream. Thus high tax rates make consumption cheap in terms of forgone income, and the saving rate declines, resulting in less investment.

The 98 percent marginal tax rate on investment income that applied in Great Britain until recently provides a good illustration. A person in that high bracket can spend $100,000 on a Rolls Royce or invest it at 17 percent. On a pre-tax basis the cost of the Rolls Royce is to forgo an income stream of $17,000 per year, a relatively high price for a car. After tax, however, the value of that additional income stream is only $340 per year (the 2 percent of $17,000 remaining after taxes), which is all the Englishman has to give up in

3. On September 20, 1977, Mr. Rousselot cited the CBO and OMB replies in the *Congressional Record.* On June 28, 1978, he had the OMB reply printed in the *Record* in its entirety, and on July 11, 1978, Rivlin's reply in its entirety.

order to enjoy a Rolls Royce—a very low price indeed. This explains the paradox of why there are so many Rolls Royces on London streets at a time when England is in economic decline. The Rolls Royces are mistaken for signs of prosperity, when in fact they are signs of high tax rates on investment income. The principle involved is most easily illustrated by this extreme example, but it operates across the spectrum of tax rates.

The other important relative price governs people's decisions about how they allocate their time between work and leisure or between leisure and improving their human capital by upgrading their skills. The cost to a person of allocating another unit of time to leisure is the current earnings given up by not working (for example, overtime on Saturday) or the future income given up by not taking courses to improve skills. The value of the forgone income is determined by the rate at which additional income is taxed. The higher the marginal tax rates, the cheaper the price of leisure. Absenteeism goes up, willingness to accept overtime declines, and people spend less time improving their work skills.

Physicians who encounter the 50 percent tax rate after six months of work are faced with working another six months for only 50 percent of their actual earnings. Such a low reward for effort encourages doctors to share practices in order to reduce their working hours and enjoy longer vacations. The high tax rates shrink the tax base by discouraging them from earning additional amounts of taxable income. The high tax rates also drive up the cost of medical care by reducing the supply of medical services. A tax-rate reduction would raise the relative price of leisure to doctors and result in more taxable income earned and a larger supply of medical services.

The effect of tax rates on the decision to earn additional taxable income is not limited to physicians in the top bracket. Studies by Martin Feldstein at the National Bureau of Economic Research have found that in many cases the tax rates on the average worker leave almost no gap between take-home pay and unemployment compensation. Feldstein found that a 30 percent marginal tax rate made unemployment sufficiently competitive with work to raise the unemployment rate by 1.25 percent and to shrink the tax base by the lost production of one million workers. Blue-collar workers are not yet in the top tax bracket, although they are getting there. Many blue-collar families are taxed at 40 percent and higher, tax rates that once applied only to millionaires. But it is not necessary to go that high in the brackets to encounter disincentives. Take the case of a carpenter facing only a 25 percent marginal tax rate. For every additional $100 he earns, he is allowed to keep $75. Suppose his house needs painting and he can hire a painter for $80 a day. Since the carpenter's take-home pay is only $75, he would save $5 by painting his own house. In this case the tax base shrinks by $180—$100 that the carpenter chooses not to earn and $80 that he does not pay the painter.

Studies by Gary Becker at the University of Chicago have made it clear that capital and labor are employed by households to produce goods and services through nonmarket activities—for example, the carpenter paints his own house. Goods and services produced in this way are not subject to taxation. Therefore the amount of capital and labor that households supply in the market is influenced by marginal tax rates. The higher the tax rates, the more likely it is that people can increase their income by using their resources in nonmarket activities or in the underground economy. A clear implication of household economics is that marginal tax rates influence the amount of labor and capital that is used to produce taxable income.

Every year the Tax Foundation in Washington reminds us that the average taxpayer has to work the first four months and several days of the year for the government in order to pay taxes before starting to work for himself. But that is not the way it happens. The first part of the year taxpayers work for themselves. They begin working for the government only when their income reaches taxable levels. The more they earn, the higher up they move in the tax brackets and the more they work for the government until rising marginal tax rates discourage further work. The progressive income tax is perverse because it mismatches effort and reward. Each additional effort comes on top of existing effort, so the disutility to the individual of additional effort is high. But since the income from the additional effort goes on top of existing income, it is taxed at higher rates. So as efforts rise, rewards fall.

The progressive income tax was devised to "soak the rich." In practice it works as a barrier to upward mobility and discourages people from making their best effort. As a result, the tax system has made it more difficult for the average taxpayer to achieve financial independence. It is this barrier to success that supply-side economists want to remove. The greater the extent of private success, the smaller the need for public assistance and the lower the burden of government. Supply-side economics is not an antigovernment position. It simply accepts the fact that government is costly by nature and maintains that the greater the incentives and opportunities to earn income, the smaller will be the size and burden of government.

The debate with the Keynesian policymakers was not about whether tax cuts pay for themselves. It was about whether fiscal policy works by changing relative prices or by changing spending, and whether people respond to better incentives by working more and saving more.[4] If so, then the Keynesians were making the wrong policy choices by ignoring these supply-side effects.

Economists measure the degree to which the labor force, savers, and investors respond to higher rewards with a concept called "elasticity." If the elasticity of response is high enough, private saving will rise by the amount that tax rates are cut. In this case, the tax cuts would finance themselves through increased saving. At a lower elasticity, saving would still rise, but by an amount smaller than the tax cut. For example, saving might rise by 40 cents for every dollar that taxes were cut. In this case 40 percent of the tax cuts would be paid for by increased saving. If saving did not respond at all to a higher after-tax rate of return, then cutting tax rates would not cause the saving rate to rise. The Keynesians believed that the saving rate is not affected by the after-tax rate of return. As we shall see, some even argued that cutting taxes would cause people to work less and to save a smaller percentage of their income. In economic jargon, they argued that the elasticity of response was zero or even negative.

4. See Paul Craig Roberts, "Econometric Models, Economic Policy and Politics," *Congressional Record*, February 22, 1977, p. H 1308; "Econometrics and Politics," *National Review*, May 13, 1977, pp. 549–551; "Political Econometrics" (letter to the editor), *Wall Street Journal*, July 25, 1977; "The Breakdown of the Keynesian Model," *The Public Interest*, 52 (Summer 1978), pp. 20–33; "The Economic Case for Kemp-Roth," *Wall Street Journal*, August 1, 1978; "Caricatures of Tax-Cutting," *Wall Street Journal*, April 24, 1980; "Reagan's Tax Cut Program: The Evidence," *Wall Street Journal*, May 21, 1981; "The Tax Cut Will Help Saving," *Fortune*, August 24, 1981; David Meiselman and Paul Craig Roberts, "The Political Economy of the Congressional Budget Office," in *Carnegie-Rochester Conference Series on Public Policy*, vol. 10, ed. Karl Brunner and Allan Meltzer (New York: North-Holland Publishing Co., 1979), pp. 283–333.

Similarly, if people respond strongly enough to the better incentives of lower tax rates, they could generate enough new income or tax base for the government to recover the revenues that it lost by lowering the tax rates. This is the Laffer curve argument. Some tax cuts do pay for themselves in this way. The 1978 reduction in the tax rate on capital gains paid for itself, just as Senate Finance Committee Chairman Russell Long said it would, in spite of the Treasury's prediction to the contrary. Enough new capital gains were realized to make up for the lower tax rates. Similarly, some tax cuts pay for themselves in increased private saving. The accelerated capital cost recovery (ACRS) provision in the 1981 Reagan tax cut caused business-sector saving to rise (at least) by the amount of the revenue loss to the Treasury (most of the provision was repealed in August 1982 in a futile effort to reduce the budget deficit). In this case, government may collect less tax revenue and have to borrow more in the capital market, but the business sector has higher cash flow and needs to borrow less, so there is no upward pressure on interest rates.

The case for supply-side economics does not depend on whether tax-rate reductions fully pay for themselves in increased revenues or higher saving. Almost any reduction in marginal tax rates will partly pay for itself through higher revenues and partly through higher saving. If, for example, 40 percent of the revenues lost by cutting tax rates feed back to the Treasury from a higher economic growth rate, and 40 percent are covered by a higher saving rate, then 80 percent of the gross revenue loss would be paid for by the supply-side effects. That would leave only 20 percent to be covered by reducing the rate of growth of government spending. Thus tax cuts do not have to be paid for dollar for dollar in spending cuts in order to avoid deficits.

These were the supply-side effects that were being left out of policymaking. It meant that the policymakers could not tell the difference between a tax rebate, which encourages spending, and a reduction in marginal tax rates on new income, which encourages production; between lower average tax rates, which do not improve incentives, and lower marginal tax rates, which do; or between a deficit that uses up private savings and one that increases private savings. To Keynesians all of these policy options affected the economy in the same way—spending would increase.

The Washington establishment realized that the supply-side argument was a fundamental challenge to its concept of economic policy. By the time the Keynesians lost the debate, they had made some strange arguments against supply-side economics. For one, in her reply to Rousselot, Rivlin admitted that cutting tax rates would make leisure more expensive in terms of forgone earnings. Nevertheless, she said that cutting tax rates might actually cause people to work less. Since cutting taxes would let people make the same amount of money with less work, they might take their tax cut in the form of more leisure. In other words, she argued that people have a targeted level of income, and if you make it easier for them to reach their target, they will work less.[5] That would mean that if you make it harder for people to reach their target, they would work more. In Rivlin's version of supply-side economics, the way to get people to work harder is to raise their taxes!

Lester Thurow, professor at the Massachusetts Institute of Technology, has used this same reasoning to argue for a wealth tax. He assumes that people have a targeted level of wealth regardless of the effort they have to make to acquire it. Therefore, the more wealth is taxed; the harder people work in order to reach their target, and the revenues pour into the government's coffers. Here we have a sort of reverse Laffer curve, which might be named the "Thurow curve." Although Laffer may overestimate the response, he at least has people responding to better incentives in normal ways. The Rivlin-Thurow economic model is one in which people respond to better incentives by working less and to worse incentives by working more.

Rivlin argued that people would respond to a tax-rate reduction "by reducing their working hours ... and still maintaining their after-tax income." It is possible for an individual taxpayer to respond in the way Rivlin says, but if the population as a whole worked less, total income would fall and, therefore, so would individual income. The reason Rivlin lost the debate is that she could not be right without proving that her own Keynesian fiscal policy would not work either. Keynesians cut taxes in order to encourage higher spending, which they believe causes more real goods and services to be produced. But if people work less when their taxes are

5. The same argument is made about saving. If you cut taxes, people can make their target by saving a smaller proportion of their income—so the saving rate falls if you make saving more profitable.

cut, the total production of goods and services must fall, and higher spending would simply drive up prices.

It is a feature of our times that the view that better incentives cause people to work and save more was branded "voodoo economics" by Vice-President George Bush, a Republican, while the view that people work and save more the higher they are taxed enjoyed the favor of mainstream economic thinking. Modern economists pride themselves on their ability to speak in mathematical language. Yet here were economists making the mathematically impossible argument that taxpayers as a group could respond to a tax cut by working less, enjoying more leisure, and still have the same real incomes. A personal income tax cut per se does not make it possible to produce the same amount of real goods and services with less labor. Supply-siders have been ridiculed for making excessive claims for tax cuts, but not even Lafferites ever claimed that tax cuts are such powerful medicine that they make it possible to produce the same amount of goods and services with less labor and no increase in capital investment. Supply-side economists were accused of voodoo, but it was the other side that had found the alchemist's secret by which a tax cut could transform nonwork into a factor of production.

In her reply to Rousselot, Rivlin stated that "the models do tend to neglect the influence of tax rates and other incentives on aggregate supply and capital formation." Bert Lance and OMB did not hedge at all. Lance wrote to Rousselot on March 22, 1977. In clear, unambiguous language (something very rare in Washington), the OMB director stated: "It is true, to be sure, that these models do not include relative price effects caused by changing the individual income tax rate."

The campaign against Lance that later developed was in a way regrettable. It weakened a new Presidency at a time when an image of stability and strength was needed to counter a dangerous image of American weakness. The destruction of President Nixon, defeat in the Vietnam war, and arms negotiations that seemed to sanction Soviet nuclear superiority made the U.S. a less certain force in the world. An Ayatollah able to mobilize millions of people at will was not likely to take heed of an American leader who could not even protect his best friend. Much of the world must have perceived

Lance's troubles as flowing from his loyalty to Carter and not from his banking practices. The Washington establishment always works to isolate the President and to reduce him to ineffectiveness by driving away his loyal aides—if he succeeds in getting any appointed in the first place. It may be that the most dangerous position in Washington is that of loyal aide to the President. The town runs on envy and competitiveness, and none of the other players competing for the limelight wants any president to succeed. Naive pundits say that the economic and foreign policy problems of the modern world are too difficult for any president to handle successfully. But the truth is that these problems are minor in the scheme of things. The problem faced by presidents is that they are neither loved nor feared, but envied. The Washington establishment attempts to alleviate its envy by reducing presidents to a state that can be pitied.

The OMB staff report stated that it "is correct that Chase, DRI and Wharton econometric models do not include any relative price effects from an individual income tax rate reduction—no incentives to work longer, to work harder, to save more, to take greater risk, to be more innovative, etc. Disposable income is increased, which raises consumption, and that is the only direct effect." Paul O'Neill, deputy director of OMB, told Senator Taft the same thing:

Econometric models with which I am familiar, such as Wharton, Data Resources, and Chase take into account the impact of rising taxes upon aggregate demand but they generally do not take into account directly the effects of rising real tax rates upon work effort and saving. This is characteristic of short-run forecasts of the economy and represents a weakness of such models.[6]

Rousselot recognized an issue when he saw one. Scarcely a witness appeared before the Budget Committee that did not get grilled by Rousselot about tax-rate reduction, supply-side effects, and econometric models. Usually he pursued them beyond the hearing. On January 28, 1977, he asked the committee's recent witnesses to respond further for the record. Letters asking about the supply-side effects of reducing tax rates went to Treasury Secretary Blumenthal,

6. Letter dated December 27, 1976, to John R. Stark, executive director of the Joint Economic Committee. The letter provided answers for the record to questions from Senator Taft relating to Paul O'Neill's testimony on December 2, 1976.

Chamber of Commerce Chief Economist Jack Carlson, Council of Economic Advisers Chairman Charles Schultze, OMB Director Bert Lance, CBO Director Alice Rivlin, Joint Economic Committee Chairman Richard Bolling, Andrew Biemiller of the AFL-CIO, Otto Eckstein of Data Resources, and Richard Everett, director of economic forecasting for the Chase Manhattan Bank.

Rousselot pointed out to Everett, for example, that witnesses frequently tell the Budget Committee that "the reason people produce is that people buy." Such a statement indicates a particular view about how the economy is affected by a stimulus. It emphasizes the effects of stimulus on the demand side of the economy where it raises disposable income and total spending, thereby indirectly stimulating production as a response to the additional buying. "According to this theory," said Rousselot, "a stimulus in the form of a tax rate reduction does nothing more than give people more disposable income, which leads to more spending." Rousselot wanted to know if production was affected by other factors, such as profitability and after-tax rewards. If so, would not tax reduction affect the economy on the supply-side?

Some of the witnesses were too Keynesian to understand what Rousselot meant. But he elicited the right answer from Otto Eckstein. On February 22, 1977, Eckstein wrote to Rousselot:

I agree with your statement that a tax reduction enhances the supply of work effort and the incentives to invest. From this point of view, it is important to design fiscal measures so they reduce the marginal tax rates on households and business and reduce the distortion that the current tax system creates to private decision-making.

The Senate Finance Committee

The admission that economic policy ignored the supply-side of the economy was not enough to make supply-side economics respectable. That took an entrepreneur and a canny Democratic politician. The entrepreneur was Michael Evans, and the politician was Russell Long, chairman of the Senate Finance Committee.

Evans accepted the criticism of the econometric models. Normally, you might expect a person with a multi-million dollar stake in what was being criticized to be defensive.[7] But Evans responded with a proposal to build a supply-side model. The proposal was an inch thick and in my hands by June 1977. By then I was on the Senate staff working for Orrin Hatch on the Joint Economic Committee. The question was what to do with Evans' proposal. Hatch and I had been trying since April 19, 1977, to get Senator Jacob Javits, the ranking Republican on the Joint Economic Committee, to sign a joint letter to Chairman Richard Bolling asking for hearings on the econometric models. My criticism of the models had put me in touch with a number of distinguished academic economists who were willing to testify that the demand-side models were providing misleading policy prescriptions. Keynesian doctrine had a more powerful hold on economic policy than its declining academic reputation could justify. I believed that public hearings on the models would break the grip of the big spenders on the nation's fiscal policy.

Hatch, a freshman senator, had already been making himself unpopular in spending circles. On March 29 he told the Senate:

Today in the United States the budget of government is larger than the value of the national income of France or Germany. It is six times the size of the GNP of Sweden and 50 percent of the total production of the Soviet Union. In the United States government takes from Americans in taxes a sum greater than the combined value of every marketable good and service that the total population of France can produce in one year. Does anyone really believe that the American people receive in return from government services equal in value to the total production of the French nation? No one believes this. Yet it does not stop us from continually expanding the size of government. That is what shows whose interests are represented in Washington.

On May 13, 1977, when the Senate was dealing with the conference report on the first budget resolution for fiscal year 1978, Hatch was increasing the pressure. "Once again," he protested, "we have made it clear that the people who work and produce exist, in our eyes, only to fund our spending programs." He went on to point out:

7. Apparently at least one effort was made by one of the other model builders to organize a common front against my criticisms. See Michael Evans' letter to *Wall Street Journal*, August 30, 1979.

Five times this year the Congress has voted down permanent reduction in the personal income tax rates. Each time those of us who pushed for a tax reduction were told that there was no room in the budget. There was not any room in the budget for the spending programs either. But that did not keep us from spending. Any time that there is no room in the budget for spending, we find room in the deficit. This time there is a $60 billion deficit to accomodate the spending programs that could not find room in the budget. This Congress has never explained why there can be spending programs, but not tax cuts, when there is no room in the budget. However, this Congress has made it clear that it prefers spending money to cutting taxes. I do not share this preference, and neither do the American people.

Whether it was these outspoken challenges to the establishment of which Javits was a member, or Javits' staff denying a potential rival access to the committee forum, or simply Javits not wanting to annoy Bolling with the esoteric concerns of a new senator, Hatch was stonewalled on his request for model hearings.[8] If we could not get the committee even to hold hearings, we were not likely to get the committee to fund a new model that would help make the case for a new policy. Another avenue had to be found.

"When our tax law becomes counter-productive, it seems to me that we ought to do something about it." That was Russell Long, chairman of the Senate Finance Committee, lecturing witnesses at a hearing before the Subcommittee on Taxation on June 14, 1977. Long wanted to cut the tax on capital gains and was very concerned about the Treasury's static revenue estimates, which "have a way of being very, very far off base because of their failure to anticipate everything that happens." Tax law is supposed "to make money for the government," but "we are defeating our own purpose" because "we are moving on bad advice." The Treasury, Long complained, was always telling him that cutting taxes lost revenues and raising taxes gained revenues. He gave the example of the investment tax credit that brought money into the Treasury instead of losing revenues. The same was true of other taxes. He did not think it had cost the government any money when the top bracket was cut from 90 percent to 70 in the 1960s. Nor was the 70 percent rate a revenue

8. Javits never signed the joint request for hearings, but on July 13 he forwarded Hatch's request to Bolling. Hatch did not succeed in getting Bolling to hold hearings on the models.

raiser. "It would be my guess if you would reduce your top rate to 50 percent, you actually would make money."

Here was a powerful Democrat speaking supply-side language. His own experience and common sense contradicted the simplistic Treasury view that higher taxes meant higher revenues and vice versa. Long was convinced "that something has to be done to try to find somebody who knows more how to put the answer in the computer so that it comes out the right way." That was exactly what Michael Evans was proposing Chase Econometrics be employed to do.

Working through Senator Carl Curtis, the ranking Republican on the Finance Committee, Evans' proposal was brought to Long's attention. It was a lengthy process. Senators are so overburdened by the size and complexity of government that it is hard to get them to focus on anything other than a vote that directly affects their constituents. Ironically, it was the big spenders in the Senate who helped Curtis and Long to concentrate on acquiring a supply-side model. The spenders had been handing out the money faster than the economy could generate tax revenues and were worried about their programs running dry. Spending advocates like Kennedy and Muskie began arguing that the tax law was full of loopholes and that the money going out through these loopholes was the same as the money being redistributed through the spending programs. All of these "tax expenditures" should go through the Appropriations Committee, just like other expenditures. Here was a clear assault on the handout power of the Finance Committee. It was going to be curtailed, and the increased revenues were going to augment the handout power of the Appropriations Committee. That got the Finance Committee's attention.

In his letter to Senator Long, Curtis wrote:

As you know, the Finance Committee has never been able to get accurate revenue estimates for the tax changes that we consider and make. There have been occasions when the estimates produced by the econometric models have contradicted common sense. The inability to get accurate estimates has sometimes made it difficult for us, in the face of opposition, to do what is best for the future growth and prosperity of this country.

Long acted, and Michael Evans was given a contract to produce a supply-side model for the Senate Finance Committee. The level of threat posed by the tiny band of supply-siders to the Washington establishment made a quantum leap up the scale. The word went out that the wily Russell Long was a supply-sider and that he was arming himself with a weapon under construction by one of the "big three" econometric firms. That did a lot for the credibility of the supply-side movement. Few people in the policy process knew what supply-side economics was, but they now knew it was something.

The Finance Committee was the first committee to "go supply-side." The second was the Joint Economic Committee, which declared for supply-side in 1979 in a unanimous report. In the meantime Orrin Hatch bore the brunt of the battle in some bloody fights with the Senate Budget Committee.

The Senate Budget Committee

It proved to be much more difficult to organize the Senate Republicans around the new supply-side strategy. One major stumbling block was Senator Henry Bellmon, the ranking Republican on the Budget Committee, and the committee's minority staff. They were aligned with committee chairman Edmund Muskie. The official reason for the cooperation was that Bellmon was committed to the new congressional budget process and was not going to risk endangering it with partisan wrangling. Should anything happen to the budget process, the senator was said to be convinced that spending would go out of control. It apparently did not strike Bellmon that by justifying $60 and $70 billion deficits even in boom years, the budget resolutions themselves were putting spending out of control.

Among the frustrated Republicans who wanted to fight the Democrats on the issues, the story went around that Bellmon had sold out to the Democrats. The problem with this explanation is not just that it sounds ad hominem, but that it does not explain the lack of willingness to fight among many other Senate Republicans at that time. A different explanation is that a nonideological minority party, which is what the Senate Republicans were, does not have any fight in it. Thoroughly used to not running things, they do not make waves in exchange for occasionally being given something in appreciation for their cooperation. Only the truly committed swim upstream. The person who plays it safe does not collect the enemies who might eventually do him in.

This explains the position of minority staffers as well. A minority staffer is not only outnumbered and outgunned. In addition, the majority has effective ways of punishing a trouble maker. For example, information can be withheld. When the staffer cannot keep a senator apprised of committee developments, it looks as if he is not doing his job. The staffer's senator may find that there is never room in the committee's hearings schedule for a witness from his home state, or that the majority staff has especially strong arguments against his amendments. It is a much simpler life to keep your feet up on your desk, cooperate, and keep your boss fully informed. He may not be able to affect anything, but at least his ego will not have to contend with being denied information and minor requests. Whatever the reason, the minority staff on the Senate Budget Committee was more willing to resist Hatch than Muskie. Before the supply-siders could carry the policy fight to the big spenders, they had to hack their way through Senator Bellmon and his minority Budget Committee staff.

There were other obstacles. Big spenders were responding to the supply-side push for tax cuts by adopting the fiscally responsible tones of orthodox Republicans. Whenever tax cuts fought their way onto the agenda, the big spenders became born-again budget balancers. We are for tax cuts, they would say, but we cannot vote to worsen the deficit. Such statements usually came after they had just worsened the deficit by voting large spending increases.

In the first budget resolution for fiscal year 1978, the Democrats found room in the deficit for a 12.5 percent increase in spending, putting the projected deficit over $60 billion in the third year of economic recovery. When the second budget resolution came up September 9, 1977, a small band of supply-siders decided to expose the opposition to tax cuts for what it was. The plan was that Senator Roth would first offer an amendment to the budget resolution making room for a 10 percent reduction in personal income tax rates, with no offsetting spending cuts. When that was voted down because it would add $11.4 billion to the deficit, Senator Hayakawa would next offer the same tax cut paid for by a specific menu of spending reductions. When that was voted down, Hatch would then offer the same tax cut paid for with an across-the-board reduction in the spending projections of 2.5 percent. That would still allow a $40 billion increase in spending over the previous year or a 9.5 percent increase in federal spending. Hayakawa and Hatch were brave enough to risk the wrath of the spending constituencies in order to call the bluff of the Democrats (and some of their fellow Republicans).

A jealous Republican staffer, acting in the time-honored competitive way, alerted the majority leader's staff to what was afoot. The next thing we knew, Hatch had been called to the floor, Roth was nowhere in sight, and Robert Byrd, the majority leader, was demanding that Hatch call up his amendment first. It makes interesting reading in the *Record* to watch this freshman senator, miffed at being called to the floor with his scheme endangered, firmly and courteously stand his ground under tremendous pressure from the majority leader. Hatch fended off Byrd by calling up Roth's amendment for him and speaking to it until Roth arrived.

Born-again budget balancers began popping up everywhere on the floor of the Senate. Muskie opposed the Roth amendment because "it would face us with an increase in the deficit for 1978 of over $11 billion." Even worse,

it would result in a permanent tax cut which would close options or sharply reduce our options, for tax reform and to deal with some of the other problems with which we are confronted, such as the cost of national health insurance, the cost of welfare reform, some of the energy problems we face, some of the mass transportation problems we face, and some of the environmental problems we face.

Senator Bellmon did not like the Roth amendment either. Although "every member of Congress desires relief for the American taxpayer," he intoned, "we are equally desirous of balancing the budget and bringing our deficit under control." This from a man who was quite prepared for federal spending in 1978 to rise 39 percent more than inflation (as measured by the Consumer Price Index). Down to defeat went the Roth amendment, with 18 Republicans, 4 Democrats, and Harry Byrd (Independent) voting in favor of it.

Next was the Hayakawa amendment, and down it went with only 15 yeas. Now it was Hatch's turn to offer his amendment, and a stunning thing occurred. The debate was entirely between Hatch and Bellmon. Not a single Democrat, not even Muskie, rose to take on Hatch. They left Republican Henry Bellmon to do their work for them. Bellmon proceeded like a merciless trial lawyer, accusing

Hatch of wanting to cut $2.75 billion from the defense budget and $3.36 billion from social security—money that "goes directly out to the retired people." "There is 2.5 percent waste in every spending program," replied Hatch. Not so, said Bellmon. Down went the Hatch amendment with 19 yeas and 64 nays. Shortly thereafter, the inspector general of Health, Education and Welfare reported that HEW alone had lost $7 billion in waste, fraud, and mismanagement—over 4 percent of its budget and 61 percent of the tax cut that Hatch proposed.

It was during the debate on Roth's amendment that Hatch's fight with the Senate Budget Committee began over the econometric models. Hatch said that the Senate was being misled by the models and that economic policy was not taking into account the supply-side incentive effects of fiscal policy. Muskie denied it.

John Rousselot noticed the dispute, and on September 20, 1977, he informed the House of the statements he had received from CBO and OMB acknowledging that the models did not contain supply-side effects. On September 23 Hatch called the Senate's attention to Rousselot's remarks and sent a note to Bellmon. At this point Bellmon's staff miscalculated. They sent a letter to Hatch implying that the issue was too technical for senators, "involving error terms and regression coefficients." It was incorrect, Hatch was told, to say that the models do not take into account the supply-side effects. "Moreover," Bellmon's staff had him say, "based on preliminary discussions, I am beginning to believe that Mr. Rousselot may have overstated the response intended by Dr. Alice Rivlin." Rousselot of course had not overstated anything, since he quoted Rivlin directly.

Hatch came down on Bellmon and his committee staff like a ton of bricks. But he first did his homework. Bellmon's letter defending the Keynesian models was sent out to leading economists at Carnegie-Mellon, Stanford, the University of Rochester, and other universities. No support could be found for Bellmon's position, which economists variously described as "literally not correct" and "laughable." On November 23, 1977, Hatch sent his reply. He told Bellmon that his defense of the Keynesian models suggested that he and his staff were unfamiliar with matters of fact that were a matter of record. "Since many of us are convinced that Republicans would be more effective if they ceased supporting faulty econometric models that serve as ramps for Democratic spending programs, I would like to bring these matters of fact to your attention."

It was a very hard letter, but Hatch had little choice. He was being buffaloed. He could drop the issue, but he had the confidence to try to set the matter straight. To get the matter into the open, he sent copies of his letter to other senators. The minority staff of the Budget Committee panicked and made another mistake. Such a show of confidence by Hatch and his staff might infect other senators and staffers and leave Bellmon cooperating with Muskie all by himself. The minority staff director resorted to subterfuge. He sent out a memo on December 6 stating that "Michael Evans of Chase Econometrics is so disturbed by the Hatch comments that he is coming to Washington next week to clarify the issue." In fact, Evans was coming to Washington for exactly the opposite reason, to tell the congressional staff that the models ignored supply-side effects. Evans demanded a retraction and on December 21 wrote to the minority staff director: "I was quite pleased to hear that you have verbally retracted your erroneous statement concerning the purpose of my recent trip to Washington. I hope you have come to realize that we know very little about the impact of tax rates on aggregate supply and that an investigation of this area could, quite possibly, have vast policy implications." The letter was copied to Senator Hatch. To forestall any further attempts at misrepresentation, the Joint Economic Committee minority staff sent out memos on December 13 and December 19 reporting on the outcome of the meeting with Evans, whose "belief is that the major *econometric models do not capture the supply-side effects of macro-economic policy.*"

It was easier to win the battle than to occupy the conquered territory. Vested interests were not going to give way to fact alone, and there were not enough supply-siders to enforce the victory. The policy process continued to be dominated by policies that had visible short-term effects on aggregate demand, without considering their longer-term effects on incentives and productive capacity. The battle rolled on, and there was no end of ammunition for the supply-siders.

In December 1977 the Congressional Budget Office published a report titled "Closing the Fiscal Policy Loop: A Long-Run Analysis." CBO argued that economic growth, like full employment, depends on spending—which means not saving. For the economy to grow in real terms at an average annual rate of 5.16 percent over the next five years and balance the budget by 1982, there had to be a lot of spending. The threat to the necessary spending would be a personal saving rate that rose above 6 percent of disposable income. If the saving rate went above 6 percent, an increasing federal deficit would be necessary to offset the harmful saving so that the growth goal could be met. CBO was saying straight out that saving was a threat to economic growth. The report had obvious implications for the Kemp-Roth bill. Previously CBO had argued that lowering marginal tax rates would not succeed in raising the saving rate. Now CBO was completing the circle. If the Kemp-Roth bill were to succeed in raising the saving rate, it would be at the expense of its growth aims and the revenue feedbacks that higher growth promised.

CBO with its 200-person staff had the capacity to overwork the handful of supply-siders, but supply-siders rose to the occasion. At hearings before the Joint Economic Committee on June 13, 1978, Senator Hatch remarked that "we seem to have a magic formula here, if only it worked, whereby the less we save the more we demand, and the more we demand the faster we grow." Where, in other words, was investment in this formula, and how was investment to take place without saving? Rousselot asked the witnesses what they thought of the CBO view that saving is basically a bad thing because it reduces spending. Evans, no timid soul himself, replied: "The CBO study is actually a landmark in incompetency." The *Wall Street Journal* editorial page said the same thing on August 1, 1978.

The fight over the economic models went on so long and so hard because more was at stake than economic reputations. The real issue was political power. A supply-side tax cut would reduce the size of government relative to the private sector. It would be an inroad on the power that had been concentrated in Washington, and the prospect of a decline in political clout is not something to be cherished by the establishment. The political careers of many liberals depend on government action replacing private action. In the Keynesian model a sluggish economy is a good excuse for expanding government. In a supply-side model it is not.

In 1979 Hatch was appointed to the Senate Budget Committee. During committee discussions of the second budget resolution for

1980, Hatch had wanted to question the staff about the economic analysis on which the budget projections were based. He indicated that he was willing to defer his questions if the committee would arrange for hearings on the models, and on September 12, 1979, he wrote to Muskie reminding him that the chairman had agreed to take his request under consideration. Two weeks later on September 26 Hatch met with Alice Rivlin to discuss the analysis underlying the models used in the economic projections. The next day he again wrote to Muskie reminding him of his request for hearings. His meeting with Rivlin, Hatch said, had "reinforced in my mind the need for the Budget Committee to hold some hearings." On October 19 Hatch again wrote to Muskie reminding him of his request for hearings, in which he had been joined by Senator William Armstrong, a Republican from Colorado, who had become interested in the matter.

On October 24 Muskie answered. The work of the committee, plus upcoming Senate debates on energy, the windfall profits tax, and SALT II, would make it very difficult to schedule hearings any time soon. Instead Muskie offered Hatch hearings on limiting so-called uncontrollable spending, a matter about which Hatch had expressed concern earlier in the year.

What Hatch did not know at the time was that on October 4 John McEvoy, the staff director of the Senate Budget Committee, had already sent a memo to Muskie concerning Hatch's request for hearings. McEvoy had mixed feelings about Hatch's request. On the one hand he was tempted to have Hatch "off on this tangent, which few people know or care about outside the economics profession, rather than to leave him with time to become engaged with something that might be more serious." On the other hand, CBO Director Rivlin "doesn't really want to have hearings and would like us to put Hatch off somehow. She says that the critics of the models CBO uses for forecasting are an extreme right-wing claque who should not be given an audience, lest it legitimize their views and give Hatch a forum which ought to be denied him if we could."

Two years and seven months after it had been established that the economic models being used to formulate national economic policy did not take into account supply-side effects, the big spenders were still protecting their monopoly on public policy. Instead of facing the economic issue on its merits, the liberals attempted to deflect it by branding supply-siders "an extreme right-wing claque" pursuing ad hominem and ideological concerns. Hatch, McEvoy said, was "beyond the pale." What that meant, of course, as McEvoy made clear, was that Hatch had not gone along with Bellmon's cooperation with Muskie, always finding room in the deficit for more spending but adopting the fiscally responsible stance of a budget balancer whenever tax cuts were mentioned. McEvoy saw Hatch's fight for a change in economic policy as a "vindictive campaign against the [budget] process and Senator Bellmon."

Had the econometric models been able to stand any close public scrutiny, none of the subterfuge would have been necessary. Hearings would have been held and the "right-wing claque" discredited. The problem for the spenders was that the supply-siders held cards that could not be discredited in a straightforward manner. The econometric models were short-run in their outlook. They overlooked the effects on capital formation, work attitudes, productivity, long-term economic growth, and the price level of policies that focused on manipulating demand in the near term. The models were convenient for liberal politics, but over time they had gradually reduced the American economy to a state of "stagflation." Although McEvoy passed on to Muskie Rivlin's suggestions on how to manage the hearings if they had to be held, there was really no way to prevent the facts from coming out if hearings were held.

It is clear that Hatch, a junior Republican senator, was putting tremendous pressure on "business as usual." Such a thing was not supposed to happen. Muskie was gradually being worn down by frustration over this maverick. One day in committee, during the preparation of the first budget resolution for 1981, Muskie lost his temper in a dispute over defense spending and called Hatch "paranoid." When Hatch again brought up the question of the economic models, Muskie stormed from the room.

Hatch is tenacious but not rude, and Muskie's rudeness annoyed him. What Muskie did not know was that someone had anonymously sent Hatch a copy of the McEvoy memo. Hatch had not known what to do with it but now, duly provoked in the eyes of his committee colleagues, he laid it on the table. It was clear to all that Hatch's open campaign in behalf of an issue had elicited a personal campaign against him behind his back.

Senator Hatch had defeated a powerful chairman in his own

committee. It may have been this defeat that caused Muskie to resign his powerful Senate position to become a lame-duck secretary of state for part of the last year of the Carter Administration. It was a straw, perhaps, that broke the back of a proud man who was stymied by the growing success of the supply-side pressure on the spending machine. For two years Muskie had witnessed growing defections from the ranks. Marjorie Holt's substitutes to the first and second budget resolutions for fiscal year 1979 were only narrowly defeated in the House by less than a handful of votes, in spite of a Democratic majority of 115 seats. In the Senate, Democrats themselves had taken to tax and budget cutting with the Nunn amendment to the tax bill. It was clear that neither chamber had much stomach left for openly voting against a policy of cutting taxes and spending. And 1979 had begun with an entire Senate committee defecting from the Keynesian ranks.

The Joint Economic Committee

Between the years 1977 and 1979, the Joint Economic Committee of Congress underwent a change that put the committee in the forefront of economic thinking. As early as 1977, when the Democratic majority's economists were still plugging for more spending stimulus to keep the recovery alive, the Republican minority was advocating new ideas about economic policy.

In its 1977 annual report JEC had been in line with the Keynesian thinking of the Carter Administration and the Democratic majorities in both houses of Congress. The economic stimulus program of President Carter, as implemented by Congress in the third budget resolution for 1977, called for a one-time tax rebate and additional spending for job-creating programs resulting in a deficit of $70.3 billion. The Democratic majority on JEC, chaired by Representative Richard Bolling of Missouri, reported that the stimulative spending measure for 1977–78 "constitutes a necessary and desirable shift in the direction of fiscal policy."[9]

The 1977 JEC report went further than the Carter Administration in its spending-level recommendations for 1978. The 1978 Carter

9. *Annual Report,* Joint Economic Committee of Congress, 1977, p. 37.

budget provided for a deficit of $57.7 billion. The JEC majority felt that this was not enough. They recommended additional spending stimulus, which would bring the 1978 deficit to approximately $70 billion. The Democrats did

not welcome the continuation of large deficits. The alternative is worse, however, since it implies sluggish growth and continued high unemployment, with all their attendant social evils. We do not believe this deficit is inflationary, nor will it crowd the private borrowers out of credit markets or reduce private economic activity, given the present underutilization of the Nation's labor resources and private plant capacity (p. 43).

As a harbinger of the future, Senator Bentsen disagreed with the committee recommendations in a footnote.

Following Senator Kennedy's lead, the majority members of the committee urged a more activist role on the Council on Wage and Price Stability. "It would be foolhardy," the report said, "to believe that wage and price stabilization can be achieved without concerted efforts by the Government." The committee recommended measures such as requiring advanced notice of price increases and delays of "wage and price increases that could have serious inflationary effects on the economy" (p. 49). While the Democrats shied away from formally endorsing mandatory controls, their recommendations amounted to virtually the same thing.

The Republican minority view in the 1977 JEC report agreed with the Democratic majority on the need for stimulus in 1977 and 1978, but disagreed on what kind of stimulus was needed. The Republicans felt that a permanent tax reduction would be more useful than a one-time "pep-pill" tax rebate. They advocated moderate money supply growth as opposed to the higher growth that the Democrats wanted. And while they agreed with the majority on the need for increased business investment, they "disagree with the implication that increased demand alone will bring this about; such a view pays little heed to the need to assure workers an adequate wage and investors an adequate return" (p. 68).

The Republican members argued that the problem lay with supply and not demand:

We have had nearly $250 billion in deficits to stimulate demand over the last seven years, and the economic results have been less than perfect.

What has been stimulated instead is inflation. In fact, each dose of ill-timed government stimulation to fine-tune the economy has only created more inflation, more recession, and more stimulation, in a vicious circle (p. 71).

Committee Republicans warned that failure to focus on supply would lead to an early renewal of inflation, since expanded demand drives prices higher. Recognizing the importance of a permanent tax reduction, JEC minority members noted the positive influence a tax cut would have on incentives and on saving and investment, thereby accelerating job formation and economic growth.

Differences on economic policy continued with the publication of the 1978 JEC annual report. Democrats were beginning to see the weaknesses of their own suggestions of 1977, but they were, for the most part, in favor of plunging ahead with the same Keynesian demand-management policies. In their minority views, Republicans developed and refined their arguments for permanent tax reductions, monetary restraint, and an easing of the regulatory burden.

In the 1977 JEC midyear economic report, the Democrats had recognized that "inflation is the principal impediment to the recovery of the economy." Nevertheless, in 1978 they were suggesting additional stimulus for 1979. The additional stimulus this time was to come from an expansionary monetary policy. The majority thought that fiscal policy could no longer bear the "brunt of support" for the economy. Monetary policy should shed its preoccupations with attempting to slow inflation and to salvage the international condition of the dollar.

In the recovery from the 1975–76 recession, investment had lagged behind consumer spending. The problem of stimulating investment, the majority felt, could be solved by an expansionary monetary policy. Rapid growth in the money supply would provide enough money to finance both the public and the private debt, thereby eliminating any danger that a large budget deficit might crowd out private investment.

Even though the majority members of the committee were still constrained by Keynesian concepts, they were not in 1978 blind to the questions that were left unsolved by their policy recommendations: "Excess unemployment," they wrote, calls for expansionary policy, but this risks renewed inflation, while a high rate of inflation calls for restrictive policy, thereby risking high unemployment. Unfortunately, during the 1970s, inflation has hampered the implementation of the Employment Act by fostering the adoption of economic policies that slow economic growth and increase unemployment (p. 49).

The majority strongly condemned any attempt to deal with inflation through demand restriction, because of the "intolerable cost in terms of lost production and employment." They continued to be constrained by the "Phillips curve" tradeoff between inflation and unemployment and by relatively unsophisticated views of inflation that ignored expansionary monetary policy as a major culprit.

Since the majority endorsed monetary expansion and condemned demand restriction, the only vehicles left to deal with inflation were indexing (of spending programs but not the income tax) and income policies. The former seeks to soften the effects of inflation on the recipients of government benefits by increasing their benefits to match price increases. The latter attempts to control inflation by holding down the wages of taxpayers. The majority largely reiterated their suggestions of 1977, urging a stronger Council on Wage and Price Stability. (Senator Lloyd Bentsen, in an appended "Additional Views," dissented from the recommendations of his Democratic colleagues. He wrote: "We should know by now that wage and price controls cannot be imposed on our economy without exacting a heavy cost in the form of serious misallocation of resources, inefficient production, and the potential domination of our daily lives by faceless government bureaucrats.")

In contrast, the Republican minority had answers to the most difficult questions of the day. The minority views in the report argued that the problem was not how to stimulate demand without sparking further inflation, but how to increase productivity to overtake inflation. The way to increase productivity was to increase the incentives to work, invest, and save: "Anyone hoping for more rapid economic growth must be concerned with savings. Only that part of national income which goes into savings is available to cover investment and the government deficit." The minority went on to observe that "a higher rate of investment is necessary in the short run to bolster our current economic expansion. But in the long run as well, we need massive capital outlays" (pp. 94–95).

The JEC minority noted the importance of marginal income tax rates (the tax rate paid on the last dollar of income earned). Marginal income tax rates had been rising because inflation pushes taxpayers into higher tax brackets. In the minority's opinion, "it is very likely that marginal tax rates have risen to the point where they are causing a substantial reduction in this country's growth rate" (p. 98). In the name of economic growth, therefore, the Republicans strongly favored permanent tax reductions as opposed to one-time tax rebates.

Republicans agreed with Democrats in 1978 that it was essential to end the inflation that was destroying the economy. From that point of agreement, however, they went in distinctly opposite directions. Whereas the Democrats called for an income policy and monetary expansion, the Republicans said the only way to stop inflation was through "a gradual reduction in the growth rate of the monetary aggregates over many years" (p. 100). They disagreed with the majority that monetary policies had been too restrictive. "Indeed, rising inflation at home and reduced demand for the dollar overseas indicate that the dollar is, if anything, in excess supply" (p. 101). In opposition to the Democrats' solution, the minority argued that permanent tax reduction was a less inflationary way to increase investment than was monetary policy.

In his "Additional Views" Senator Roth criticized the Carter tax plan, which showed additional tax increases for nearly all income groups. He outlined his own "Tax Reduction Act," cosponsored by Congressman Kemp, to reduce marginal income tax rates for individuals across the board. Senators Hatch and McClure, in their "Additional Views," noted the shortcomings of econometric models in neglecting the effects of fiscal policy on supply.

Dissatisfaction with the worn-out Keynesian policies reached new heights with the appearance of the 1979 annual report of the Joint Economic Committee. Led by Senator Bentsen, the new chairman, and Representative Clarence Brown, JEC produced its first unanimous report in twenty years. It was a breath of fresh air. Stagflation, said the report, is the result of policies that have stimulated demand while retarding supply. The Democratic majority, including such liberals as Kennedy and McGovern, signed the report, thereby endorsing the supply-side approach that the Republican minority had been working toward for two years.

In the chairman's introduction, Bentsen recognized "an emerging consensus in the committee and in the country that the federal government should put its house in order and that the major challenges today and for the foreseeable future are on the supply side of the economy." Stagflation, the simultaneous drain on the economy by inflation and unemployment, had grown to become the single biggest problem facing America. The 1979 report suggested stimulating economic growth through investment and productivity gains. Increased productivity was to be achieved through spending restraint, moderate monetary policy, and reduced tax and regulatory burdens. The standard Keynesian notions that investment is inflationary, that saving represents a drag on the economy, and that spending will lead to economic growth regardless of the level of tax rates were absent from the report.

Previously JEC had tended to view inflationary policies as beneficial to economic growth. In 1979 this was replaced by the supply-side view. JEC now argued that inflation was very bad for economic growth because the replacement costs of the plant, equipment, and inventory used up in production are greater than the value of the depreciation allowances. The understatement of expenses causes profits to be overstated and overtaxed, thus reducing the earnings on investment. Less investment means less output. Fine-tuning demand is incapable of doing anything about this serious problem, since "even if demand is high, capital spending and the supply of output in general may be low if the after-tax real rate of return is inadequate." Supply-side incentives, concluded the committee, had "been badly neglected as a way of fighting inflation."

The 1979 annual report created a new ballgame. Here was the Congress' premier economic committee shifting the focus of economic policy to the supply side. "The greater the tax burden on a factor of production, the smaller the quantity of that factor that will be offered to the market. The greater the tax burden placed on production, the less production there will be." Policymakers must "alter the policy mix to encourage supply, reduce disincentives and raise the reward to production."

It could not have been encouraging to Muskie that JEC had declared against the kind of spending stimulus that the Budget Committee was so adept at providing. How was Muskie to fend off the tenacious Hatch when an entire joint committee of Congress controlled by the Democrats had crossed over to the supply side? Of course, part of the crossover was just politics. Democrats had noticed the success that supply-siders were having with the issue. The Republicans had beat them to the voters with the personal tax cuts, so the committee's Democrats put together a supply-side package to market to big business. Republicans on the committee, such as Rousselot, pointed out that their Democratic colleagues were more interested in cutting business taxes than personal taxes. The Democrats did partly succeed in making an alliance with big business, and the alliance did succeed in holding the 1981 personal tax cuts hostage to a generous business tax cut. In fact, they did better than that. When Ronald Reagan signed the tax bill in August 1981, the business part was retroactive to the previous January and the individual tax cuts, which had been the cutting edge of the movement, were delayed until 1982 and 1983.

In addition to the politics, however, JEC's crossover was sincerely motivated. Many members understood that it was necessary to clean up the incentive structure for economic growth and to throw out the penalties on production that hindered the nation's success. In 1980 JEC followed up its pathbreaking report of the previous year. The title of the 1980 report—"Plugging in the Supply Side"—illustrates the prominence supply-side economics had achieved.

The 1980 report reaffirmed the recommendations of the previous year. "America does not have to fight inflation during the 1980s by periodically pulling up the drawbridge with recessions that doom millions of Americans to unemployment." As Chairman Bentsen put it in his introduction to the report, "steady economic growth, created by productivity gains and accompanied by a stable fiscal policy and a gradual reduction in the growth of the money supply over a period of years, can reduce inflation significantly during the 1980s without increasing unemployment." "Traditionally," the committee said, "tax cuts have been viewed solely as countercyclical devices designed to shore up the demand side of the economy," but now a tax cut was needed to increase saving and investment. JEC again recommended that government spending should decline as a percentage of GNP, and that a regulatory budget should be adopted to control the enormous costs being inflicted on the economy by regulation.

The 1979 and 1980 JEC reports were, like the Holt and Nunn amendments of 1978, Reaganomics before Reagan. The bankruptcy of Keynesian policy and its inability to provide solutions to the basic economic problems confronting the country was the explanation for JEC's conversion to supply-side economics. The failure of the old policies is dramatically reflected in the 1978 report. The recommendations of the majority proved weak and inconsistent, particularly on the issues of inflation and productivity. In contrast, the minority views offered a coherent and practical solution to the economy's woes.

The JEC's 1979 annual report seriously inconvenienced the traditional Republicans and liberal Democrats who tried to interpret the 1978 elections in a way that would push the tax-cut issue off the stage. Running on tax cuts, Republicans had enjoyed their greatest success in years, winning 57 percent of the Senate races, capturing six governorships, and gaining 300 seats in state legislatures. Yet pundits were writing about "almost universal" agreement that the Republicans had made a political blunder of the first magnitude by basing their campaign on the Kemp-Roth bill. The pundits who were trying to ensconce this verdict were a self-serving crowd. There were economists campaigning to have their issues adopted instead, contenders for the 1980 Republican presidential nomination who were not associated with the tax-cut issue, and big spenders who could find no other way to defuse tax-cut politics than to become born-again budget balancers. In the midst of all these self-serving declarations of the political failure of the tax-cut issue, JEC unanimously declared for supply-side. It knocked the stuffing out of the campaign to paint the tax-cut issue as a political blunder, but it was not to be the last time that traditional Republicans, liberal Democrats, and the media would gang up on the tax cuts.

"We are meeting here today at a rare moment of opportunity for supply-side economics," testified economist Otto Eckstein. The long effort to call attention to how the econometric models were warping the country's economic policy and growth potential finally paid off, and on May 21, 1980, the Joint Economic Committee held hearings on the models. The witnesses were the three major model builders, Otto Eckstein, Michael Evans, and Lawrence Klein; their customer, CBO's Alice Rivlin, who stressed that she was just a buyer of the standard services with no model of her own; and a supply-sider, Norman Ture, who had made the first efforts to develop a supply-side model.

Senator Bentsen called the hearing to order. He disavowed the Keynesian tradeoff between inflation and unemployment, stating that he was "convinced that we do not have to put people out of work to control inflation." The goal of the next decade, he said, "should be to fight inflation and unemployment through supply-side incentives to put more goods on the shelf." He and the ranking Republican, Clarence Brown, announced that the era of the quick fix was over. The committee wanted to know from the model builders if they had got around to plugging in the supply-side.

In most respects it was a different world from the one I had come upon several years before. Rivlin, flanked by her econometricians, moved quickly to "associate myself strongly with the general tone of your remarks, Mr. Chairman, and Mr. Brown's, about the importance of supply and productivity." The models, she said, are designed primarily for analyzing the short-run effects of policies and "cannot be relied on to predict the outcome of proposed policies that would fundamentally change the structure of the economy." The models had not been helpful in analyzing many tax changes, including the effect of marginal tax rates on work attitudes and saving. But the model builders were moving to incorporate the hitherto missing supply-side effects. "The DRI model," she testified, "shows somewhat larger effects from tax cuts than in the past," and "the Evans model is expected to show even larger effects." She now saw supply-side tax cuts as important tools for achieving higher economic growth.

Eckstein testified that "the mistake we have made over the last 20 years is that we have always looked at the short-run demand effects, and have thereby ignored what we are doing to the long-run growth potential of the economy." He admitted that "one of the things that we did not do very aggressively was to focus on the question of the effect of the tax system on the supply of labor, the supply of saving."

But when Klein's turn came, the clock was turned back to pre-February 1977: "I think there is a great misconception that econometric models have neglected supply." It was all "loose talk and rhetoric." It became clear that Klein still had no idea what supply-side economics was. He thought it involved input-output tables showing the physical flow of resources in the economy—for example, X number of new houses requires Y new gallons of paint. "The heart of supply-side modeling," he said, is "the whole problem of interpreting the energy crisis, the oil embargo, the high rise in oil prices, and limitations on the availability of other natural resources." Here was a Nobel laureate who did not even know what the discussion was about. "The problem that we face is that there is a tendency to identify supply-side economics with tax incentives on worker productivity and worker effort." Klein was out to redefine supply-side economics. There could not be much to the supply-sider's own version of it, Klein thought, because cutting taxes lets people reach their targeted income level faster. Repeating Rivlin's erroneous arguments of three years earlier, Klein said that people might simply take their tax cut in the form of increased leisure. "It is very difficult to repeal the law of economics called the 'backward bending supply curve of labor,' " so the net effect of the tax cut might be to reduce work.

It was obvious that Klein, adviser to Washington policymakers, had not followed the economic policy discussion of the previous three years. As a result, he confused the effect on labor supply of an increase in productivity or technology with the effect of a reduction in marginal tax rates. An improvement in the tools and technology with which labor works allows more goods and services to be produced with fewer working hours. In such a case, it is possible for workers to enjoy more leisure and more goods and services as part of a rising living standard. But reducing personal income tax rates cannot result in higher income unless people respond to the better incentives by working more. If everyone responded to a tax cut by working less, total production would fall. Therefore, people cannot maintain their living standard if they respond to a tax cut by increasing their leisure.

Except for Klein, the witnesses had adapted to supply-side economics. Eckstein testified that under current law the economy was facing large tax increases (the scheduled payroll tax increases), and it would be dangerous not to offset them with tax cuts. "It is very hard to see how you could not make some moves for 1981, since you will be looking at major tax increases on January 1st." He warned against only partially offsetting these tax increases. His model showed that a reduction in personal income tax rates together with a tighter monetary policy would increase real GNP and lower infla-tion. Two years later Eckstein had forgotten these remarks. On April 29, 1982, we were on a panel together at the annual meeting of the Eastern Economic Association. Eckstein argued that the Reagan tax cuts, which barely offset the higher taxes from social security and bracket creep (see Table 1), were massive and went too far. He criticized the "contradictory" policy of lower taxes and lower money growth that he had endorsed in his JEC testimony and that Reagan had adopted. Five months later he changed his mind again, and the *Washington Post* quoted him: "Let's face it. In the end it turned out that [the tax cut] was not enough to lift the economy" (September 4, 1982).

Consistency is not a feature that characterizes the politics of eco-nomic policy. The survivors of Washington's policy debates are the quick-change artists who can doff and don their policy positions while they dance around the issues. Brown and Rousselot did not let Rivlin's dancing go unremarked. Brown told her that she sounded very supply-side, but what about that memo to Muskie, which had recently surfaced, denouncing supply-siders as a "right-wing claque"? Rivlin answered: "I cannot be responsible for people mis-quoting me." Brown then asked her if his impression was correct

Table 1. Net Tax Cut (−) after Bracket Creep and Payroll Tax Increases (in current dollars)

Income	1981	1982	1983	1984	1985	1986	1987	1988
$15,000	145	88	56	32	90	111	116	122
$20,000	199	108	21	−34	40	65	68	72
$25,000	253	139	−34	−107	−22	6	5	4
$30,000	306	171	−49	−136	−37	−4	−5	−6
$40,000	517	318	52	21	180	265	373	477

Table based on the administration's economic assumptions as of April 1982 and assumes cost-of-living increases to keep real pre-tax income constant over the period.

"that you are anxious to try to embrace consideration of the supply-side economic arguments in the budget model?" She replied that "any reading of CBO reports and discussion of the last couple of years, or particularly the last few months, would indicate that we are intensely interested in the supply-side."

It was too much for Rousselot, who remembered "very well just a few years ago when I was on the Budget Committee writing you letters and receiving letters in return, a kind of downgrading of the whole idea." Rivlin invited him "to look back at those letters." "Funny you should bring it up," Rousselot replied. "I have them right here. Do you want me to read them?" The room laughed.

The point of this story is not to poke fun at Alice Rivlin, who ably represented the Keynesian point of view, but to show that by May 1980 no one wanted to be on the wrong side of supply-side economics. By then even Klein had declared himself a supply-sider, although he had his own definition of what that meant. It was only after the President's own men had mismanaged the tax-cut issue, as I feared they would,[10] that it again became fashionable to criticize supply-side economics. The Washington policymaker has a finger ever in the wind. If supply-side economics is blowing, everyone is going to take credit for it, even to the exclusion of the responsible parties. In the celebratory awards that accompanied the Reagan Administration's tax-cut victory, the supply-siders were left out. Even the Treasury's award went to a man who was in no way identified with the supply-side movement or was ever more than lukewarm toward it. I remember telling one of my deputies, a man who had spent five years of his life fighting hard and brilliantly for the issue, not to be upset that his role was not acknowledged. I recommended an apropos movie, *The Dragonslayer,* that was playing at the time. When the fearful beast was slain, everyone who said it could not be done was taking credit, and the real victors were pushed off the stage.

These standard forms of personal competition sometimes result in more than injustice. At the JEC hearings on the economic models, Michael Evans had testified that personal tax cuts have strong posi-

10. See my "Political Economy" columns in *Wall Street Journal* on October 24, 1980, December 18, 1980, January 22, 1981; and my article, "Reaganomics: A Change?" *New York Times,* November 9, 1980.

tive effects on the economy. The Kemp-Roth bill combined with a limit on government spending (holding it constant in real terms) would allow the budget to be balanced by 1984. (Evans, of course, did not anticipate that the tax cuts would be delayed while the Federal Reserve implemented a recessionary six-month freeze on the growth of the money supply.) A year later the Treasury was locked in a policy dispute with the Office of Management and Budget over the effects on the economy of the President's economic program. As assistant secretary for economic policy I requested that the Treasury subscribe to Evans' model in order to counter OMB's negative image of the President's program. My request was blocked by my old comrade-in-arms, Norman Ture, then a Treasury undersecretary, on the grounds that Evans' model was not an authentic supply-side model. That left the initiative in OMB's hands, and the Treasury was reduced to trying to keep the fires OMB was starting from consuming the President's program.

3

The Spreading Revolution

REGARDLESS OF THE DEFECTS OF THE ECONOMETRIC models, the supply-side revolution would not have occurred in a successful economy. Supply-side economics became an issue because the economy's performance had been deteriorating for over a decade. As Chart 1 shows, economic performance previously deemed unacceptable became unattainable as both inflation and unemployment rates rose. As an example, the year 1979 capped a four-year period of expansion, but the unemployment rate in that year was nearly one full percentage point higher than the recession year of 1970. The deterioration in the economy's performance was worrisome, and it created an environment in which new policy ideas could get a hearing.

Americans are accustomed to being "people of plenty," but developments over the past decade indicate that this reputation is no longer deserved. Statistical measures show that the engine of plenty is running down. The rate of growth of labor productivity has declined rather drastically since 1968. The growth of output per work-hour averaged 3.1 percent annually between 1948 and 1968 and declined to 2.1 percent between 1968 and 1973. From 1973 to 1980, productivity growth in the private business sector averaged only 0.6 percent per year, one-fifth of the rate over the twenty-year period ending in 1968. In 1979 and 1980 productivity growth was negative, that is, productivity actually fell.

Not only has U.S. productivity growth slowed, it has lagged far behind the performance of our leading trading partners. When I was a student studying economics and management, we were told that

INFLATION AND UNEMPLOYMENT RATES

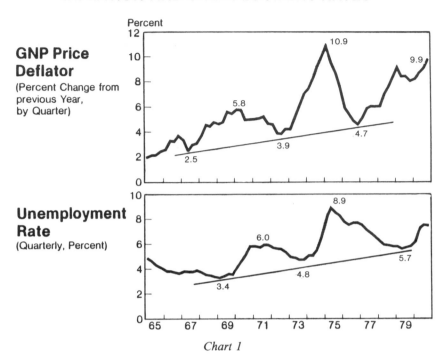

GNP Price Deflator
(Percent Change from previous Year, by Quarter)

Unemployment Rate
(Quarterly, Percent)

Chart 1

we did not have to worry about high American wages. American workers were much more productive than their foreign counterparts because they had much more capital with which to work. That is something we can no longer take for granted. International productivity comparisons for the manufacturing sector prepared by the U.S. Department of Labor show the United States with a 1.7 percent rate of growth in 1973–1981, compared with 6.8 percent for Japan, 4.6 percent for France, 4.5 percent for Germany, 3.7 percent for Italy, and 2.2 percent for the United Kingdom. Only Canada, with its 1.4 percent rate of productivity growth in manufacturing, lagged behind the performance of the land of plenty.

The consequences of declining productivity growth are well known. Our products become less competitive in markets both at home and abroad, and pressures for protection rise. Declining productivity growth means a slower rise in living standards, and when it is combined with taxflation—the combination of inflation and rising marginal tax rates—it becomes a fight just to hold on to existing living standards.

As inflation rose from less than 2 percent a year in the first half of the 1960s to 13.3 percent in 1979, people sought to protect their purchasing power by arranging for their wages and salaries to rise with inflation. However, since our tax system taxes nominal or money income, and not purchasing power, the higher wages and salaries pushed people into higher tax brackets. Since the IRS took a bigger and bigger bite out of each pay increase, many people experienced a constraint on their living standard. Data from the Bureau of the Census show no increase in median family income from 1969 to 1980.[1]

There are some obvious reasons for the productivity slowdown. The capital-labor ratio, a measure of the plant and equipment available to the average worker, has been falling. The decline reflects both increased growth of the labor force and a slowdown in the rate of capital formation. The decline in the growth of capital per worker means slower productivity growth. The decline in productivity is not unrelated to economic policy. For fifteen years macroeconomic policy has been directed at managing aggregate demand. Taxes and expenditures were manipulated to move the economy toward target levels of spending. It was taken for granted that the nation's ability to produce—the supply side of the economy—depended only on adequate demand.

By focusing on demand, policymakers in Washington overlooked the rising disincentives to produce additional income. The combination of inflation and a progressive income tax pushed potential savers into higher tax brackets and reduced incentives to save. A median-income family of four faced a federal marginal tax rate of 17 percent in 1965. By 1981 the rate was 24 percent—a 41 percent increase in the rate of tax on additions to the family's income. If social security taxes and state income taxes are added in, the median income family is in the 40 percent bracket or higher. A family with twice the median income saw its top federal bracket nearly doubled, rising from 22 percent in 1965 to 43 percent in 1981. The sharp upward rise in marginal tax rates had an adverse effect on saving, because for most people income from saving and investment is added on top of wage and salary income and automatically taxed at the top rate.

1. *Economic Report of the President*, 1982, table B-27, p. 264.

The adverse effect on saving was compounded by government-imposed ceilings on interest rates, so that many households could only obtain negative real after-tax rates of return on their savings, that is, they got less than the inflation rate. The personal saving rate dropped. From 1976 through 1980 the personal saving rate averaged only 6.1 percent, one of the worst five-year periods in the postwar era, and substantially below the 7.8 percent average rate from 1966 to 1975. The decline in the personal saving rate reduced the funds available to the capital market by $130 billion over those five years.

The rising marginal tax rates also undermined work attitudes and the incentive to upgrade skills, since the after-tax reward for extra effort was low. The results were a rise in absenteeism, growing unwillingness to accept overtime work, and a decline in the effectiveness with which the existing capital stock was utilized. In a hearing before the Joint Economic Committee on May 21, 1980, Representative Clarence Brown took issue with the claim that tax rates do not significantly affect the work attitudes of full-time employees. There had recently been a six-month strike at International Harvester in Ohio, and one of the issues was the ability of the company to assign overtime to its employees and expect them to report to work. Owing to high marginal tax rates, the employees did not want compulsory overtime. Brown said that he knew tax rates affected employees' work attitudes because "I have had them explain this issue to me on a very personal basis in short Anglo-Saxon expressions."

The combination of inflation and tax-depreciation law caused the cost of replacing the plant, equipment, and inventories used up in production to be understated. In the nonfinancial corporate sector, the replacement value of inventories and fixed assets were understated by $262 billion over the 1976–1980 period. This impaired business saving and, together with the decline in personal saving, the funds available to the capital market were reduced by an amount larger than the accumulated federal budget deficits over the five-year period.

The understatement of depreciation overstated corporate profits, raising the effective rate of corporate taxation above the statutory rate. As Table 2 shows, when book depreciation allowances are adjusted to a replacement cost basis, corporate profits have been taxed higher than the statutory rate for more than a decade, averaging 56 percent in the 1970s and reaching 77 percent in 1974.

The stop-go demand-management policies during the 1970s created additional uncertainty. No one knew for sure when the policy of expanding demand would give way to contracting demand, and vice versa. This additional element of uncertainty compounded the difficulties of planning, thus raising the "hurdle rate of return" that must be met before new investment commitments are made. All these factors, along with government regulation and inflationary money growth, combined to reduce the rate of private capital formation, to curb business investment in research and development, and to divert resources to nonproductive purposes and into the "underground economy." The overall result was the marked deterioration in our productivity performance that the record shows (see Chart 2).

Over these same years the indictments of our economic institutions have been severe. The market economy is too often portrayed not as an institution that allows individuals to better themselves, but

Table 2. Effective Corporate Tax Rates

1960	54.1%
1961	53.4
1962	47.0
1963	46.2
1964	43.3
1965	42.0
1966	43.3
1967	43.3
1968	49.3
1969	53.8
1970	58.4
1971	53.6
1972	50.4
1973	55.9
1974	76.8
1975	53.9
1976	53.6
1977	49.7
1978	50.9
1979	56.4
1980	58.6

Nonfinancial corporate profits tax liabilities as percent of corporate profits with inventory valuation adjustment and depreciation of fixed assets adjusted to replacement costs at double-declining balance over 75 percent of Bulletin F service lives.

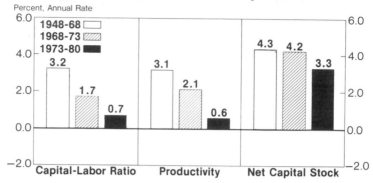

Rates of Growth in the Capital-Labor Ratio, Productivity, and Real Net Capital Stock

Percent, Annual Rate

Legend:
- 1948-68
- 1968-73
- 1973-80

Capital-Labor Ratio: 3.2, 1.7, 0.7
Productivity: 3.1, 2.1, 0.6
Net Capital Stock: 4.3, 4.2, 3.3

Note: Capital-labor ratio is real net capital stock (gross stock less replacement requirements and pollution abatement expenditures) in the private business sector divided by the civilian labor force (excluding government).

Productivity is output per hour of all persons in the private business sector.

Chart 2

as a relentless machine for grinding the poor and unfortunate under the heel of greed. Allegations of market failures and social costs helped to transform our economic institutions. New rights have been created which give some people claims, known as entitlements and transfer payments, to the income of others. Relentlessly over the years the positive incentives of a productive society have been increasingly crowded out by the perverse incentives of a transfer society. As transfer programs became competitive with production as the source of income for larger numbers of people, more and more work effort was allocated away from producing income toward acquiring income transfers through political action. By drawing resources away from the production of new income, the expansion of the transfer economy contributes to economic decline.

The growth in transfer income contrasts starkly with the stagnation in the real earnings of a full-time worker after federal income and social security taxes are deducted. Unpublished Treasury Department estimates show that real after-tax earnings for the typical worker did *not* increase between 1967 and 1981. Between 1972 and 1981 they declined by 0.7 percent per year. Between 1976 and 1981 they declined by 1.3 percent per year. In contrast, while the real after-tax median earnings from a normal workweek of a full-time married male remained unchanged between 1967 and 1981, real social security benefits increased by 20 percent.

The tax system together with inflation encouraged the accumulation of debt instead of equity. Many people found that the only way they could "save" at all was to go into debt and rely on taxflation to push up the value of their homes and depreciate the value of their mortgages. Businesses were equally encouraged by the tax system into becoming debt-dependent. Their depreciation allowances were confiscated by taxflation, which reduced their cash flow and curtailed internal financing. Since payments to equity must be made from taxable income but debt service is tax deductible, business became increasingly debt-dependent. Concerns arose that the monetary policies necessary to control inflation and to change these perverse incentives could result in liquidity problems and threaten the asset values that underpin the debt structure.

While higher taxes were lowering our standard of living, a new tax was taking shape on our external relations with the rest of the world. I have called it the weakness tax.[2] It will grow as the world perceives and exploits our loss of economic, military, and diplomatic supremacy. Weakness leads to accommodation, and accommodation signals to the world that aggressive demands on the United States earn a high rate of return. As we respond to demands with negotiations and concessions, the demands multiply. To let one's power slip is to experience increasingly uncomfortable and hard demands. Because an incentive structure has been established that encourages others to make demands of us, the situation will be difficult to rectify.

When I began my professional life, the United States was unquestionably the world's richest nation. But when the 1981 *World Bank Atlas* was published in early 1982, the U.S. ranked ninth in terms of per capita income, a fall of three places from the previous year's report. There are problems with the conventional measures of international per capita income comparisons, and it is probably not true that we are only number nine on the list of the richest nations. Nevertheless, the World Bank report challenges the perception of Americans as people of plenty.

If there is decline, it is not inevitable. Economic performance is

2. See my "Political Economy" column, *Wall Street Journal*, March 20, 1980.

affected by policy. If the wrong policy over a number of years has worsened our economy's performance, a better one can improve it. The political opponents of tax reduction claim there is no evidence that supply-side economics can do any better than the Keynesian policies that led the economy into decline. Actually there is strong evidence in behalf of supply-side economics. The Mellon tax cuts of the 1920s, named after Treasury Secretary Andrew Mellon, whose full-length portrait presides over the secretary's conference room at the Treasury Department, produced a noninflationary economic boom.[3] Tax revenues increased, particularly from the rich, and Mellon was able to pay off 36 percent of the national debt during the decade of the 1920s.

Closer to our own time there are the Kennedy tax cuts, which took effect on January 1, 1964, and January 1, 1965, and reduced marginal rates on personal income by an average of 20 percent. Since almost all the economists in the United States in the 1960s and 1970s were Keynesians, the Kennedy tax cuts have been studied from the demand-side point of view. The economic boom that resulted has been interpreted as a consumption-led expansion caused by higher spending. In actual fact, after the tax cut went into effect, *people spent a smaller percentage of their income.* Chart 3 relates consumer spending to disposable income.[4] The dotted line shows the path consumer spending would have taken if people had continued consuming the same percentage of their incomes after the tax cut as before. The solid line shows actual consumption expenditures. By 1967 consumption was at least $17.5 billion below the previous trend—a sum larger than the size of the personal income tax cut (measured in constant dollars).

If consumers were spending a smaller percentage of their income, they had to be saving a larger share. And, indeed, the empirical record shows that personal saving rose sharply. Chart 4 shows the behavior of personal saving and the saving rate. There was a marked increase in the real volume of personal saving following the

3. See "The Mellon and Kennedy Tax Cuts: A Review and Analysis," a staff study for the Subcommittee on Monetary and Fiscal Policy of the Joint Economic Committee (Washington, D.C.: U.S. Government Printing Office, June 18, 1982).

4. See Paul Evans, "Kemp-Roth and Saving," *Weekly Letter,* Federal Reserve Bank of San Francisco, May 8, 1981. The Treasury reestimated Evans' work and confirmed the validity of the chart. See Paul Craig Roberts, "The Tax Cut Will Help Savings," *Fortune,* August 24, 1981, pp. 44–45.

Real Consumer Expenditures

Actual Compared with Predicted Values
from a "Keynesian" Consumption Function

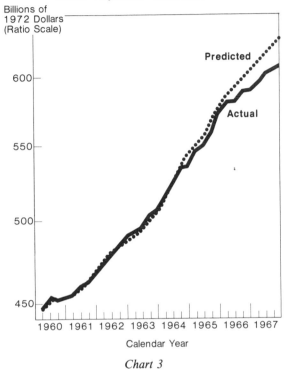

Chart 3

tax cut, and the saving rate, which had been declining during the early 1960s, also rose sharply. It remained high for a decade until rising marginal tax rates pushed it down.

Table 3 is a Treasury estimate of the impact of the Kennedy tax cut on personal saving. In 1964 real personal saving rose $6.6 billion above the trend growth prior to the tax cut. The gain in saving was 74 percent of the size of the tax cut. In the next two years saving increased $10.2 and $10.8 billion above the previous trend, a gain equal to 72 percent of the tax cuts. In 1967 saving was $19 billion above the previous trend—a gain equal to 121 percent of the size of the tax cut.

During the debate over President Reagan's tax-reduction program, critics said that saving would not increase much because people would only save a small part of their tax cut. The critics were

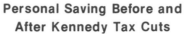

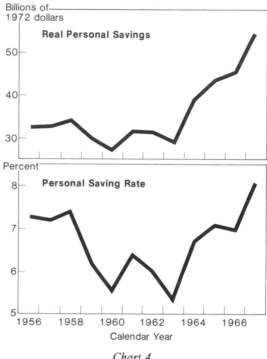

Chart 4

thinking only about how much of the difference in withholding would be set aside in savings. They ignored the effect of better incentives on both the rate of saving and the rate of economic growth. A higher saving rate applied to a higher growth in income can produce a substantial rise in saving. That explains why the gain in saving in 1967 was larger than the tax cut.

The rise in saving, by releasing real resources from consumption, assisted a rapid growth of business investment. In real terms capital spending had grown at an annual rate of 3.5 percent during the 1950s and the early 1960s through 1962. During the remainder of the 1960s real capital spending rose over twice as fast, rising 7.3 percent annually. While growth was high in the corporate sector, small business investment posted the greatest acceleration.

The acceleration in investment greatly enhanced the economy's ability to produce. The net stock of capital had grown by 3.8 percent annually between 1949 and 1963, but with the tax cuts it rose to 5.5 percent for the remainder of the decade. Keynesians claim that the investment boom resulted from the investment tax credit, but the sharp rise in investment could not have taken place if consumers had not released resources from consumption by saving a larger share of their incomes.

The saving response makes clear that if a widening budget deficit had resulted from the tax-rate reductions, the larger saving pool would have removed its sting. As it turned out, the federal budget moved close to balance in 1965. It was only after the expansion of federal expenditures to pay for the Vietnam war and Great Society programs that the budget moved into deficit. Chart 5 shows why the budget position was favorable in spite of—or because of—the tax cut. In real terms, federal revenues increased sharply and far outdistanced the trend growth in revenues.

In testimony before the Joint Economic Committee of Congress on February 7, 1977, Walter Heller made these same points. He told the committee that the 1964 tax cut

Table 3. Gains above Trend in Real Personal Saving after the 1964 Tax Cut (billions of 1972 dollars)

Year	Trend real disposable income without tax cut[a]	Trend real personal saving without tax cut[b]	Actual real personal saving[c]	Gain over trend in real personal saving with tax cut[c]	Gain in real personal saving as percent of tax cut[d]
1964	$559.1	$32.4	$39.0	$ 6.6	74%
1965	576.4	33.4	43.6	10.2	72
1966	594.3	34.5	45.3	10.8	72
1967	612.7	35.5	54.5	19.0	121

a. Values of real disposable income that would have developed had the trend of 1959–1963 been maintained.

b. Real personal saving that would have been associated with that income path had households maintained the 5.8% saving rate of the 1960–1963 period.

c. Actual real personal saving and the difference between that actual volume and the calculated values of the pre-tax cut trend (second column).

d. Ratio of the gain in saving above trend to the real value of the personal tax cut. The saving gain in 1964–1966 was about three-fourths of the tax cut, while the increment to saving in 1967 exceeded the value of the tax reduction by 21%.

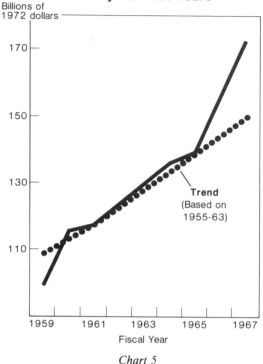

Chart 5

was the major factor that led to our running a $3 billion surplus by the middle of 1965 before escalation in Vietnam struck us. It was a $12 billion tax cut which would be about $33 or $34 billion in today's terms, and within one year the revenues into the federal Treasury were already above what they had been before the tax cut.

He concluded: "Did it pay for itself in increased revenues? I think the evidence is very strong that it did."

Keynesians credit the 1964 tax cut with raising GNP $25 billion by mid-1965 and $30 billion by the end of the year.[5] Another

5. See Arthur Okun, "Measuring the Impact of the 1964 Tax Reduction," in *Perspectives on Economic Growth,* Walter Heller, ed. (New York: Random House, 1968), p. 47; Lawrence Klein, "Econometric Analysis of the Tax Cut of 1964," *The Brookings Model: Some Further Results,* James Duesenberry, ed. (Chicago: Rand McNally, 1969), pp. 459–472; House Budget Committee, *Economic Stabilization Policies: The Historical Record, 1962–76* (Washington, D.C.: U.S. Government Printing Office, 1978).

Keynesian, Edward Denison of the Brookings Institution, estimated the gap between actual and potential GNP to be only $12 billion— the size of the Kennedy tax cut. Obviously, a $12 billion gap does not leave enough room for a $30 billion expansion based on increased demand and unused capacity. Denison is an expert on estimating these gaps. If this estimate is a ballpark figure, the substantial expansion that followed the Kennedy tax cut had to be based on a supply-side response to the higher after-tax rates of return to productive activities.

The Keynesian advisers to President Kennedy wanted to stimulate the economy in order to move it up to its full potential. They chose a policy that they thought would stimulate consumer spending, and the conventional wisdom today still holds that it was a consumption-led expansion. However, the empirical footprints show that what the policymakers really got was a burst of saving and investment activity that spurred the economy beyond a fuller utilization of existing resources to faster growth of the ability to produce. Far from being a consumption-led expansion, real consumer spending actually declined as a percentage of income. Saving, investment, and tax revenues rose sharply. As Stanford economics professor Paul Evans has said, "the critics who assert that there is not a shred of evidence [for supply-side economics] just have not looked for it."[6]

The Holt Amendment

Evidence alone counts for little in Washington, but supply-side economics proved to be good politics as well. On March 15, 1978, Jack Kemp and Albert Quie, who later became governor of Minnesota, offered the Kemp-Roth bill as an amendment to the Humphrey-Hawkins full-employment bill. The amendment was defeated on a 194–216 vote, which was surprisingly close considering the huge majority that the Democrats enjoyed in the House. A swing of only 12 votes and Kemp-Roth would have passed in the early spring of 1978.

The supply-side tide was rising, and on May 3, 1978, it swept over the Democrats for the first time. The occasion was the Holt amendment to the first budget resolution for fiscal year 1979. Marjorie Holt, a Republican from Maryland, combined the Kemp-Roth tax

6. Evans, p. 3.

cuts with a limit on the growth of government spending, holding 1979 outlays to an 8 percent increase over the 1978 level. Her plan would have balanced the budget within five years.

I had left the Budget Committee minority staff in 1977 to help Orrin Hatch fight the supply-side battle in the Senate. By 1978 I was working two shifts in order to help Holt and Rousselot revive the tax-cut effort on the part of the House Budget Committee minority. The fight was getting a little easier because tax cutting was catching on. Both President Carter and the House and Senate budget committees had tax cuts in their budget proposals for 1979. They also had federal spending growing at 11 percent, far above their inflation projection of 7 percent. The result was government spending growing 57 percent faster than the rate of inflation and a 1979 deficit in the $60 billion range. By holding the growth of spending to 8 percent, the Holt amendment provided a larger tax cut and a smaller deficit of $48 billion.

On the Republican side the fight was carried by Holt, Rousselot, Conable, Burgener, Regula, and Latta. The Democrats' resistance came from Mitchell, Simon, and Giaimo, the Budget Committee chairman. The Democrats quickly moved to label the Holt amendment, which provided a $38 billion increase in federal spending, a budget cut. They did this by measuring the spending level in the amendment against their own higher proposal, rather than against the previous year's level. Parren Mitchell instantly invoked the widows and orphans. He claimed that the Holt amendment, which dealt only with aggregate spending and revenue figures, was going to cut "$400 million for Title I of the Urban Rural Poverty Concentration Initiative for Elementary and Secondary School Children" and "eliminate $144 million in the Federal subsidy for educating handicapped children." Even worse, with an 8 percent limit on spending growth, "we could not even consider a new proposal—the entire Middle-Income Student Assistance Act, which so many members of the House have shown an interest in." Obviously, if the middle class were not overtaxed, it would not need student assistance. The Republicans did not tolerate the nonsense about "spending cuts," so Giaimo refined the argument and reminded the House that an 11 percent increase in spending would buy more votes than an 8 percent increase. He was for a larger tax cut too, he said, but let us not kid ourselves into believing that we can vote additional moneys for veterans, additional moneys for defense, additional moneys for tuition tax credits, additional moneys for agriculture, for energy, for health, for social security and income security, for general Government, and on and on, and at the same time vote for a good-sounding amendment, a wish-type of amendment, if you will, to reduce spending and reduce taxes.

Giaimo always threw a one-two punch, and after the politics came the economics. He could wield Keynesian arguments every bit as deftly as Republicans had learned to wield supply-side ones. The larger tax cut in the Holt amendment, he said, would be canceled by the lower level of government spending, so "we would not get the needed stimulus" and "would be deluding ourselves." The economy would slow down, and revenues would decline. Unemployment would rise, pushing up budget expenditures, and the deficit would widen. Giaimo was trying to keep Republicans in that Keynesian box where tax cuts were a weaker stimulus to the economy than an increase in government spending. By this time, however, supply-side economics had dismantled the box.

The Republicans had the upper hand on another issue as well. They had learned that the budget resolution was a fiscal policy process, and now Conable was telling the Budget Committee chairman that the Holt amendment "has to do with whether or not this committee is going to set fiscal policy." The Democrats were allowing the appropriations subcommittees to determine the aggregate level of spending. Then the Budget Committee would subtract the revenues and arrive at the deficit. The deficit would then be justified on the basis of Keynesian fiscal policy as a necessary stimulus to the economy. In this procedure, fiscal policy was a rationale for whatever level spending reached. The Republicans wanted to do it differently by first deciding the aggregate spending figure and then handing it over to the Appropriations Committee to divide up as it saw fit. The Republicans argued that not only would this procedure provide better control over spending, but it would also protect members of Congress from pressure from special interests to raise appropriations. As Burgener said, the only way Congress could avoid the upward pressure on the budget from having to accommodate special interests was by setting the aggregate spending level first.

The House of Representatives found the case for "a good-sounding amendment" compelling. When the vote was tallied, the Holt amendment had won. But the Democratic leadership knew what to do. Pressure was applied and, as the *Congressional Record* shows, "Messrs. Brown of California, Carr, Fithian, Flippo, Ammerman, Benjamin, Gaydos, and Mattox changed their vote from 'aye' to 'no.' " The big spenders squeaked by 197–203, but their era had ended.

When the House Budget Committee reported the second budget resolution on August 8, it resembled the Holt amendment more than it did the first budget resolution. Spending had been held to Holt's level, and the deficit was even lower. Even so, in committee the Democrats were able to defeat by only one vote the Holt amendment to the second budget resolution. The amendment's outlay, revenue, and deficit figures were not much below those in the Budget Committee's resolution. However, it provided for a larger tax cut and curtailed the increase in budget authority, which governs spending in future years, by $30 billion.

When Holt called up her amendment on August 16, the debate was between the same people and over the same issues. The Republicans argued that fiscal policy had to take precedence over accommodating the spending constituencies. They believed it was neither fair nor good economics for government spending and the tax burden to grow faster than the incomes of the taxpayers. Parren Mitchell, a Democrat and an advocate of more income redistribution, called the amendment "the Holt Hit at the Hopeless." But the moralism rang false in the face of the massive increases in income-redistribution programs over the years and reports from the General Accounting Office and the inspector general of Health, Education and Welfare of large-scale waste and fraud in these programs.

The big-spending Democrats had another problem. The week before they had voted down, 177–240, the Kemp-Roth amendment to the Ways and Means Committee tax bill by cloaking themselves in the robes of the fiscally responsible. Member after member declared that they favored the tax cut, but since Kemp-Roth did nothing to control government spending their concern over the deficit precluded their voting for it. Now Holt was reminding them that her amendment, combining the Kemp-Roth tax cuts with limits on spending growth, was exactly what they had said they would vote for.

The screws were turning on the spenders, and the Keynesian analytic was breaking down under the challenge. Giaimo argued that the reduction in the rate of spending growth would only partially compensate "for the inflationary pressures of a Kemp-Roth type tax cut." He seemed to be arguing that private spending was more inflationary than government spending—exactly the opposite of his previous argument that tax cuts provide less stimulus to the economy than higher government spending. The Democrats were defeated, and there was barely enough discipline in their 115-vote majority to defeat the Holt amendment, 201–206. The Democrats could still outvote the Republicans but could not stop them from setting the agenda and controlling the direction of national policy.

The Nunn Amendment

The combination of Kemp-Roth with limits on the growth of spending was proving to be irresistible. In October 1978, the tax bill was brought up in the Senate. Except for reducing the tax rate on capital gains, the bill ignored the deterioration in economic incentives that higher taxation was causing. In an effort to improve the bill, the Kemp-Roth tax cut was offered as an amendment. It was defeated 36–60, and a proposal to index the tax system against bracket creep was also defeated. Opponents claimed that they could not vote for tax cuts unless they were matched by spending reductions. Otherwise the deficit would swell and inflation would accelerate. Of course, few of them had trouble voting for an equivalent deficit as long as it was produced by higher government spending.

Senator Sam Nunn, a Democrat from Georgia, borrowed a page from the Holt amendment. He and Senator Lawton Chiles, a Democrat from Florida, with some help from Republican staffers put together an amendment to reduce federal taxes and spending and to balance the budget by 1982. The Nunn amendment combined across-the-board reductions in personal income tax rates with a proviso limiting the growth in federal spending to the rate of inflation plus one percent. The combination would reduce the government's share of GNP to 20.2 percent in 1982 and balance the 1982 budget.

When the Nunn amendment came up in the Senate, it became obvious that a bandwagon was rolling. Russell Long gave it his support, and the *Record* shows that Robert Dole and Howard Baker asked unanimous consent to be added as cosponsors. Roth was quick to endorse it as one of the original sponsors. Even Henry Bellmon was on board. Muskie complained that the Nunn amendment would "tie the hands of future Congresses and reduce the flexibility of the budget process in establishing a revenue floor." But no one was listening. Senators were shouting "vote!" Kennedy tried to nitpick the distribution of the tax cut. Magnuson, the chairman of the Appropriations Committee, said he was going to vote for it but warned senators not to "come downstairs to room 128 and ask us for more appropriations." Moynihan tried to portray the Nunn amendment as "an extraordinary change in the budgetary arrangements of political democracy," and tarred it as a form of inept planning "pursued in the centrally planned economies of the Soviet bloc." Keynesians had run out of arguments, and on October 9, 1978, the Nunn amendment swept the Senate 65–20. Curiously, Lloyd Bentsen, who was only a few months away from becoming a supply-side hero, voted against it.

When the Nunn amendment passed, Orrin Hatch made a short speech immediately following the vote, in which he paid tribute to "the long efforts of Mr. Roth and Mr. Kemp." Accompanying the speech was the morning's editorial from the *Wall Street Journal* putting a positive light on the spread across party lines of supply-side economics. I knew that it was not possible to succeed with an issue unless people were let on board. In Washington, even that is often not enough.

Three days later the House voted 268–135 to instruct its conferees to the House-Senate conference on the tax bill to support the Nunn amendment. Supply-side economics had passed both houses of Congress and was on the verge of becoming the economic policy of the United States. But the Carter Administration resisted. Treasury Secretary Blumenthal told the conferees that President Carter would veto the tax bill if it contained the Nunn amendment. When that word went out, the organized lobbyists, who had lobbied for other provisions in the bill, went to work against the Nunn amendment in order to protect their gains from a veto. In an effort to save it, sponsors of the Nunn amendment proposed a modified version that would allow the President to cancel the scheduled tax cuts if economic conditions warranted it. But the Carter Treasury refused the weaker version as well. The conferees settled on a compromise stating that the goals of the Nunn amendment should be attained "as a matter of national policy," and all that was left was words. It was not to be the last time that political manipulation would undo a supply-side victory.

When the conference report on the tax bill came before the Senate, a motion was made to recommit the report with instructions to the conferees to insist on the Nunn amendment; it was defeated. The year ended with the economy moving closer toward a crisis. The supply-side remedy would require a new President.

The idea has been spread that Kemp and the supply-siders captured the heart and mind of Ronald Reagan while he was still a candidate for the Republican nomination. As the story goes, respected Republican advisers were too wary of their reputations to get very close to a right-wing contender for the Republican nomination. There had been the Goldwater debacle, and people with connections to the Republican establishment did not want to risk their credibility in the competitive circles in which they moved. This left Reagan to be captured by "Lafferite snake-oil salesmen."

The story is a form of misinformation that reduces the supply-side revolution to a happenstance. It helps opponents to depict supply-side economics as a fad that got out of hand. The notion that supply-side economics owes its all to Laffer's conversion of Kemp and Kemp's conversion of Reagan replaces a powerful broad-based movement with a quirk.

By the autumn of 1978 a majority of the Congress had clearly demonstrated that supply-side economics was irresistible. It could no longer be voted down openly. The year 1979 found the Democratic leadership in the House changing the rules affecting the budget process in an effort to ward off the Holt amendment. Unable to defeat it, they changed the rules to prevent it from being offered.[7] By

---

7. See "Cancelling Votes with Rules," *Wall Street Journal* editorial, January 31, 1979.

the time of the campaign for the 1980 presidential nomination, only the impervious did not see that Kemp-Roth was a winning political issue that could not be defeated except by subterfuge. When Reagan won the nomination, the Republican establishment moved to influence him by pressing to make a balanced budget the main political and economic issue. It was the same fight all over again that the supply-siders had gone through in Congress. The irony is that President Reagan placed the men he had defeated for the nomination—men who had ridiculed his economic program—in charge of his White House staff and, thus, in control of his administration.

Whatever Reagan's trials and tribulations turn out to be, he inherited a Congress that had already passed his economic program on the strength of floor amendments. On August 21, 1980, two months after candidate Reagan had endorsed a ten percent reduction in individual income tax rates and faster depreciation writeoffs for business, the Senate Finance Committee attached an amendment to a bill that permitted the duty-free entry of six bronze bells for the Foundry United Methodist Church of Washington, D.C. The Finance Committee used this minor bill to put forward a major piece of legislation: the Tax Reduction Act of 1980, which contained personal income tax rate reductions and faster depreciation write-offs for business.

Russell Long was maneuvering to position his party on the right side of the issue. However, Majority Leader Robert Byrd wanted to stall in the hope that Carter would win the election and the tax cuts could be kept bottled up. Byrd was finally forced to allow a procedural vote on whether the Senate would take up the Finance Committee's tax cut prior to the election. Uncertain whether a tax cut would help them or be read as an endorsement of Reagan's economic program, the Senate Democrats voted to leave the tax cut until after the election. The election gave control of the Senate to the Republicans, which was perhaps the electorate's way of saying that they were now supply-siders too. By the time Ronald Reagan entered the White House, only an incompetent administration could have lost the tax-cut battle.

4

Reagan's First Months

RONALD REAGAN CAMPAIGNED FOR THE PRESIDENCY ON A supply-side platform. It gave him an employment policy that did not rely on inflation and government programs. It gave him an anti-inflation policy that did not rely on the pain and suffering of rising unemployment. And it gave him a budget policy that eliminated the deficit through economic growth instead of balancing the budget on the backs of taxpayers. Reagan was a different kind of candidate because he emphasized the capabilities of the people and the American economy. He campaigned on a message of hope that sparked a rebirth of confidence in the people. Reagan's optimism was so unfamiliar to the Republican establishment that its candidate, George Bush, called it "voodoo economics."

The political themes of failures and limits, themes that had created and reinforced insecurities in the people leading them to accept more government programs and controls over their lives, were not a part of Reagan's message. He spoke the language of an American renaissance. His message invigorated the hopes of people whose lives, pocketbooks, and prospects were cramped by a politics that closed all frontiers except those serviced by the federal budget. Here was a man breaking all of the ingrained political rules, and he was winning.

The new policy caused resentments among some Republicans who thought of themselves as belonging to "the responsible party" in contrast to "pie-in-the-sky" Democrats. Being responsible meant "being honest with the voters" and telling them forthrightly that a dose of pain and suffering would be necessary to straighten out the economy. Their feelings of responsibility were heightened by having paid the price for this policy in lost elections and charges of insensitivity to the poor. The change in policy devalued the heavy burden they had carried and left them with diminished roles. They saw themselves being displaced by the supply-side crowd of "wild men," which was the portrait that Jude Wanniski painted of all of us. People so threatened in this way were not willing to support the new policy.

The Republican establishment was eager to find a handle on Ronald Reagan. Not only was he perceived in some quarters as a political Neanderthal, but he was also winning over the people with his message that they could again be self-reliant instead of dependent on government. Even worse, as an outsider he was a threat to the establishment's control over the party.

During the campaign Reagan said he would balance the budget. It was a traditional Republican theme and one that the Lafferite version of supply-side economics made too easy. Reagan meant that a balanced budget would be a result of a program of economic growth designed to restore economic prosperity and self-reliance. He did not mean that a balanced budget was his principal aim or a constraint that would dictate his economic policy. He certainly did not mean that he would balance the budget on the backs of taxpayers or by permitting a further decline in the country's defense capability. Nevertheless, the establishment saw its handle and moved quickly to grab hold of it. The more a balanced budget could be emphasized, the greater the chance to bring austerity measures into the picture as an alternative approach to balancing the budget. The austerity policies could then be used to subdue the new economic policy of Reagan and Kemp. Ironically, the Laffer curve played into the hands of the establishment. It made Reagan and Kemp over-confident about a balanced budget and left them unaware of its potential as a tool of counterrevolution.

Early Threats

I had left the Senate staff in the autumn of 1978 to join the editorial page of the *Wall Street Journal* as associate editor and columnist for "Political Economy," a new feature on the editorial page. I welcomed the opportunity to restate supply-side economics. Wanniski, who I replaced, had helped make supply-side economics an issue. But as a journalist he had sensationalized it and left the impression that Jack Kemp was the only person in Washington who wanted to cut taxes. That perhaps was the right tactic to use in order to bring public attention to a new idea. But now that supply-side economics was noticed, it needed credibility and a broad base.

Two years later I was back in Washington as a member of President-elect Reagan's Task Force on Tax Policy. The Republicans had gained the White House, the Senate, were a larger minority in the House of Representatives, and supply-side economics was on the national agenda. The Democrats had no alternative policy, and some in the Senate were stauncher supply-siders than many of their Republican colleagues. The danger to Reagan's program came from other sources. Some business lobbyists regarded grabbing as much of the tax cut as they could as a competitive game.[1] Establishment economists were determined to protect themselves from being depreciated by a new approach to policy. And Republicans with presidential aspirations did not want to wait on the sidelines while a supply-side team played the politics of a successful American renaissance. Rather than an open fight with the Democrats, it was clear that the real fight would be within the Republican ranks.

The fight began almost immediately. Early in January 1981, prior to the inauguration, a small group met under the leadership of David Stockman to work out the economic assumptions and budgetary implications of the Reagan economic program. Stockman, stooping and prematurely grey, was a crisp conversationalist. He had the dry and ascetic looks associated with religious idealists and, as a consequence, few were prepared for his tremendous ambition and competitiveness once he was in a position of power. Stockman had played the role of his former boss, John Anderson, in mock debates to prepare Reagan for the real thing and was considered to be in the supply-side camp. He wanted to be director of the Office of Management and Budget, a position that Jack Kemp helped him obtain. When Stockman's appointment was announced, our minds were put

---

1. The U.S. Chamber of Commerce was one of the notable exceptions.

at ease. With Stockman at OMB, myself as assistant secretary of the Treasury for economic policy, and Norman Ture as Treasury undersecretary, supply-siders believed that the President's program was safe. It did not occur to any of us that Stockman was not really committed to the program.

Other members of the group included Alan Greenspan, Alan Reynolds (who decided that Stockman was relying on Greenspan too much and dropped out after declining the job of chief economist at OMB), Norman Ture, Steve Entin (who had fought the battles with me in the Congress and would be one of my deputies in the Treasury), and myself. At first we met in a spacious committee room in the Longworth House Office building near Stockman's congressional office. The room was too large for us, and we seemed swallowed up by Washington even before we began. Later we met in the old executive office building next door to the White House in a smaller, ornate room made available by OMB. The group grew to include Beryl Sprinkel (undersecretary of the Treasury for monetary affairs), Martin Anderson (domestic policy adviser to the President), Murray Weidenbaum (chairman of the Council of Economic Advisers), and a few others.

All the conflicts that were later to threaten Reaganomics were played out in preliminary form in those temporary quarters where we met as victorious colleagues working toward nothing less than the restoration of the American economy. Many studies have been made and a great deal written about the interaction of people in group decisions. No doubt the outcome is affected by analytical arguments and empirical evidence, but just as often these are foils for individual egos and the competitive drive to prevail over others. In such a process it is difficult even for the participants to comprehend exactly what happened and why. Turf, personal rivalries, and political aspirations are as likely to determine the response to a point of view as the soundness of the argument, the skill with which it is put, or the national interest. During those six weeks from early January to mid-February, it became obvious that the debate over economic assumptions was being distorted by jockeying over priorities between turf-interested parties. For many of the participants the fellowship fell apart before it formed, and in the crucible of self-interest that remained, the President's economic program was always at risk.

Reaganomics

The President-elect wanted to get on with his business of using incentives to rebuild the U.S. economy. He ruled out both wage and
price controls and the continuation of demand management—the
economic cycle of fighting inflation with unemployment and unemployment with inflation. In place of a stop-go monetary policy
ranging from too tight to too loose, there would be steady, moderate,
and predictable growth in the money supply. And instead of pumping up demand to stimulate the economy, reliance would be placed
on improving incentives on the supply side.

This is the policy package that became known as Reaganomics.[2]
Its controversial feature is its belief that the economy can enjoy a
rise in real gross national product while inflation declines. Monetary
policy would first stabilize and then gradually reduce inflation,
while tax cuts would provide liquidity as well as incentives and prevent the slower money growth from causing a recession. By creating
the wrong incentives and damaging the cash flow of individuals and
businesses, the tax system had produced a nation of debt junkies.
With the economy strung out on credit, it had to be carefully reha-
bilitated so as not to produce a liquidity crisis.

A decade of taxflation (inflation and rising marginal tax rates)
had taken most of the gains in individual incomes, leaving people
no recourse but to turn to debt to finance their gains in consumption. Since the interest on debt is tax-deductible, being in debt was
the only way for people to get some of their income back from the
government and experience a rise in living standards. Businesses
were equally encouraged by the tax system to go into debt. The only
way out of this dilemma is to improve production incentives and the
cash flow of individuals and businesses, while gradually reducing
the rate of money growth. The tax cuts had two purposes. One was
to lower tax rates and improve incentives. The other was to prevent
a reduction in money growth from causing liquidity problems in the
private sector. With incentives restructured, money growth would

2. The term "Reaganomics" originated, I believe, in the title that a copyeditor put
on an article, "Reaganomics: A Change?" that I wrote for the *New York Times* (November 9, 1980) a few days after the election of Ronald Reagan. In the article I predicted that President Reagan would have a hard time preventing his policy from being
reversed. I did not like the copyeditor's title because it seemed to imply that the President's economic program was an idiosyncrasy.

be used to finance the growth of real goods and services rather than to bid up the prices of houses and commodities.

Ronald Reagan was no exception to William Simon's observation that "as soon as a President is elected, he is captured by the past."[3] The Reaganomic view that real GNP and employment can rise while inflation declines conflicted with a bogus but nevertheless influential concept called the "Phillips curve." The Phillips curve purports to show a mathematical relationship between inflation and unemployment, claiming that economic policy cannot reduce one without boosting the other. A looser formulation known as "core inflation" claims that inflation is so thoroughly embedded in the economy that it can be wrung out only at enormous economic cost. Although the Phillips curve has proven inaccurate as a forecasting tool, it and the core-inflation concept still influence economic forecasters.

Alan Greenspan, later supported by Murray Weidenbaum, argued that an administration forecast that conflicted with these concepts would lack credibility with economic forecasters. Both men were unwilling to make a clean break with the outmoded concepts that had hampered the economy's performance and produced the political change that brought Reagan to office. Their refusal to break with the past was itself a threat to the President's economic program. The President was not likely to succeed with his proposals to fundamentally alter the tax, monetary, budgetary, and regulatory policies of the United States if he could not show that his new policies would make a difference in the economy's performance.

It was frustrating for a policy revolution to find itself in the chains of old concepts like core inflation and the Phillips curve. It meant that if we were going to project much of a decline in inflation, we could not project much real economic growth. Conversely, if we were going to project a higher rate of real economic growth, we could not show much of a decline in inflation. Greenspan was insistent on these rules, although they had not applied to him when he was chairman of the Council of Economic Advisers in the Ford Administration.[4] It was never clear whether Greenspan himself be-

3. See my "Political Economy" column, "Constraints on Change," *Wall Street Journal,* October 24, 1980.
4. While serving as CEA chairman, Greenspan had projected real economic growth averaging 6 percent annually over five years and an inflation rate cut nearly in half.

lieved in core inflation or whether he was saying that what we could project was controlled by the forecasting authority enjoyed by the concept. He reminded us that a widely used forecasting model had a 12 percent inflation rate and that five-sixths of it was core inflation. That meant monetary policy at best could lower the inflation rate only from 12 percent to 10 percent.

Both the monetarists and the supply-siders objected to Greenspan's position. We felt that he was chaining us to the past. If the Reagan Administration's economic projections had to abide by concepts like core inflation, then either supply-side or monetarist policies—or in some measure both—had to be dismissed in advance as ineffectual. Monetarists could not project lower inflation as a result of slower money growth if supply-siders were projecting higher economic growth as a result of better incentives, and vice versa.

The media devoted a lot of space to stories about tension and conflicts between supply-siders and monetarists. In terms of the Phillips curve or core inflation, we had to be in conflict, and that is the way the press presented it. But of course neither the supply-siders nor the monetarists believed in either concept. We were united against the traditionalists, and that was the true conflict. We believed that the Phillips curve and core inflation were rationales for the failure of Keynesian demand-management policies, and that they had no meaning or applicability in the new policy context that we were working to create. From this perspective there was no inherent contradiction in Reaganomics. However, the press had latched onto an attractive theme and was not going to give it up. Monetarists and supply-siders continued to read about how they were at each other's throats, while in truth we were jointly fighting to fend off policy traditionalists and political manipulators.

The Deficit Takes Over

The core-inflation argument had another unfortunate result. It provided Stockman with an opening to elevate the deficit and to make it the dominant concern of economic policy. In the first weeks we had been trying to determine how tax and monetary policies would affect real output and inflation. The budget deficit was treated as a residual of the economy's performance. It would gradually be eliminated by a policy of economic growth. None of the supply-siders within the administration were Lafferites promising that the tax-rate reductions would pay for themselves in higher revenues. All we promised was that some of the revenues would be recaptured from the larger tax base resulting from economic growth. We assumed there would be a deficit but that it would be easier to finance because of a higher saving rate. We were trying to estimate the combination of revenue reflows, increases in private-sector saving, and reduction in the growth of federal spending that would eliminate the deficit as an *economic* problem.

Stockman grew restive under this approach to the deficit. The way the discussion was going, the administration's success indicators were shaping up to be the inflation rate, the saving rate, and the rate of real economic growth. This left Stockman with a less central role because a budget director cannot take credit for tax and monetary policies. Stockman wanted his own success indicator. In the campaign the President had said he would balance the budget, and that goal was being urged by members of the Republican establishment as a means of keeping themselves in the policy center.

Stockman began arguing that the deficit was a *political* problem. Since there was no provision in the budget for showing an increase in private-sector saving as an offset to a budget deficit, people would not see the progress we were making. The lingering deficits, however, would be bottom-line items and would worry the markets. The Democratic opposition would attribute the red ink to the tax cuts and attack us as fiscally irresponsible—a Republican weapon that had never worked on Democrats.

Stockman would have set off alarm bells if he had argued that the deficit was an economic problem that precluded taxes from being cut or inflation curtailed until the budget was balanced. To express such a point of view in the early days of the policy revolution would have been heresy. The idea that tax cuts and lower prices were rewards to be given *after* the budget was balanced was too clearly the establishment point of view. Instead, Stockman warmed to the core-inflation argument. Core inflation would keep up the inflation rate, and that would mean higher nominal GNP and higher tax revenues. With higher tax revenues he could project a balanced budget, and once projected it would become a constraint on the whole program.

Since Greenspan and Weidenbaum were already arguing for core inflation, Stockman tipped the balance. With the deadline approaching for announcing the President's program, it was a difficult situation for less senior members of the group. A pragmatic posture is intimidating because it occupies the one position that makes all others extreme. Suddenly "ardent" supply-siders and "extreme" monetarists were confronting a "pragmatic" Stockman. It did not help matters that some of us had political holds on our appointments from a Republican senator who turned out to be an ally of Stockman. The message was clear. Still, there was no way for lesser officials to overrule a man who had direct access to the President. Any more fussing and we would have been painted in the media as people who thought deficits unimportant, and our own party would be causing difficulties at our confirmation hearings in the Senate.

Beryl Sprinkel, who was slated to be the undersecretary of the Treasury for monetary affairs, pointed out to Stockman that our money-growth assumptions were too low to support the nominal GNP that Stockman needed to show a balanced budget. Stockman said that we should not be concerned and to go ahead and put the higher GNP figures in the economic projections. He had been focusing on the 1981 and 1982 budgets in order to get our spending reductions before the Congress and had not yet had time to identify the budget cuts for 1983 and 1984. He would find the cuts later, and at that time we would lower the nominal GNP numbers to make them consistent with our monetary assumptions. In the meantime, core inflation substituted for the missing budget cuts and gave Stockman his balanced budget.

The feat launched Stockman as a hero with the President by delivering tax cuts, increases in defense spending, and a balanced budget, all in one package. Stockman may have been anxious about the hidden deficit, but his aides later claimed that he expected Congress to deliver only half of the tax cut, thus making him whole on his balanced budget.

By hiding the deficit, Stockman elevated a balanced budget into even more of an issue than he intended. It sent a signal that the administration placed such importance on a balanced budget that it would resort to producing one by hook or by crook. This confused some people about our priorities. The size of the budget deficit be-

came the overriding measure of the administration's success or failure, eventually threatening to turn the Reagan presidency into a re-
play of the policy flip-flops that had destroyed the Carter
Administration. It would have been wiser and easier to forecast a
deficit and to have kept the emphasis on restructuring incentives
and reducing inflation. The economy had experienced deficits for
the past two decades and would not have panicked over their continuation, especially if spending were brought under control and incentives restored.

Once the deficit became an issue, the supply-side tax cuts, hitherto
the centerpiece of the program, were moved to the side. The January
beginning dates for the tax cuts were delayed until July. Then the
first installment was further delayed until October and cut in half,
all in the name of a balanced budget. There would have been further delays had the President not put his foot down. The delays
guaranteed that the tax cuts would be overtaken by the recession
and that there would be large recessionary deficits prior to the loss
of revenues from the tax cuts. Recessions produce deficits as a matter of course. Since employment and incomes fall, the Treasury col-
lects less revenue. At the same time, budget expenditures for
income-support programs rise. A recession means that the deficit
projections must rise. If the size of the deficit has been made the
overriding measure of performance, the indicator would read "failure" before tax cuts can take effect. It is hard to hold on to a program that is perceived as a failure.

Holding On

Indeed, it was hard to hold on to the program long enough to get it
passed. Appointed officials who might be reluctant to advocate policy ideas different from the President's could instead talk to the
press. And there were plenty of outsiders who wanted to get their
oar in and turn policy in their direction.

By the week of the inauguration, the media were reporting divi-
sions both within the administration and among outside advisers
concerning the President's economic program. The press reported
that a number of conservative advisers, if not a majority, were opposed to one or more elements of the Reagan tax-cut proposal; the

timing, the size, and the shape were criticized. Reagan stuck by the Kemp-Roth tax cut, which cut marginal rates across the board by 30 percent over a period of three years. The first 10 percent reduction in tax rates was to be retroactive as of January 1, 1981. The second and third stages would take place on January 1, 1982, and January 1, 1983.

On January 23, 1981, the *Washington Post* was pleased to report that Alan Greenspan had testified before the Joint Economic Committee that the tax cut should be delayed until midsummer 1981. Postponing the debut of the tax cut "could decrease the drain on fiscal 1982 federal revenues by more than $35 billion." The other witnesses before the committee stressed spending reductions. The push was on to replace the President's program with austerity. Only Richard Rahn, the chief economist for the U.S. Chamber of Commerce, gave equal weight to the need for tax cuts.

That same day Leonard Silk informed *New York Times* readers of "G.O.P. Rifts on Tax Policy." Arthur Burns, the former chairman of the Federal Reserve Board, had told the Senate Budget Committee that he would not cut taxes at all at this time. Silk recognized the President's firmness on the tax-cut issue, but he felt that the administration may have already been planning an escape hatch to back out of the tax cut. The escape hatch was the discovery that the budget was in much worse shape than anyone had thought. The Carter Administration had left a $55 billion deficit on the new administration's doorstep, and it would be hard to cut spending in 1981 when the year was already a third over (the fiscal year 1981 began in October 1980). "It will therefore be difficult for the Reagan Administration to put through its big tax cuts without worsening the deficit, possibly by $20 billion to $30 billion," said Silk.

The call to cut spending first in order to "permit" tax cuts was echoed on February 2, 1981, by Federal Reserve Board Chairman Paul Volcker. Volcker said if tax cuts alone were approved, the board would continue to maintain tight control over the growth of money and credit, which would lead to higher interest rates. He expressed interest in what was reportedly Stockman's suggestion of a "trigger" to allow the tax cut to go into effect only as spending reductions were achieved. Steven Rattner of the *Times* quoted Volcker: "I've been very encouraged in my conversations with

members of the Administration and Mr. Stockman in particular."
Rattner pointed out that Volcker's position was at odds with Treasury Secretary Regan, who said tax cuts could not wait until after
the budget outlays were reduced. Already Regan seemed to be one
of the few senior officials supporting the President.

On February 6, 1981, an article by Steven Roberts appeared in
the *New York Times:* "G.O.P. Admits Need to Revise Tax Cuts."
Senator Dole of Kansas, the new chairman of the Senate Finance
Committee, had told him that the tax-cut plan would have to be altered somehow to attract enough votes from the Democratic side.
"In recent visits to Capitol Hill," the *Times* correspondent wrote,
"White House aides have been told that this plan [Kemp-Roth] is
politically unrealistic." Republican leaders expected the plan to be
cut in half and that it would also have to include a "Christmas tree"
of tax goodies for special interests. To make room for these items,
the personal tax cuts would have to be scaled back.

The editorial page of the *New York Times* was also extremely critical of the President's tax-cutting plans. A January 30 editorial,
"Taming the Inflation Monster," found a dangerous inflation lurk-
ing in the tax cut. The President lacked wisdom: "It is not his tenacity that is in question but his wisdom. For at a time when inflation is
still untamed, such a tax cut risks making it worse." Later the President's critics would take the opposite view and claim that his tax
cuts caused a recession.

It was in the middle of the concern about inflation that core-inflation advocates decided to lock in a higher inflation forecast by
leaking it to the press. At 4:00 p.m. on February 11 a newswire item,
citing "sources who asked not to be identified," reported that the
Reagan Administration was less optimistic than a week ago about
inflation. The next day bond prices tumbled.

On February 18, 1981, the White House released the details of the
new economic program. The following morning the *Times* supported the President's program for one day in an editorial titled
"Who Has a Better Plan?" But soon the *Times* was again attacking
the tax cuts, this time for not being targeted enough toward investment. By February 26 the newspaper wanted the people's tax cuts to
be given instead to big business: "If lower taxes are to turn the
economy around, they should not be simply dribbled out to consumers but passed into hands that will directly invest the money in

job-producing enterprises." Later the "too small" business tax cuts became "excessive." On Sunday, July 25, 1982, just after the Republican Senate essentially repealed the tax cut for business, the *Times* congratulated the Republicans for rolling back "part of the enormous tax cut rashly given to businesses last year."

The editorial board of the *New York Times* could not grasp the supply-side logic behind the personal income tax-rate reduction. All it saw was a "murky notion" with "no textbook or history book to support it," and the *Times* was not alone. I had foreseen this problem. Unlike the Keynesian policy that it was displacing, supply-side economics came out of the policy process itself and not out of the universities. The previous fiscal revolution that swept Washington was preceded by years of preparation. Keynesian economics had been enshrined in the universities for more than a decade before it reached Washington. A generation of journalists, congressional staffers, and government economists had been taught its precepts and basic principles. Everyone knew what it was before it became policy.

However, the luxury of long preparation was denied to supply-side economics. Its time had come before many professors had learned what it was. Keynesian policies still worked in the classroom and textbooks, but they had ceased to work in practice. Over the years the government had assumed more and more responsibility for the economy. One day the government woke up to find that its policy had worn out. Fortunately, a new policy was ready, but the only people who were thoroughly familiar with supply-side economics were those who had participated in the congressional debates or were readers of the editorial page of the *Wall Street Journal*. It was important that people learn about the new policy, especially journalists who would be reporting on it and White House staff and cabinet secretaries who would be defending it. The missing textbook that the *New York Times* was asking for needed to be provided.

The Economic Report

The administration had an opportunity to explain supply-side economics in the report that the White House released in February 1981, on the new economic program. Every year the Council of Economic Advisers, with input from the Treasury, OMB, and the

White House, prepares the *Economic Report of the President.* President Carter had issued the 1981 report just before leaving office. Because of the change of policy that it envisaged, the Reagan Administration decided to issue a report of its own. An official presidential report explaining the logic and rationale for the new policies would be an important document. A great danger to the new economic program was the lack of appointed people who could explain it. Since so few could, the media—and those government officials who compete for power by leaking and planting stories in the media —were free to make what they would of the President's policy.

The opportunity to explain was lost. At first, things started off on track. George Gilder, the author of *Wealth and Poverty,* was commissioned to write the introduction to the report. Gilder's work reflected the President's own hopeful themes. David Stockman himself had declared on Gilder's book jacket: "*Wealth and Poverty* is promethean in its intellectual power and insight. It shatters once and for all the Keynesian and welfare state illusions that burden the failed conventional wisdom of our era. It recovers the classic truths about the sources of prosperity and growth—just in time." In spite of this endorsement, Gilder's introduction was sentenced to the trash can. About all that remained in the final report was a statement that "the U.S. economy faces no insurmountable barriers to sustained growth."

The Treasury's supply-side explanation of the tax cut was purged as well. We found ourselves fighting hard just to prevent the economists on the CEA staff from explaining the tax cuts in Keynesian terms. The last draft save one still contained language suggesting that the purpose of the supply-side tax cut was to stimulate demand in order to take up the slack in the economy. We were preparing the manifesto of the Reagan revolution, and we could not get rid of the symbols and jargon of the old order.

As Treasury officials discovered from calls from reporters seeking confirmation or stirring up trouble, someone on the White House staff was encouraging the view that the final report was a rebuff to supply-siders. Since the President himself was a supply-sider, that interpretation would mean that he was not well served by the report. Many reporters are no longer careful about their sources, and fingers pointed to Richard Darman, a top aide to James Baker, the

White House chief of staff, as the source. Whoever it was, he was following the time-proven rule of undercutting cabinet departments in order to build the power of White House staff. On February 20, 1981, Evans and Novak reported in their column that White House officials were suppressing the supply-side explanation of the economic program. Murray Weidenbaum was reported to have cut out all but the most inane references to supply-side economics.

He probably did, but for a different reason. Weidenbaum, a traditional economist, was unsure of his role in an administration dominated by monetarists and supply-siders. Although he never really believed in the President's program, as his remarks to Joseph Kraft shortly after his resignation make clear,[5] Weidenbaum was attending to more important things. He was defending his turf. Economic reports of presidents are always drafted by the Council of Economic Advisers, and Weidenbaum was not going to lose his function to Treasury, OMB, or George Gilder. The same CEA staff that had written Jimmy Carter's economic reports was writing Ronald Reagan's, and in the same way.

The Treasury Department's Office of Economic Policy fought to keep Reagan from being captured before he could achieve some changes. As draft after draft flew back and forth between Treasury, CEA, OMB, and the White House, Tim McNamar, the deputy secretary, was Treasury's liaison. Like many people who come to government from the business community, he was a seeker of consensus. Consensus, of course, worked against change by compromising the President's policies. On more than one occasion I had to remind the administration that the President himself knew what he wanted to do and was waiting for us to do it, not to arrive at agreement among ourselves about what he should do. People are so unaccustomed to leadership that the President's officials did not recognize the President's. On February 14, 1981, I sent a memo to McNamar:

I think it is extraordinary that in the first Reagan economic report (even if a mini-report), the first explicitly supply-side President ever elected to office provides no explanation whatsoever of the new policy that he is the carrier of and for which he has made so many claims.

5. See Kraft's column in *Washington Post,* Sunday, July 25, 1982.

I was urging him to take the President's program seriously. Perhaps he did, but the issue was resolved by leaving economic analysis out altogether and providing only a description of the program. Later we heard that Vice-President Bush told his staff that the White House took all of the "Kemp language" out of the report and White House releases so as not to inflame a jealous House of Representatives. By "Kemp language" Bush meant supply-side economics. The President had exhorted us that policy was to prevail over politics, but here again was the usual victory of politics over policy.

The document that was to have been the first official explanation of Reaganomics hit the streets on February 18 with no rationale for the program or the economic analysis underlying it. Not surprisingly, both news producers and news consumers were left in the dark as to what it was all about. The unexplained policy was left open to criticism and speculation in the press and ultimately to Stockman's own damaging claim in the *Atlantic Monthly* that the President's program was only a disguise for trickle-down economics. A year later in March 1982 Martin Feldstein, who later succeeded Weidenbaum as chairman of the Council of Economic Advisers, declared: "The changes in tax rules and in monetary and fiscal policies can do much to end the poor performance of the past decade. It's very unfortunate therefore that the new policy has been so poorly explained by the Administration."

On February 17, the day before the report was to be published, Treasury was still fighting off an attempt to describe budget cutting as "the centerpiece of our program," while the tax-rate reduction, the true centerpiece, was described as "the second element of the program." We rewrote the paragraphs and described each element of the program—the reductions in tax rates, spending, regulation, and money growth—as "one element," "another element," and so on. Since there was a lot of "team" talk, our objections had to receive at least pro forma consideration. But someone in the White House was determined that tax reduction should be assigned less importance from the beginning. The final published report described budget cutting as "the leading edge of our program." Austerity was taking over the program even as it was being launched. By the third week of the administration, it was clear as day that the team concept served to dilute the influence of Reaganites on policy.

The President nevertheless had an important victory. Although the report projected a balanced budget by 1984, nowhere in the report was a balanced budget listed as a *goal* of the Reagan Administration. A balanced budget would be a *result* of achieving the four goals or elements of the program. The budget goal was explicitly defined as the reduction of federal expenditures from 23 percent of GNP in 1981 to 19.3 percent of GNP in 1984. Later the media forgot how the administration had specified its aims. After the tax cuts had been delayed, after monetary policy had gone off course, and after Congress had refused some of the spending reductions, the administration's economic projections no longer showed a balanced budget in 1984. The media let loose a barrage of stories about the failure of the Reagan Administration to achieve its "principal goal" of a balanced budget. We showed many reporters the February 18, 1981, statement of our goals, but it did no good. The story was Ronald Reagan's failure, and that was that. Media that were able to turn the Tet offensive in Vietnam—a crushing defeat for the Viet Cong— into an American defeat could work their will as well with Reaganomics.

It is disturbing how little support there is in the media for any form of American success, outside of sports. The media have a proclivity to harp on internal administration "splits" and "defeats" and to encourage competitiveness among policy officials by speculating on who has influence and power and who has not. I knew that such working conditions for policy officials could erode the program. The President's officials would be battling against each other rather than for his program. Who is out to get whom would become the question of the day, and the fundamental changes that the President wanted would fall by the wayside. Yet, from the start, administration officials themselves were encouraging the development of these corrosive working conditions by leaking policy decisions to the press (sometimes before they were even made). With the leak would go an interpretation that the decision was a "policy defeat" for some part of the administration. Too often it was the Treasury and the supply-siders who were being defeated, as if our policy were different from the President's. The administration was not three weeks old before there were two important instances of this. Both the decision not to reduce the top rate on investment income from 70 to 50 percent

during the first year and the administration's economic projections
were represented as Treasury defeats.

The Politics of the Top Bracket

The tax system discriminated against investment income. Income
from wages and salaries could be taxed up to 50 percent, but income
from saving and investment could be taxed as high as 70 percent.
Even the terminology discriminated, with income from saving and
investment labeled "unearned income." The 30 percent reduction in
the tax rates would bring the 70 percent rate down to 50. The question was whether to bring the rate down all at once the first year or
to phase the reduction over three years (like the rest of the personal
tax cut). Many economists believed that investment and the economy would get an added boost from dropping the top rate in one
stage. There was a political cost, however, in that the President
would be accused of favoring the rich and giving them their tax cut
first. The decision was made to forgo the added kick to the economy
in order to avoid the political demagoguery.

What happened next was unfortunate. Instead of simply not including the proposal in the tax package, the White House staff
leaked the decision as a rebuff to the Treasury. At 4:27 p.m. on
February 13, 1981, the Dow Jones wire service reported: "The
White House said President Reagan had rejected a Treasury proposal to reduce the maximum tax on unearned income." I had spent
lunch that day explaining to Norman Jonas and Steve Wildstrom of
Business Week that the economic program was on track, and now
here was an announcement of a high-level split between the President himself and the Treasury.

As I watched the late afternoon news reports erase my credibility
with *Business Week,* I wondered whose staged show I was watching.
Treasury had not made the issue into a presidential decision. We
had learned from our office of legislative affairs that Congressman
Brodhead, a liberal Democrat, was going to include the measure in
the Ways and Means Committee bill, whether the administration
proposed it or not. Since this was likely to be the case (and was),
Treasury had never bothered to resolve its own ambivalence. We
liked it economically and worried about it politically.

Secretary Regan was not amused either. No cabinet member likes to read in the press that his department has been overruled by the President, even when it is true. When it is not true, it is even more upsetting. The White House produced the following excuse: the decision not to reduce the top rate all at once offered the opportunity for some image making. After all, went the explanation, here was a President whose friends were millonaires and who went to black-tie affairs with an elegantly dressed first lady. Something needed to be done to counter the rich-man imagery. The President could score points with the public if it seemed that he had overruled his advisers and decided on his own against cutting taxes for the rich.

The naiveté of White House public relations was shocking. The President seemed to be in the hands of people who were likely to squander his most valuable asset—his sincerity. It was dangerous for the White House to telegraph a (false) sensitivity to a falsely drawn rich-poor issue. What the White House was really demonstrating was a willingness to accept the constraints of the other side's ideology on the President's program. That was poor politics, since it could invite a stronger resistance to the President's program. In the past, the cost of getting any tax cut usually was income redistribution and tax rebates for people who do not pay taxes. Since we were trying to restructure incentives, it was not wise to encourage the thought that, under enough pressure, the White House might give way on the marginal tax-rate reductions in the higher brackets.

The Policy-Split Game

Besides, our real problem was different. There had been stories in *Business Week* and the *New York Times* about policy splits in the administration. Treasury was worried by these stories. The fundamental policy changes that were necessary to restore the American economy would be difficult to achieve. Stories of splits in our ranks prior even to our being confirmed in our positions by the Senate were signaling to opponents that the President lacked unity among his team and was ripe to be handed defeats. The stories of policy splits were being fed to the press by White House staff—from "people around Baker," reported my friends in the media. Baker, of course, was White House chief of staff James Baker III, the millionaire Texan whose smoothness had helped him to gain his position. As *Business Week* (December 7, 1981) noted, Baker has a "history of working against Reagan on behalf of President Ford and then Presidential candidate George Bush." After losing his own campaign for attorney general in Texas in 1978, Baker became Bush's campaign manager for the 1980 GOP nomination. People around Baker were Richard Darman, his deputy, and David Gergen, White House staff director and later director of White House communications. Gergen is the towering figure seen on TV after a presidential press conference pushing Reagan out of the room before he does too much impromptu communicating with reporters. Neither of the three could be said to be knowledgeable about policy, and they certainly are not Reaganites. Darman, a protegé of Elliot Richardson, has been described by *Time* magazine (August 12, 1982) as "Baker's alter ego." *Time* quoted "one wary colleague" as saying "philosophically, he is not where the President is." But it made no difference. They had decided they were going to run the show by manipulating the press, and they had the positions from which to do it.

I realized that if the President was going to get anywhere with his economic program, I was going to have to take a lot of risks. Something had to be done about the policy-split theme. Complaining to Baker was not one of the options. So on Thursday morning, March 19, 1981, my article, "The Keynesian Attack on Mr. Reagan's Plan," appeared in the *Wall Street Journal:*

Every morning when I pick up my *New York Times* I expect to read in Steven Rattner's reports that I have abandoned supply-side economics. After all, he even reported that Jack Kemp himself had abandoned his own bill in disagreement over an inconsequential detail.

Mr. Rattner has established himself as leader of a corps of reporters trying to drive permanent wedges into any crack of disagreement that policy discussion inevitably generates. The object is to isolate the supply-siders. Last week Hobart Rowen, a *Washington Post* commentator long identified with the liberal Keynesians, said it wouldn't be long before supply-side economics is back on the shelf. Critics sense that if they can blunt and deflect the intellectual cutting edge of the Reagan program, the rest of it can gradually be chopped up with the familiar interest groups and income redistribution arguments.

But in spite of all the journalistic smoke, the supply-siders still have on their side the Office of Management and Budget,[6] Treasury, and the President—not exactly what you would call a hunkered-down position. And the Reagan tax bill is still very much alive. The problem isn't in controlling the policy but in controlling the explanation of it.

It was now out in the open. Everyone knew that Rattner covered the White House and that his stories about policy splits originated there. Soon afterward, the *New York Times* reassigned him to London.

The article had not been cleared. Since no mechanism had been set up, no policy had been violated. Clearing the article in advance would have been an invitation for someone to edit it, and its message would have been lost. It was uncertain how the White House staff would respond, but I knew that if I let them muzzle me, I would be less effective for the President, and he was certainly not overloaded with officials loyal to his policies.

At the Treasury staff meeting on March 20 Don Regan whispered to me his congratulations and then asked, "How's your press across the street?" "The White House loved it," I said, meaning the Reaganites who welcomed this counterattack. Secretary Regan left the staff meeting early and turned it over to McNamar, the deputy secretary. I heard alarm bells. I was sitting at the opposite end of the conference table from McNamar, with Andrew Mellon staring down the table at him impassively from his full-length portrait behind my back. In his portrait Mellon appears invulnerable. Not a bad posture to adopt, I thought, as I saw the muzzle floating down the table toward me.

"Craig," said McNamar, "I don't want you to take it personally, but in the future we need to clear articles with Ann in Public Affairs." Ann McLaughlin was the assistant secretary for public affairs, and she owed her job to McNamar. I was not sure whether he was speaking for Don Regan, himself, Jim Baker, or all three, but I knew that once I uttered the expected "Sure, Tim," I would find my pen clipped.

"When the editorial board of the *Wall Street Journal* and I make a decision," I replied, "I'm not likely to run it by Ann." Beryl Sprinkel, the undersecretary for monetary affairs, suppressed a grin

6. My claim that OMB was in the supply-side camp must have amused William Grieder, the *Washington Post* editor who was taping David Stockman's weekly confessions of disloyalty which later appeared in the *Atlantic Monthly.*

and mustered a gruff voice to declare: "It was a damn good article." That was the end of it. I went on explaining, defending, and interpreting the President's economic program in the *Wall Street Journal,* the *New York Times,* the *Washington Post,* and *Fortune.* It was clear that I had far more allies outside the administration than within, so my decision to protect the independence of my pen was sound. I estimated that I could help to keep the President out of the establishment's cage for a year. By the time I resigned a year later, Bob Bartley, the editor of the *Wall Street Journal,* told me that I had earned a reputation as a guerrilla warring for the President's program behind the lines of his own administration.

Rosy Scenario

When the economic projections were published on February 18, 1981, they showed real economic growth of 4.2 percent in 1982, 5.0 percent in 1983, and 4.5 percent in 1984 (see Table 4). They were promptly labeled "rosy." A joke went around: "Who is the highest-ranking woman in the Reagan Administration?" "Rosy Scenario!" In fact, the promised payoff was exceptionally modest. Chart 6, comparing our five-year projections of real economic growth to the economy's actual performance during the Carter Administration, had to be omitted from the February 18 document in which the new Reagan policy package was announced. The real growth rates that Reagan was promising turned out to be *lower* than those the economy had achieved during 1976–1978. The chart invites the obvious question: Why fundamentally change the tax, monetary, and bud-

Table 4. Summary of President's Economic Scenario

	1981	1982	1983	1984	1985	1986
Real GNP growth	1.0%	4.2%	5.0%	4.5%	4.2%	4.2%
CPI change	11.0	8.2	6.2	5.4	4.7	4.2
GNP deflator	9.9	8.2	7.0	6.0	5.4	4.9
Govt. % of GNP	23.0	21.6	20.1	19.2	19.2	19.3
Monetary base growth	8.0	6.4	5.4	4.4	4.0	3.4
Unemployment rate	7.8	7.2	6.6	6.4	6.0	5.6
Interest rate (T bill)	12.0	9.3	8.0	7.2	6.2	5.7
Productivity growth rate	0.6	1.8	2.3	2.2	2.0	2.0

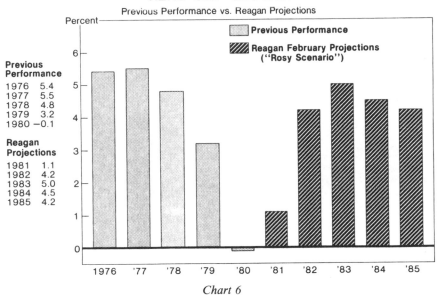

REAL GNP GROWTH

Previous Performance vs. Reagan Projections

Previous
Performance

1976	5.4
1977	5.5
1978	4.8
1979	3.2
1980	−0.1

Reagan
Projections

1981	1.1
1982	4.2
1983	5.0
1984	4.5
1985	4.2

Chart 6

getary policies of the United States if the change does not improve the economy? Reagan's scenario was not rosy enough to justify the political battle over the program.

It did not take much research to establish that Rosy Scenario was a member of previous administrations and not Reagan's. Our outlook should have been named "Blue Sue." As Chart 7 shows, we were projecting less real economic growth with a major tax reduction than Presidents Ford and Carter had projected with tax increases. Furthermore, their optimistic growth projections had not prevented them from projecting a substantial decline in inflation. Yet both Charles Schultze, who had been CEA chairman in the Carter Administration, and Alan Greenspan, who was Ford's chairman, were joining in the media's criticism of our projections. But as Chart 8 shows, the Reagan February projections displayed only a slight improvement over the projections that Schultz had prepared for the Carter Administration the previous month. Nonetheless, the media and the politicians managed to create a general perception that the Reagan Administration had come up with more optimistic projections than had ever been seen before.

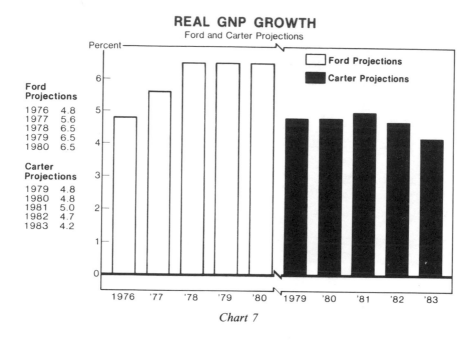

Chart 7

The hyperbole flew fast and loose. On March 9, 1981, the *Washington Post* charged that Reagan's "scenario lies far beyond the limits of any past experience in this country or any other industrial democracy." But as recently as 1976–1978 the economy had produced real growth rates of 5.4, 5.5, and 4.8 percent. On the very day that the *Washington Post* made its ridiculous claim, Treasury learned from Aritoshi Soejima of the Japanese Ministry of Finance that Japan's recent economic history contradicted the *Post*'s assertion. In 1974 Japan had an inflation rate of 24.5 percent and a real growth rate of −0.6. Five years later Japan's inflation rate was 3.6 percent, and its economy was growing 5.9 percent (Table 5).

The Japanese experience also contradicted the charge that it was not possible to increase real economic growth while reducing the growth in the money supply. In 1973, prior to the 1974 jump in the inflation rate, the Japanese money supply increased 22.7 percent as a result of accommodating the jump in energy prices from the first oil shock. Stunned by the inflation, the Japanese brought money growth under control. In his address to the Mont Pelerin Society held at the Hoover Institution in September 1980, Yoshio Suzuki,

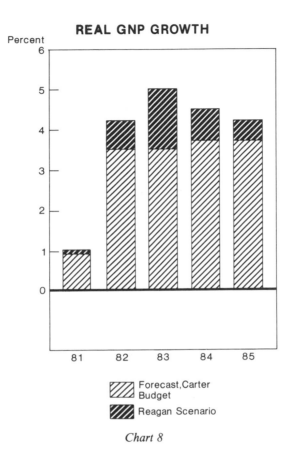

Chart 8

adviser to the Bank of Japan, attributed the success over the five-year period to "the transformation of monetary policy," which did not expand the money supply to accommodate the second oil shock.

But the myth of the rosy forecast stuck. It has become a commonplace that the Reagan Administration overpromised and oversold its

Table 5. Japanese Economic Performance

	1974	1975	1976	1977	1978	1979
Real GNP growth	−0.6%	1.4%	6.5%	5.4%	6.0%	5.9%
Consumer prices	24.5	11.8	9.3	8.1	3.8	3.6
GNP deflator	20.1	8.6	5.6	5.6	3.9	2.1

program. As time passed, a tale grew that there was an even rosier set of projections prepared by the Treasury and that David Stockman had to intervene to save the administration from embarrassment. There was indeed a more optimistic set of numbers, but the Treasury had not prepared them. As *Business Week* reported on February 23, 1981, the "even more bullish forecast" was "prepared for the Office of Management and Budget by economic consultant John Rutledge, president of Claremont Economics Institute." The advocacy of Rutledge was "led by Lawrence Kudlow, the chief economist at the Office of Management and Budget," reported the *New York Times* (February 13, 1981).

From the standpoint of the recession that developed, the administration's projections were rosy. But the projections did not assume a serious recession. Neither did anyone else's. Indeed, throughout the spring and summer of 1981 when we were trying to get the program passed, the air was full of charges that it would be wildly inflationary. Among many, Walter Heller was convinced that the proposed tax cuts would inject too much inflationary purchasing power into the economy. He asked in the *Wall Street Journal* on February 10, 1981, "How can the economy absorb that big an expansionary punch without aggravating our already intolerable inflation?" A few days later *Washington Post* columnist Hobart Rowen declared that the tax cut was "so big that traditional Republicans and many Democrats regard it as dangerously inflationary." So did Rowen: "Even if Congress were to pass budget cuts that matched the tax cuts dollar for dollar, there is nothing in the fiscal program—in the view of those not addicted to supply-side theory—that works against inflation."

Over the succeeding months, the inflation hysteria grew. On May 11 Senate Finance Committee Chairman Dole told the *New York Times* that he personally continued to fear that the tax cut would be inflationary. At a July meeting of the board of governors of the Federal Reserve System with its economic consultants, Alan Greenspan expected that a restrictive monetary policy would be overwhelmed by the tax cuts, and inflation would explode. Monetary policy was the junior partner, Greenspan said, and could "do nothing other than a weak rear-guard action." There can be little doubt that the inflation hysteria encouraged Volcker to overreact by clamping down too tightly on money growth.

Almost every week during 1981 brought new complaints from Herbert Stein, who was certain that the administration was going to send the economy up in the smoke of inflation. So was the *New York Times,* which on July 29 editorialized again that "the Great Tax Cut of 1981 ... promises more inflation." An old-fashioned Keynesian belief in the predominance of fiscal policy combined with politics and Washington competitiveness to whip up an inflation hysteria even while the economy was plummeting into recession. When the Federal Reserve let money growth temporarily turn up sharply in the spring of 1981, it was taken as confirmation that the Reagan Administration intended to monetize deficits.

The February 1981 projections were not a forecast. They represented an estimate of the effects on the economy of the full implementation of the Reagan program. The scenario was based on three important assumptions. One was that personal income tax rates would be cut 10 percent in January 1981, 10 percent in January 1982, and 10 percent in January 1983. The scenario was never adjusted to reflect the delay of the tax cuts. Another assumption was that federal spending would be brought under control and would decline to 19.3 percent of GNP by 1984. The other assumption was that the Federal Reserve would provide moderate and predictable growth in the money supply.

Monetary Policy

The assumptions underlying our February projections were stated explicitly many times. For example, the February 18 report states: "the economic scenario assumes that the growth rates of money and credit are steadily reduced from the 1980 levels to one-half those levels by 1986." Secretary Regan, Undersecretary Sprinkel, and I are on the public record in testimony before Congress stating that our monetary assumption and the policy we requested from Federal Reserve Chairman Paul Volcker was a gradual 50 percent reduction in the growth rate of the money supply spread over six years. Yet, oddly enough, when I testified before the Senate Budget Committee on March 5, 1982, Chairman Domenici was surprised to hear my statement of the administration's monetary assumption. He seemed to think that we had supported the very tight monetary policy during 1981, when Volcker collapsed the growth of the money supply to zero for six months of the year. I wondered who in the administration had been keeping Domenici abreast of events.

We were never utopian about our projections, knowing that they were no better than our assumptions. We thought we had a fighting chance to restructure the tax code and to reduce the growth rate of federal spending. Our biggest concern was monetary policy. The day after the Reagan inauguration, Treasury was asked to prepare a short memo on the subject of the new President's message to Volcker. The memo read:

There is no way the President can carry out the main points of his administration . . . unless the Federal Reserve provides the right kind of monetary policy. The right policy is stable moderate and predictable money growth . . . Volcker should manage the affairs of the Fed so that uncertainty is reduced . . . There is no excuse for failure. If the Fed fails, the Reagan Administration fails.

Unfortunately our fears were realized. Instead of evenly spreading the reduction in money growth over a six-year period, the Federal Reserve delivered 75 percent of the reduction in the first year. In November 1981 the Treasury staff reported that the main monetary measure, called M1-B, which consists of currency plus all kinds of checking accounts, had *fallen* over the previous six months, for only the second time since 1959–60. There was actually less money in the economy in October than there had been the previous April. The growth in M1-B over the year was meager, roughly equivalent to figures for the recession years of 1970 and 1975. This was ferocious tightness indeed and, with the tax cut delayed, recession was inevitable.

The administration's monetarists were worried that the Federal Reserve would overshoot its targets and deliver too much money. I was worried that they would undershoot and deliver too little. If the Federal Reserve brought on a recession before the administration could get its tax and budget reductions passed, it could be the end of the Reagan program. Falling revenues and a widening deficit would jeopardize the tax reductions, and rising unemployment would make it difficult to hold down expenditures. These concerns led me to send a memo on the economy to Secretary Regan on March 9, 1981. "The economy and forecasts of its performance might interact in decisive ways with the success of the President's economic policy package in Congress," the memo began. The recent unemployment number looked fairly good on the surface, "but employment gains on the payroll survey slowed to 51,000 after averaging 275,000 over the previous six months." Most of the forecasters had shifted away from predicting a 1981 downturn, but "it is possible with their Keynesian orientation that they are paying insufficient attention to the monetary side of the equation." Specifically:

The monetary base has been flat since mid-November. It had been growing at an 8 to 9 percent annual rate for the last several years and 10 percent this past summer and early fall. There is no recent parallel for such an abrupt slowdown.

Conceivably, monetary developments could force the economy down sooner and more sharply than expected on the current forecast.

"It is possible," I concluded, "that the Fed's past behavior has booby-trapped the Administration's economic policy package."

As it turned out, the recession hit after the program passed but before the delayed tax cuts were scheduled to take effect. The recession nevertheless came close enough to endanger the tax cuts with the deficits it brought in its wake. On July 20, 1982, in an editorial, "What Comes After Reaganomics?," the *Washington Post*, pointing to the recession, declared the supply-side tax cuts a failure—this in the very month that the first 10 percent reduction went into effect. The *Post* justified its haste in dismissing an untried policy by declaring that supply-siders had promised that the anticipation of a future tax cut would bring about an investment and economic boom in advance. It had not happened, so it was time for a new policy.

The *Post* conveniently overlooked that the Federal Reserve had produced a recession prior to the tax cut. In addition, the *Post* was shooting from the hip on the principle of the matter. The argument that anticipation of a tax cut would produce a boom in advance was made by Martin Feldstein, Harvard professor and the president of the National Bureau of Economic Research. In a *Wall Street Journal* column of August 7, 1980, "Dawdling with Incentives," I rejected this argument, calling it "the responsible economist's version of the Laffer curve." Anticipating a tax cut would have *adverse* effects on the current economy. People would shift income earning activities to the future when tax rates would be lower, and they would shift tax deductions and credits to the present when their value is highest. The result would be to worsen the economy and the deficit in the present. The reasoning was theoretical, but it was later validated by the practical advice that accounting firms and tax lawyers gave their clients.[7] Since I knew the tax-rate reductions would be phased in, my concern that anticipation might cause a temporary dip in the economy was one reason I did not want any tight money prior to the tax reductions. I was not the only supply-sider making this point. Once it was known that the tax cuts would not be effective retroactive to January 1981, the supply-side forecasting firm, H. C. Wainwright Economics of Boston, predicted the recession while others were forecasting inflation. Subscribers who listened to Wainwright escaped being caught with too much debt in a recession, when cash flow is poor.

In the March 9 memo I warned Secretary Regan that a recession could also cause our inflation program to fall apart. From their experience with policy in the past, people have learned to expect that a recession will be followed by monetary expansion. Therefore, their inflation expectations could move up in advance of the recovery. This would keep interest rates high during the recession. The high interest rates could cause a retreat to ad hoc policies and defeat the President's economic program. In 1979–80 I had predicted that, unless there was a change in policy, interest rates might remain high in future recessions—a fact of which T. Rowe Price reminded its clients on April 2, 1982. My March 9 memo to Regan ended with a one-sentence paragraph: "The landmine which might exist in the downturn in the money numbers is the reason an early due date from the President to the Congress for passage of his economic policy program is imperative."

7. On public television the very day the tax bill was signed, newscasters MacNeil and Lehrer interviewed tax accountants who explained how to take maximum advantage of the tax cut by postponing income and bringing deductions forward to the present tax year. On August 25 Sylvia Porter's column began: "Millions of you, in occupations ranging from salespersons to physicians to lawyers can shift portions of your income from 1981 to 1982. Start arranging to do so now, and you will be able to cut your federal income taxes substantially." On October 26, 1981, *Business Week* wrote about the "flood of advice on postponing income and accelerating deductions."

*   *   *

The Reagan Administration made a fundamental error when it released its February 18 projections without a base-line forecast to show the state of the economy under a continuation of the old economic policies or how the economy would be if Reagan's policies were not enacted. Without a published, official standard of comparison, journalists and critics could choose their own standards for comparison, usually to our disadvantage. I pushed hard for a base-line forecast, but could spark no interest elsewhere.

Many kinds of harmful interpretations resulted from the absence of a base-line forecast. One of the most damaging was the revenue-loss estimate, the figure that would be used as the measure of the size of the tax cut. Without a base line the revenue losses had to be computed by using Reagan's higher GNP projections as the tax base. This exaggerated the size of the tax cut. The proper procedure would have been to apply the higher tax rates of the then current law to the lower base-line GNP forecast to get a measure of tax revenues in case there were no tax cut. Then, to obtain a measure of revenues under the Reagan program, the proposed lower tax rates should have been applied to the higher GNP projection made possible by the stimulus of better incentives. The difference between the two would be the revenue loss. But since there was no base-line forecast, the proper procedure could not be followed and the revenue loss came to an exaggerated $765.5 billion.

In a memo to Undersecretary Ture on January 31, 1981, I argued against preparing revenue estimates "based on a growth path that current tax law precludes." The President needed to be protected from the unrealistically large figure of $765 billion. Publishing this figure in isolation would create the impression that the government was losing $765 billion. The tax cut needed to be put in perspective by comparing the year-by-year growth in revenues under the Reagan proposals with the growth in revenues projected in the last Carter budget. In spite of the tax-rate reductions, federal revenues were projected to rise by 57 percent over the 1981–1986 period. Under the Carter proposals revenues were projected to rise by 95 percent. In view of the lower spending and lower inflation that we planned, we did not need such a large growth in revenues. This way of presenting the tax cut would not produce any panic.

Nevertheless, the $765 billion figure was hurled out into the

media. Why I do not know. Ture and I had been fighting battles together for years. Perhaps he had too many fires to fight to be respon-
sive to this problem. More likely the bureaucrats in the office of tax
policy, who wanted to close loopholes rather than cut tax rates, dug
in their heels and refused any change from "standard procedure."
On yet another front we were captured by the past.

The War Against the President's Program

Reagan made a fundamental mistake in failing to appoint to the senior White House staff, to CEA, and to OMB people with a direct
stake in the success of his policy. Instead, a group of advisers were
assembled whose careers were vested in a different approach to economic policy. People who believe in the Phillips curve or in fighting
inflation with unemployment cannot at the same time believe in
supply-side economics, and people who believe in core inflation or
that deficits cause inflation cannot believe in monetarism. The President had a program based on one set of principles and advisers who
believed in a different set.

All the supply-siders were in the Treasury where they could be
isolated, and isolation was not long in coming. By February 1981
many journalists were writing that Stockman was stealing the economic show to the chagrin of Treasury Secretary Regan. On February 22 Hobart Rowen devoted his Sunday column in the
Washington Post to "Kudos for Stockman's Budget Blitz." "Until
the workaholic Stockman took over," he wrote, "the Reagan program was mere rhetoric." Rowen claimed that Regan was "chafing
in a second fiddle role in the Stockman band" and that the Treasury
secretary "has yet to live up to his billing as the President's chief
economic spokesman." Five days later, on February 27, Rowen further distanced Stockman from Regan and the supply-siders: "Even
if one can't support all of Budget Director David A. Stockman's
spending reduction exercise, by and large it is much more convincing than is the totally untested "supply-side" tax program that Congress wisely will reexamine and almost surely modify drastically."

The separation and realignment of Stockman became more pro-
nounced with the appearance of an article by Steven Rattner in the
New York Times (March 4, 1981). Here it was said that Stockman
had sided with Weidenbaum in suppressing overly optimistic pro-

jections prepared by supply-siders. He was reported to have helped to delete an attack on the Federal Reserve in the economic report and to have opposed the retroactive tax cut in favor of a six-month delay. "While Mr. Weidenbaum has long been seen as pragmatic, Mr. Stockman has confounded those who considered him an ideologue by displaying a similar sense of pragmatism and political reality." On the other hand, Secretary Regan "has played only a modest role in shaping policy, and he has disappointed even his supporters in his performance as economic spokesman." But that was to be expected, since he was saddled with the "most ardent" supply-siders. "Failing to pick his own team," declared Rattner, "is among the complaints voiced about Mr. Regan's tenure."

It is not necessary to read between the lines to understand what this campaign was all about. Stockman, who was increasingly playing the role of the traditional balanced-budget Republican, was being praised by liberal journalists who had spent their lives ridiculing such an economic posture. Regan, who was attempting to present the President's own supply-side perspective in policy debates, was made to look weak and ineffective. If Regan looked bad, however, it was not all his fault, since he was surrounded at the Treasury by "ardent" supply-siders. In the subtle, shifting world of Washington politics, imagery means a great deal to egos and power. Reports of an omnipotent Stockman and an ineffectual Regan were intended within the administration and in the press to isolate Regan from his subcabinet and to make him toe the line with the traditionalists. Regan was torn between his ego and his loyalty to the President, which accounted for the up-down performance of the Treasury in the policy debates.

The campaign to lionize Stockman continued. A UPI story on March 23 began: "David Stockman, David Stockman—it's the highest rated show on Capitol Hill these days." The article went on to say that Stockman was in such great demand because he was the chief architect of the budget cuts and because of the poor performance of the cabinet secretaries. While Stockman's budget-cutting show was playing to rave reviews, the attacks on the tax-cut portion of the Reagan program continued. On March 4 Paul Volcker showed the Federal Reserve's lack of support for the President's program by calling the administration's outlook too optimistic.

Another behind-the-scenes campaign had developed as well. It involved the image of White House domestic policy adviser Martin Anderson. The February 2 issue of *Business Week* reported that Anderson was going to serve as a conduit for advice to the President from Alan Greenspan and Arthur Burns, both of whom were critical of supply-side economics. A *New York Times* report by Steven Rattner on March 10 placed Anderson in the anti-supply-side camp. The March 16 issue of *Business Week* (which appeared the same day as Rattner's article) gave Anderson credit for helping to kill the proposal to lower the maximum tax rate on investment income, supposedly a defeat for supply-siders. In addition he was said to be opposed to the appointment of New York businessman Lewis Lehrman, a supply-side advocate, to the Council of Economic Advisers. From the way the press was telling the story, it seemed as if Anderson would do anything in his power to stop the supply-siders. Anderson and I had been colleagues in the Hoover Institution at Stanford University. We were both Reaganites, and we shared many of the same views. If he and I were to team up, Treasury supply-siders would have a direct communication link to the White House. At the same time he would be backed up by Treasury staff resources, which would strengthen his policy input. Someone wary of the potential alliance was attempting to drive wedges before it could form.

In the early days of the Reagan Administration, there were disturbing signs of disarray on other policy issues as well. One of President Reagan's first actions was to warn his cabinet against letting "the permanent government"—the bureaucracy—take control of policy. In spite of this warning Department of Transportation Secretary Drew Lewis gave signs of being captured by his bureaucracy in the first hours of appointment. On January 28, scarcely eight days into the new administration, Lewis called a meeting of cabinet secretaries. I went to the meeting with Regan. As we were being driven over to DOT in the dark blue Buick he had as a Treasury car, we had a few minutes to speculate about what was afoot.

When the meeting began, the secretary of the Treasury was stunned to find that he had been called to a meeting to listen to Deputy Assistant Secretary Charles Swinburn, a Carter holdover, present his case for auto import quotas against the Japanese—a protectionist policy in direct contradiction to the free market principles of the Reagan Administration. Treasury telephoned Darrell Trent, the deputy secretary, and Judith Connor, the assistant secretary, and asked them what DOT had in mind. Treasury was assured that DOT had no intention of pressing for quotas. The department had inherited the Carter Administration's "Goldschmidt Report," which it needed to discard without generating a lot of internal problems with the bureaucracy. DOT was setting up a task force so that Treasury could take over the analysis. The task force would also keep Congress from legislating quotas by making it look as if the administration were doing something about the Japanese car problem. Shortly afterwards Drew Lewis told reporters that it was administration policy to do something for the auto industry, and he had a full-scale campaign going in the press for import quotas.

Over the next month Reaganites watched incredulously as the auto-import issue pushed the President's economic policy package off the agenda. By the first week in March, Treasury's attention had been completely diverted from cutting taxes to resisting the rush toward protectionism. A government that was supposed to be bringing a policy revolution was deflected from its goal by a deputy assistant secretary of transportation. No one could understand why Drew Lewis did not get a call from the White House. Not only inappropriately timed, this was definitely a no-win issue for the President. Treasury, CEA, and OMB did not believe that protection would make American cars more competitive, the unions less demanding, or management more alert. If the President made the right policy decision and stood up for free trade, he would be accused of favoring the interest of Japanese workers over American workers. If he made the wrong policy decision in order to avoid the political cost, it would seem that his principles were not very strong and that he had no faith that his economic program would bring recovery to the auto industry along with the rest of the economy. Furthermore, giving in on the quota issue would open the door to a long line of other supplicants, each with its own industry-specific proposal. In its first days the administration was running the risk of having its new economic policy pushed aside by the resurrection of economic management on an issue-by-issue, crisis-by-crisis basis.

On March 13 Tim McNamar called a meeting of the Treasury auto task force. There had been a front-page article in the *New York*

Times about a split in the cabinet over the issue of import quotas on Japanese cars. The White House, said McNamar, was pointing its finger at Treasury for taking the fight to the press. It was preposterous. DOT had been openly taking the issue to the press for weeks. McNamar was telling Treasury to disengage from the battle. The official line was that a compromise was necessary for the sake of the governors of the auto states as well as for the image of cabinet government. The compromise was that the Japanese would voluntarily restrain their auto exports to the United States. Before it was over, the United States had come close to starting a trade war. Canada informed Japan that it expected similar and parallel treatment to that accorded the United States. If Japan limited auto exports to the United States but not to Canada, Canada would take unilateral action. Simone Veil, president of the European Parliament, declared that any "measures taken in favor of the United States must also be taken in favor of Europe." Europeans were fearful that Japan would increase exports to Europe in order to compensate for the loss in exports to the United States.

By the time the issue was settled, the small Treasury policy staff was exhausted. The economic program had gone nowhere. And the *Washington Post* was declaring that the lost initiative meant that the Congress would work its will on the President's economic package. The Reagan revolution had wound down before it started. It would take a tremendous effort to get it going again.

5

Preludes to Victory

MONDAY, MARCH 30, 1981, STARTED OFF ON A HIGH NOTE with breakfast at the White House with President Reagan. As an architect of his economic program, I would have liked to sit down and talk things over with him. But the breakfast was a social affair for presidential appointees and an opportunity to be photographed with the President. For Reagan it was an opportunity to see who was in his government. Presidents seldom know more than a few of their appointees and have no idea who they are relying on. The lack of contact between a president and his government was dramatized by the watchful eye that the Secret Service kept over the roomful of people bearing presidential commissions. In a brief address to the group the President again exhorted his government to put policy before politics. A man sitting next to me asked if I was new to government. It was his third administration, he explained. All of a sudden the pleasure of breakfasting at the White House gave way to a sinking feeling that the Reagan revolution was running on retreads. I felt lonely and wondered if the President did.

Later in the day I was to feel a great deal lonelier when I heard that the President had been shot. Alexander Haig's announcement from the White House—"I am in charge here"—sounded too final for hope. The early rumors were that Ronald Reagan was dead and that the White House was waiting for Vice-President Bush to arrive back in Washington before announcing the President's assassination. The Reaganites in the government telephoned each other to commiserate the tragedy and to share their sudden feelings of vulnerability, not to an assassin's bullet but to the forces of the establishment. To the extent that my sails still had any wind in them after the economic report, Rosy Scenario, auto-import quotas, and the decision to delay the tax cut, they went slack. I sat in my spacious office with its high ceiling and full-length windows overlooking the front lawn of the White House. An oil portrait of Alexander J. Dallas of Pennsylvania hung in a gilt frame over the blue leather sofa where I would informally explain and discuss the President's economic program with visitors. Dallas had been Secretary of the Treasury from October 1814 to October 1816. I tried to recall if the White House had been rebuilt by then after being burned by the British in the War of 1812 or whether the Treasury in Dallas' day had also presided over a ruin next door.

When the definite word came that the President was not mortally wounded, our spirits revived. We rededicated ourselves to the fight for the President's program. Reagan would gain a sympathy element—an attempt on the President's life is one of the few things that can still draw the nation together, and Reagan had shown extraordinary bearing by quipping, with a bullet in his lung, "I forgot to duck." Nevertheless, we knew that Reagan would be out of action during a critical period—the spring budget resolution.

Momentum and Compromise

Treasury had been concerned about momentum ever since the administration had decided to delay the beginning dates of the tax cuts in the name of balancing the 1984 budget. We wondered if that decision would turn out to be the first step away from our program of balancing the budget through increased economic growth. The rationale for the tax cuts was improved economic performance, which would bring the budget into balance. Yet, in effect, the administration had made a decision that the budget would be improved by delaying the tax cuts. If that was the case, why have the tax cut at all? If the logic behind the decision to delay were followed through, there would be no tax cut.

The deficit was also a problem for the tax cut on the expenditure side of the budget. During April the debate in Congress concentrated on budget cutting and the deficit, or at least that is how the press played it. The emphasis did not bode well for the tax cuts. Holding down the growth of spending could turn out to be a bloody business. If it was all done in the name of a balanced budget, there would be a hesitance to accept the revenue loss from a tax cut. The organized spending constituencies have grown accustomed to demanding more and more. The taxpayers, however, are not organized, although they have a few bold champions in Reagan, Kemp, and a handful of others. The politicians take advantage of unorganized taxpayers by taxing them at rich men's tax rates in order to finance the spending programs. But even that has not been enough, and the government has become unable to live within its vast means and is forced to borrow to finance its expenditures. Reaganomics intended to put the government into a position where it would have to reduce its borrowing while simultaneously accepting a cut in its income—that is the way Congress saw the President's program.

There was a great deal of talk about compromise. Jim Jones, chairman of the House Budget Committee, developed a strategy to push the President toward compromising his policy. Jones had some credibility as a tax cutter because he had played a role in cutting the capital gains tax in 1978. He developed a budget proposal that had higher spending and a lower deficit than the President's. He was trying to hold the Democrats together. The higher spending would appeal to the liberals, and the smaller deficit would attract the southern conservatives (the "boll weevils"). Jones arrived at his package by cutting taxes less. In place of the three-year tax-rate reduction, he had a one-year tax cut skewed toward middle- and lower-income brackets. Fishing for the support of business lobbyists, he hinted at more generous depreciation allowances for business than the administration was proposing.

It was a clever move by an astute man. But an extraordinary thing happened. On April 9 an editorial, "Jim Jones for President?," appeared in the *Washington Star*. Jones, the *Star* reminded everyone, "represents a single Oklahoma constituency. Unlike the President, he did not place an economic program before the country, nor was he elected by a majority of the votes of 44 states." The message was clear: Get out of the President's way. The next day, however, three Republicans joined nine Democrats to vote down the President's program in the Senate Budget Committee. Many saw the combination of Democratic opposition to spending reductions and Republican opposition to budget deficits as a threat to the tax cuts.

In Washington, principles are an imported product. They spoil soon, lasting only as long as the people do who bring them to town. It was Ronald Reagan's fate that what principles existed were operating against his program. Three freshmen Republican senators, William Armstrong, Steve Symms, and Charles Grassley, had campaigned against deficits, and they were not going to vote for Reagan's deficits or anyone else's. Domenici had made the outcome inevitable by being principled himself. He refused to accept the President's balanced budget projection for 1984 because it was based on $44 billion in unspecified budget cuts. David Stockman was still playing games with the budget while accusing Treasury of playing games with economic assumptions. Domenici adopted the Congressional Budget Office's deficit projection of $44.7 billion and lost the vote for the President's budget in his committee. (He was to lose the vote for the President's budget the next two years as well.)

With no one from the White House enforcing the President's policy in the Republican Senate, the *Wall Street Journal* spoke up for the President in an editorial, "John Maynard Domenici," on April 16: "The fundamental problem in the Budget Committee is Chairman Pete Domenici's insistence on using economic projections that assume the program will fail." The *Journal* objected to making policy in 1981 on the basis of an estimate of what the deficit might be in 1984. "If you think any of these estimates can tell you what the deficit will be in 1984, lie down until you get over it." If Senator Domenici continued to use CBO's deficit projections, the editorial warned, "they will be used to whittle back the tax cuts." Why not assume instead that the program will work? Otherwise, "we will be back in the same old rut of trying to balance the budget three years hence by allowing inflation to raise taxes."

Domenici called Secretary Regan and blamed the editorial on me. The administration was not yet three months old and already it was taken for granted that only the supply-siders in the Treasury would defend the President's tax cuts. It was demoralizing that complaints were lodged only against administration officials who were suspected of having planted *defenses* of the President's program in the press. No one called in the ubiquitous "White House officials" who were regularly sowing their doubts about the President's program.

The next day David Stockman and Jim Baker sent a letter defending Domenici to Robert Bartley. Secretary Regan did not sign the letter, perhaps because he had heard that Domenici's staff had convinced him not to work with Armstrong to reduce the deficit on the expenditure side, but to stretch out the tax cuts. Bartley was amused that Stockman and Baker chose to defend Domenici rather than Ronald Reagan, and he followed up with another editorial, "For Pete's Sake." Republicans, he wrote, "should have voted for the Reagan program and their chairman should have been careful to give them no reason for doing otherwise."

In their column of April 22 in the *Washington Post,* Rowland Evans and Robert Novak saw more in the story than a tale of misguided principles. They reported that Domenici's budget committee staff—especially Steve Bell, "a 37 year old ex-newspaper reporter, poet and self-styled Renaissance man"—was exploiting the budget deficit as a way of killing the Kemp-Roth tax cut. The charge is not implausible. If true, Bell was continuing in the tradition of the Senate Budget Committee Republican staff that had been fighting tax cuts since the days of Senator Bellmon. Normally, the staff director of the Senate Budget Committee is an important policymaker—but not if someone else has set the agenda. And Reagan, Kemp, and the supply-siders had set the agenda, leaving other policymakers with the role of implementation. In Washington, there are not many people who want to implement someone else's success. According to Evans and Novak, Bell had set an early tone of inveighing against "supply-side ideologues" and belittling tax-rate reduction. What was afoot, they reported, became clear immediately after the vote in the Budget Committee defeating the President's budget: "Domenici's staff proclaimed, with unconcealed delight, that Kemp-Roth was dead." Bell reportedly told Budget Committee staffers that, instead of working with conservative Republicans like Armstrong to reduce the deficit by controlling spending, Domenici would work with Democrats to reduce the deficit by stretching out the tax cut. According to Evans and Novak, who were admirers of Stockman at that time, Stockman was alerted to the scheme and stopped it. It would be interesting to know what argument he used, since Bell was employing Stockman's own strategy of balancing the budget by delaying the tax cuts. More likely it was the *Wall Street Journal* editorials that put the Senate Budget Committee on the spot. It was too early in the administration for Republican senators or their staff to be able to get away with undercutting the Republican President.

Holding the Fort

The Treasury and the *Wall Street Journal* editorial page succeeded in holding the fort for the President for a month while he convalesced. On April 28 he was back in the fray with an address to a joint session of Congress. It was not a day too soon. Talk of tax compromise—by which was meant a reduction in the size of the personal income tax cuts—was thick in the air. On April 12 Jim Jones leaked some real mischief. He told reporters that three Treasury officials, John Chapoton, Norman Ture, and Bruce Thompson, had expressed a willingness to compromise on the three-year tax cut, "10-10-10," and accept a one-year tax cut instead. The story was untrue and presumably the result of a misunderstanding. From his bed the President sent an order to retract the compromise offer. But the damage had already been done, and the anti-tax cut faction at the White House was off and running. An unidentified White House official told *New York Times* correspondent Howell Raines that "it would be foolish to deny that some sub-cabinet person might have hinted to Jim Jones that we might come down to one year at 10 percent" (April 14, 1981). Raines went on to report that "even before the shooting incident, Mr. Reagan was being told in Oval Office meetings that he might have to settle for a one-year tax cut, and that the President himself did not rule out the possibility that he might modify his tax plan."

White House aides apparently wasted no opportunity to tell Reagan that his chances of winning his full program on Capitol Hill were slim. Neither did they shrink from reporting the President's private meetings to the press, especially if they could make it appear that Reagan had no support for his tax cuts. For example, on April 15, 1981, the day after Raines's story, Lou Cannon reported in the *Washington Post* that an allegedly unanimous front of top administration officials was trying to get Reagan to compromise his tax program. All the talk of compromise coming out of the White House did much more for the morale of Democrats like Jones, Rostenkowski, and O'Neill than for the President's supporters. Clearly, someone in the White House was manipulating both the media and morales in an effort to generate pressures that would produce a compromise as a fait accompli. Why, the Treasury wondered, produce a compromise in advance? Were not Republicans negotiating with themselves? For all intents and purposes the Congress had passed Reaganomics in 1978, and there was no reason to expect that Congress would not pass it again. Treasury officials began to wonder if the President read the newspapers—and if he did, why he did not clean out those disloyal "White House officials" who were whittling away at his program. The irony was that the Jim Jones affair pointed to the Treasury subcabinet—the power base of the supply-siders—as the compromisers. It was a double irony in that two of the alleged compromisers were staunch supply-siders—Ture, one of the architects of the policy, and Bruce Thompson, who had been Senator Roth's tax aide. Most likely, the White House aide who ran to Reagan's sickbed with the story of Treasury's compromise with Jim Jones was the one who was planting the compromise talk in the press.

The President's April 28 nationally televised speech before Congress reined in the loose talk. Lou Cannon in the *Washington Post* acknowledged "Ronald Reagan's triumphant return to action." Reaganomics was "once more in the ascendancy." In a few words the President defeated Jones's and O'Neill's budget resolution and ensured the passage of the Gramm-Latta bill, named after Texas Democrat Phil Gramm, a former economics professor, and Ohio Republican Del Latta, the ranking Republican on the Budget Committee. Gramm-Latta was the product of the "boll weevil" and Republican coalition that supported the President's program. It provided for the President's tax and spending reductions, and on May 7 it passed the House 270–154, with all 190 Republicans and 80 Democrats voting for Reaganomics. The vote showed there was more support for Reagan in Congress than in his administration.

In his address to Congress Reagan said that we had to chart a bold new course in order to restore our economic strength and build opportunities for the people. Begin with a dream that we can do better, add faith, then "reach beyond the commonplace and not fall short for lack of creativity or courage." Some in his government

heard the message. Others fancying themselves pragmatists and re-
alists heard nothing but cant. They had fallen short before the enterprise began.

Treasury had had a hand in the President's speech. Ken Khachigian, who was filling in at Reagan's request as chief White House
speech writer until someone could be found, had sent it over from
his office in the old executive office building. The speech contained
too much emphasis on the budget deficit per se, and we warned
Khachigian that the emphasis could set a trap for the President's
program. If the deficit were to become the focus, "the President's
program will be defeated by scaling back the tax cuts or even raising
taxes." We recommended that "the emphasis should be on the fact
that government spending has been growing faster than the economy, and on reducing such a high rate of spending growth." If the
emphasis were on controlling spending, where it belonged, it could
not be met by raising taxes. This was Ronald Reagan's own view,
and it remained a theme of his speeches for the next ten months.

There were other occasional victories to relieve the distressing life
of a Reaganaut in the Reagan Administration. At the end of February the Wall Street gold trader, James Sinclair, warned his clients
against expecting higher gold prices. "We are so accustomed to
compromise," Sinclair wrote, "that we assume that strength, character and dedication are non-existent on this planet." But the Reaganites, he said, "have an intellectual dedication uncommon in U.S.
politics. Yes, they could be called fanatical as a compliment to their
dedication to a goal which they see as no less than saving America."
Higher gold prices "could only follow an intellectual default":
"Only a failure to adhere to the principles and mandate that
brought this new Administration to office will result in a substantial
price gain for gold." I sent a copy of Sinclair's newsletter to Secretary Regan with a note that we now had a reputation to live up to,
having been declared too tough and too filled with strength of character to compromise the President's program into failure.

Another victory came from unexpected quarters. In April the
Brookings Institution published a collection of papers evaluating
the influence of tax policy on economic behavior. Caroline Atkinson
wrote a brief article about the book in the *Washington Post* on April
27 giving the impression that the studies contradicted the admin-

istration's supply-side views. But in fact, as the Treasury staff reported, "many of the major conclusions provide general support for the Administration's position." Supply-siders had been criticized for thinking that people would work more and business would invest more if their taxes were cut, but now Brookings was publishing studies showing that the combination of federal, state, and social security taxes caused married men to reduce their work effort. Another finding was that the economic inefficiencies caused by high marginal tax rates were large and rose rapidly with income. Other chapters in the Brookings volume dealing with investment, stock prices, and capital gains were supportive of the reasoning behind the President's economic program.

But not even published studies helped. Journalists and academics continued to declare that there was not a scrap of evidence for supply-side economics. When pressed on this matter of evidence, it always turned out that they meant there was no evidence that tax-rate reductions would pay for themselves in each bracket. Since Reaganomics was not based on the Laffer curve, they either did not know what they were criticizing or pretended not to know in order to hold on to their strawman. The organizers of conferences would always put forth a Nobel laureate to slay the ignorant supply-siders. Invariably these men were ideologically opposed to defense spending and reducing taxes on the rich, and for them that is all Reaganomics was about. They never came prepared to make a serious case against supply-side economics.

April brought another victory. Since the February economic report, we had been trying to issue an official explanation of the economic analysis underlying Reaganomics. Stymied by the White House, we had prepared a Treasury document explaining the economics of the program. When it appeared, however, it had been turned into our personal statement by Tim McNamar, who added a note that the document had been prepared by Norman Ture and myself. Reporters quickly inquired whether this implied a Treasury Department disavowal of supply-side economics or whether Ture and I had such big egos that we had to append our names to the Treasury's seal. No one in the Treasury had objected to the document, and we wondered why McNamar had gone out of his way to create the impression that it was a personal statement. We also

wondered why with all the talk of policy splits he would risk creating the impression that the Treasury itself was split. For whatever
the reason—whether our names gave it the air of a disputed document or whether it was too academic for reporters—it did not catch
on as an explanation of the program.

By April Secretary Regan was expressing a need for the missing
explanation. The program, he said, made more sense than people
were giving it credit for. Couldn't I produce an explanation of how
the program works? Not having explained what we were doing at
the beginning, we were now at a disadvantage. I prepared a brief
account of two and a half pages, and an official explanation of the
President's economic policy package finally appeared.

The Vicissitudes of Policymaking

In Washington victories have to be privately and quietly savored. If
they are proclaimed, everyone else denies them, and they are taken
away by the common front of envy. While the press wrote about the
supply-siders' lack of influence, I had established within the administration that I was a voice for the President's program that could
not be ignored. The process of establishing this kind of posture is
not without cost. It can win the grudging respect of colleagues, but it
can also cost friends and allies. I had paid the price and was carefully husbanding my purchase, when in the middle of April Jude
Wanniski came to Washington and squandered it.

Wanniski was convinced that Jim Baker and Dave Gergen, who
had worked hard to defeat Reagan for the Republican nomination,
were supply-side supporters but would not know what policy
choices to make. What better adviser could they have than Wanniski? But how was he to promote himself as the White House
staff's supply-side adviser when the Treasury was full of supply-
siders? He arranged a meeting with Baker and Gergen and told
them that the Treasury supply-siders were afraid of them. Therefore
they could not rely on the in-house supply-siders to speak up and
make their true opinions known. They needed outside advisers,
people who would not be afraid to speak out. Wanniski recommended himself and Jeffrey Bell. Whether or not he realized it,
Wanniski had jeopardized the Treasury's influence. It was doubtful

that Baker or Gergen would be able to picture us as trembling with fear. My two deputies, Steve Entin and Manuel Johnson, were confident and outspoken, and no one thought of Ture or me as shrinking violets. Still, if Baker and Gergen got the idea that we might be uneasy about them, they could run roughshod over us.

I have told this story because it is a good example of the kind of extraneous, fortuitous events that impinge heavily on policy outcomes and often determine them. The professor in the classroom explains to his students the importance of careful statistical measurement, properly specified models, and sound economic analysis. But these things, as important as they are to the professional economist, count for little toward the making of policy. One reason, of course, is that economists themselves cannot agree. Another is that most of the decision makers do not know enough to recognize careful statistics and sound analysis. If they are presented with a choice, they will choose on the basis of personalities, or according to who tells them what they want to hear, how it will play in the press, who they want done in and who elevated, who is smooth and who is strident, or who is the best manipulator of their own personalities.

As an example of how little evidence counts, during the last six months of my stay in the Treasury the fate of Reaganomics turned on a set of spurious statistics assembled by OMB. The statistics purported to prove that government budget deficits caused inflation and high interest rates. Neither the professional staff of the Treasury, nor the Council of Economic Advisers, nor prominent academic economists who had studied the matter for years could find any such relationship. The empirical record shows that deficits and interest rates move with the business cycle, but in opposite directions from each other. At the top of the cycle, deficits are low because tax revenues are pouring in from the booming economy. Despite a falling deficit, interest rates are high because of the investment and consumption boom in the private sector. At the bottom of the cycle, deficits are large because incomes and tax collection are down but unemployment-related expenditures are up. Yet, despite a large deficit, interest rates are low because private demand for credit is down. In spite of the evidence to the contrary, the OMB statistics held sway over the government. When William Niskanen, a member of the Council of Economic Advisers, announced the results of his scientific work—that deficits per se do not cause inflation or high interest rates—at an American Enterprise Institute conference in 1981, the White House and Republican senators were incensed.

Stockman's Preemptive Move

By May it was obvious that Stockman was worried about the hidden deficit peeking out from under the cover of core inflation. Stockman's solution was to cover it up again by reducing the tax cut. He could not directly advocate cutting back on the February tax proposals that were then before Congress. That would have stirred up Reaganites and brought Kemp out against him. In addition, such a move would have undercut Stockman within the administration itself. To argue that we needed to step back from the February tax proposals would be an admission that the administration did not know what it was doing when it submitted its program. It would hand over to Congress the initiative on economic policy, and the Reagan Administration would be off and stumbling with an upfront defeat. Not even the in-house skeptics of the President's policy wanted that, because it would reflect on their ability to manage issues.

Stockman's strategy was to go after the tax cut in an indirect way. He expressed concern that high interest rates were registering the financial markets' lack of confidence in the economic program. The behavior of the markets, he said, could cause the Congress to vote against the President's tax program, despite the momentum created by the President's victory on the budget resolution (Gramm-Latta). From this way of arguing, compromise was the way to save the day, just as later a tax increase would become the way to save the President's policy. Compromise always meant scaling down the personal income tax cuts from 10-10-10 to something less. Jack Kemp and Bill Roth had had great success in having their tax bill adopted as presidential policy. Stockman could rely on the envy and resentments of some members of Congress to cut 10-10-10 and, in the process, Kemp and Roth down to size.

Since the President had said that he would not compromise, he had to be maneuvered into it. The campaign began in earnest on May 14 with a story planted on Steven Weisman of the *New York Times* by "a senior White House official" who "was interviewed on the condition that he not be identified." The story was headlined "Aide Hints at Reagan Tax Shift: Market Disarray Cited as Ground for Compromise." It began:

Washington, May 13—President Reagan, concerned by the unsettled condition of the financial markets, is prepared to accept less than the full amount of his proposed tax cut but wants the Democrats in Congress to make the first move toward compromise, a senior White House official said today.

In an interview, the official said Administration planners had become increasingly worried that the behavior of the markets would cause members of Congress to have second thoughts about voting for Mr. Reagan's tax program, despite the momentum created by the President's recent victories.

The official also said that recent disarray in the markets had shown some Reagan aides that Wall Street was afraid that tax cuts would widen the budget deficit, contributing to the fear of inflation. As a result, he said, the Administration was more willing to compromise on the size of the tax cut.

The official went on to say that "in some basic sense we have been ahead of the game politically and behind the game in terms of the responses of the financial markets." As a result "we're at a critical juncture" and need to adjust the economic program in order "to reverse the enormous lack of confidence we're seeing in the markets." The official then planted the suggestion that what was important to Reagan was the concept of a multiyear cut in the marginal tax rate for individuals, but the magnitude of the reduction was negotiable. The reporter noted that "the official suggested several times that market conditions had shaken members of the Administration, who had been hoping that legislative progress on Mr. Reagan's economic package would cheer Wall Street."

Even in its own terms, the story made no sense. If the President wanted to compromise on a smaller tax cut, he could let Ways and Means Chairman Rostenkowski know without one of his senior officials publicly calling his policies into question. The argument that the stock and bond markets were falling apart as a result of the President's economic policy would normally be the argument of the opposition party. The story was also too clever by half. Weisman presented the leak not as an effort to undermine the tax cuts but rather as the opposite. The official's comments "appeared to be part of an Administration strategy to push Mr. Rostenkowski, an Illinois Democrat, to move first on a compromise."

Treasury recognized the unidentified official by his arguments: it was Stockman. Everyone else recognized him too. *Newsweek* reported (June 15) that "some powerful White House aides are privately expressing displeasure" with Stockman for leaking

two stories to the press warning of danger in the Reagan Administration's tax proposals. One story prematurely signaled Reagan's intention to compromise on taxes; the other claimed that Reagan would have to trim $20 billion from the defense budget over the next two years to make up for the tax cuts, a decision the White House aides insist has not been reached . . . Stockman, aides say, is pushing his own proposals before he has sold them to the President.

At the time Treasury wondered about the story. Although the powerful White House aides were reported to be displeased, the only quotes from them were in praise of Stockman's "enthusiasm and brightness." "Nine times out of ten Stockman gets a first down for you," said the displeased official. It seemed the officials, for appearance' sake, were feeling more pressure to be displeased than they actually felt.

All around, it was a preemptive move. Stockman was attempting to grow a smaller tax bill by planting seeds of compromise. And he was preempting the explanation of high interest rates by associating them with the deficit and the deficit with the tax cuts. The CEA and Treasury monetarists had a different explanation for the behavior of interest rates. By the end of April it was clear that the Federal Reserve Board had allowed the money supply as measured by M-1 to rise sharply. With the board above its targets, interest rates stopped falling and began rising. Stockman seemed overly desperate to ignore the effects of the board's behavior on interest rates and overly anxious to focus the blame on the tax cuts. After all, the markets had known the size of the tax cuts since February, if not before, and interest rates had fallen until the spurt in the money supply became evident.

Don Regan was also upset. Normally a cautious man, he immediately complained to the President that Stockman was undercutting his role as secretary of the Treasury and making him ineffectual. The same day Weisman's article appeared Regan told me in his office that the President said he "would straighten out Stockman." I wondered what that meant. It seemed to me that Stockman had gone too far, not just in encroaching on the Treasury secretary's turf but also in encroaching on the President's economic policy. From what Regan said, I could not tell whether he complained that Stockman was undermining the tax cut or the Treasury's role. Before I could probe, Regan told me that he and the President had also spoken that day about "abolishing the Fed." Since Paul Volcker was in the outer office waiting to see Regan, I thought it was a piquant way to keep me off balance.

Don Regan has a winning smile that is more convincing than his scowl, and he relies more on charm than force to get his way. I was respectful of his position and addressed him as Mr. Secretary, while everyone else called him Don, and in this instance my respectful attitude made it easier for him to take me into his confidence on momentous events without telling me a thing. To this day I do not know if Regan complained to Reagan that Stockman was undermining the program or just encroaching on Treasury's turf. Neither do I know why he and the President were discussing abolishing the Federal Reserve. The secretary knew that I was too polite to embarrass him by keeping him from his appointment with Volcker while I pressed him for explanations. We both knew that the battles ahead would keep the agenda too crowded to permit a revival of the conversation.

I walked back to my office not knowing for certain whether the President intended to fight for the full tax cut or whether it was just a negotiating posture, as some administration officials were beginning to tell the media and the Congress. If Reagan were only striking a pose, then the hard fight I was waging on his behalf was going to leave me far out on a limb. On the other hand, if he was sincere, he was being undermined by some of his own officials. There was no way I could know for sure whether the "senior White House official" was speaking for the President or for himself. I had to choose between self-protection and faith. Numerous policy officials before me had undoubtedly faced the same dilemma. While I wondered about how they had arrived at their decisions, I remembered that I was fighting for a cause.

The May 13 Briefing

The Treasury had seen Stockman's arguments coming. Ironically, the day he was feeding them to the *New York Times* I was in Secretary Regan's office with a set of briefing papers arming him against them. I advised the secretary that it was a mistake for administration officials to claim that high interest rates reflected the market's belief that the President's budget and fiscal policy would fail, especially when monetary policy *was* failing. A "senior Administration economist" had recently remarked to the press that the administration's forecast of higher interest rates for the year had already missed the mark and that continued high interest rates could mean a gloomy budget picture. There were two dangers in this approach. It focused on the budget while overlooking the relationship between monetary policy and interest rates, and it risked holding our program hostage to the performance of an economy that was still laboring under the old laws and policies. Reagan's policies were not yet in effect, and they were not likely ever to go into effect if interest rates were blamed on fiscal rather than monetary policy.

I pointed out to Regan that over the years interest rates have risen and fallen with inflation. Few economic data series track each other so closely. However, in 1979 the relationship broke down. The bond markets had become sensitive to any signs of faster money growth, which was associated with more inflation, higher interest rates, and lower bond prices. Since late 1978 there had been violent swings in the money supply and a period of credit controls. Interest rates began moving directly with upward movements in the money supply, not waiting for the changes in the money supply to show up in the inflation rate. In November 1980 the Federal Reserve had the growth in the money supply down. Interest rates fell early in 1981, but money growth rose again from February through April, taking interest rates up with it. From March to May the interest rates on three-year Treasury notes rose from 13.5 percent to 15 percent. Ten-year Treasuries rose from 13.1 percent to 14.1 percent, and short-term rates exploded with three-month Treasury bills and six-month prime commercial paper rising from about 13.5 percent to 16.5 percent. The monetarists believed that the volatility of the money supply had added uncertainty and risk premiums to interest rates. There was no sign that monetary policy had settled down on a predictable course.

The monetarists and supply-siders in the administration worried that the Federal Reserve was being let off the hook and the President's tax cuts were being put on the hook. In May 1981 the argument was being made that the tax cuts would lead to an inflationary burst of consumer spending, and this fear was allegedly keeping up interest rates. (Later when inflation fell in spite of the tax cuts the argument changed: interest rates were high because the deficit was crowding out private investment. This argument became the fashionable explanation of high interest rates during a recession, when firms were experiencing a high failure rate and practically no private investment was taking place.)

To answer the argument that the tax cuts would cause an inflationary burst of consumer spending, we carefully examined the response to the very similar Kennedy tax cuts. The evidence was clear that people had responded to the tax-rate reductions by consuming a smaller percentage of their incomes, and saving and investment had expanded. We assembled some striking tables and charts, and recommended to Regan that Treasury provide a cabinet-level briefing on the evidence. At the least, we thought, it should be presented to the Cabinet Council on Economic Affairs, which Regan chaired. Nothing happened. As far as I know, the evidence in behalf of its program was never presented to the Reagan Administration, although some of it found its way into Regan's congressional testimony. It was fortunate, I thought, that I had maintained the independence of my pen, and I published the evidence in the *Wall Street Journal* on May 21 and in *Fortune* on August 24. At least the public would know the case for the President's program, even if his administration did not.

By May 1981, if not before, it was clear that a person could get nowhere within the Reagan Administration by supporting the President's program. You were expected to say that you supported the program, but if you really did it was a different matter. Although I was an architect of the President's economic program, I was never allowed to make a presentation before the Cabinet Council on Economic Affairs, which was chaired by Treasury. Regan himself seemed to have little control over the council. The council functioned as a forum for the economic policy views of OMB and CEA. Treasury was supposed to receive the agendas, review the papers that were to be presented, and prepare comments for the secretary, but in practice it was often bypassed.

Among the May 13 briefing papers was one titled "Money Growth: Supply vs. Demand." The Treasury's Office of Economic Policy was concerned about the administration's monetary assumptions. The administration was supporting a policy of progressively tighter money supply each year over a five-year period. We agreed with monetarists that the growth rate of the money supply had to be brought down from where the Federal Reserve had put it during the Carter Administration. However, looking farther out after the tax reductions had improved the profitability of work and investment, the economy would demand faster money creation because of the faster real growth of goods and services. Then the Federal Reserve would have to increase money growth at whatever rate necessary to keep prices stable. It was important for the administration to understand that whether or not any given amount of money supply growth is inflationary depends upon why the money is growing. If the money supply is growing because the government is supplying it as the means for paying its bills, inflation will result. The situation is different, however, if the money supply is growing because the demand for it to finance the growth in real output is strong. "In an expanding economy responding to better profitability," I told the secretary,

money supply growth is not an automatic indication of inflation. In such an environment, money supply growth can hold down interest rates and prevent the developing scarcity of money which could ultimately lead to actual deflation.

Ambush and Compromise

In Washington it is safer to keep a low profile, but I had fought hard for the supply-side tax cuts and made myself a target, not straight on, of course—that is not Washington's style—but from ambush.

Bob Dole was not being very helpful to the President's tax bill. He was telling everyone, particularly the press, that he did not have the votes in the Finance Committee to report out the full Kemp-Roth bill. Since White House officials were talking down the President's tax bill even more than Dole was, it fell once again to Robert Bartley and the *Wall Street Journal* to give the President a hand. On May 15 an editorial appeared asking, "Where's the Dole Bill?" The President, Bartley said, "needs Senator Dole's support," but "what he is getting is hems and haws." "The Finance chairman thinks the tax bill might 'have trouble' in the Senate. The chairman doesn't want anyone trampling on his hard-won prerogatives. The chairman is worried about this and that." Again, the message was clear: Dole should get busy and deliver the President's bill or one of his own, "if he has a better plan."

Four days later Dole sent a copy of the editorial to Regan with a letter attached. The letter read: "If I were a betting man, I would bet this editorial was inspired by your Craig Roberts." I was puzzled that Dole would think it was me rather than his own behavior that had inspired Bartley's pen. Then it occurred to me that my adversaries had seized the opportunity to inflame Dole against me. The pressure was building on what few supporters the President had.

Dole did not want 10-10-10, not only because it was Kemp's bill but also because the members of the tax committees had a lot of "Christmas tree ornaments" that they wanted to hang on the tax bill. Dole wanted 10-10-10 reduced in size in order to create "revenue room" for a host of special measures. The President wanted a clean policy bill. We were trying to prevent the economy from collapsing, and Congress wanted to buy votes. There was an obvious conflict of purpose. Looking back, it is surprising that the President and the Treasury prevailed over the administration, the Republican Senate, and the House Democrats, and got the tax bill passed.

The story that Stockman planted on Steve Weisman on May 13 revived all the tax-compromise talk that had been stopped by the President's victory on the budget resolution six days before. Treasury was concerned that the talk of compromise would strengthen Rostenkowski's and O'Neill's ability to hold out for a substantially different tax bill, one that might be long on income redistribution and short on supply-side incentives. If too much compromise was forced on the President, the bill would be inadequate to do the job. The President would have to make the bill his or accept a defeat. His political advisers would be opposed to a defeat, and public relations experts would give him assurances that they could sell the bill as a victory. Since true victories are rare in Washington, the image makers have a great deal of experience at that sort of thing. Worried by the prospect that an inadequate bill would be presented as a great supply-side victory, we fought harder for the President's program.

By Friday of mid-May talk of compromise hung heavy in the air. That morning the *Washington Post* reported that Regan had met with Rostenkowski and Dole on Thursday to work out a compromise. According to the *Post,* "sources said the Treasury Secretary hinted that the administration ultimately might agree to less than a full three-year cut if the rest of Reagan's plan was approved relatively intact." As we read the report in the Treasury press clips, we wondered if Regan had revealed a willingness to scale back 10-10-10 or whether Dole, Rostenkowski, their staffs, or someone else was putting words in his mouth. If Regan had hinted at compromise, had the signal come from the President? Or had Regan simply been reading in the press all the administration leaks about compromise and decided that he had better say the same thing? After his meeting with Dole and Rostenkowski, he left for Saudi Arabia leaving me with a flood of press calls wanting to know if Treasury had caved in.

It was a day of extravagant ambiguities. The same story that reported Regan's hint at compromise quoted the President as standing firm: "I have not changed my opinion one bit." But on the evening news there was White House deputy press secretary Larry Speakes saying "compromise is no longer a dirty word." Speakes was followed by NBC news commentator Judy Woodruff reporting that "Treasury officials had expressed surprise" at Speakes's comments, "an indication that the White House was bypassing them." That brought a whole new wave of press inquiries. Was Treasury being bypassed because Treasury would not cave in? I pointed to the President's statement and told reporters that the relevant point was that the President had not given in. One reporter found that unconvincing and took me under his wing. "The President," he confided, "will make whatever decision his government makes."

The expectation of a compromise made Secretary Regan's every move a subject of speculation. The press had reported that Regan was on a nine-day trip to Saudi Arabia and other countries. He intended to return early, leaving the remainder of the itinerary to other Treasury officials. The press, though, did not know this, and with the expectations of a tax bill compromise in the air, there were fears that the press would misinterpret his early return to mean he had been called back to negotiate the expected compromise. If no compromise was then forthcoming, the press might interpret it to mean that the administration's attempt to make a deal had failed. Such an interpretation would strengthen the other side's ability to dictate a compromise.

The compromise talk continued to build throughout the following week, with headlines like "Reagan Ready to Bend on Tax Program" (*Washington Star,* May 16); "President Called Ready to Discuss Tax Cut Accord" (*New York Times,* May 16); and "Reagan is Said Ready to Make Tax Cut Deal" (*Washington Post,* May 21). On May 18 the *Washington Star* reported that senior White House officials "maintain that they'd have a 'very good chance' of getting the President's tax proposal through the House if they launched the same all-out effort that was devoted to winning on the budget resolution." But they were unwilling to spend two months' worth of "political capital" and to engage in "hand-to-hand combat for every single vote"—something that the same senior White House officials were willing to engage in for the sake of a tax increase a year later.

The compromise talk made the Treasury wary, since the impetus for a compromise was coming from *within* the administration and from some Senate Republicans, not from the House Democrats or the bond market. Part of the problem was feelings of rivalry toward Jack Kemp, who was seen in some quarters as being too successful in providing political leadership. Part of the problem was Stockman's drive to make himself economic policy czar. And part of the problem was that lawyers and executives generally learn from their careers that the path to personal success is paved with negotiation and compromise. When they come to Washington as presidential appointees, they bring these traits with them and as a matter of course begin compromising away the changes on the political agenda. The mixture of political and personal motives and imbued

traits caused the administration to maneuver itself, alone and una-
betted, into a compromise that further delayed the first installment
of the tax cut until October and cut it in half. Again and again the
Treasury would ask: "Why is the administration negotiating with itself?"

Stockman's goal was to reduce 10-10-10 to 5-10-10 with the first
installment delayed until October. I thought that, if we had to compromise and reduce the tax cut, we should do it in a way that was
economically and politically sound. I would have settled for "10-10"
in exchange for no delays in the tax cut. There was nothing to be
gained from backloading the tax cut. The way Stockman was pro-
ceeding, the first 10 percent reduction in the marginal tax rates
would not take effect until July 1982, eighteen months into the Reagan Administration. Delaying the tax cut would leave the economy
struggling along without the supply-side benefits until the second
half of the President's term. That would be gambling the mid-term
congressional elections and, indeed, the entire economic program on
an economy that we ourselves were saying was not doing well. For
example, Jonathan Fuerbringer reported in the *Washington Star* on
May 4 that Murray Weidenbaum had "put out several statements
warning against optimism, contending that the good economic performance will not continue." (In 1981 first-quarter real GNP growth
was an unexpected 7.9 percent.) Weidenbaum was quoted as saying
that "we may even see a rise in unemployment. I'm trying to prepare
people for that." It made no sense to delay the tax cut if we thought
that we were walking into a recession. Wasn't this the way the
United States had lost the Vietnam war—by committing our forces
in dribs and drabs? If a tax cut was the medicine the economy
needed, why were we delaying the dosage, especially if we were
looking at a recession? By delaying weren't we sending a signal that
we lacked confidence in our own policy?

While the fight was going on within the administration over the
Stockman compromise, it was being offered to House Democrats as
the "Dole proposal." The House Ways and Means Committee
turned it down on May 28. After having watched the political ama-
teurs in the Reagan Administration negotiate with themselves for
four months, the Democrats were convinced that they could get a
better deal. The administration's negotiators and compromisers

were going to have to fight after all. Yet, instead of spending the two months' worth of political capital and engaging in hand-to-hand combat for the President's bill, we ended up fighting for the Stockman compromise.

The Mid-Year Review

In the midst of all the compromise talk, we were confronted with the mid-session review of the 1982 budget. OMB and CEA wanted to issue economic-growth forecasts that were lower than the projections in the February document. Treasury's position was that we could not make any forecasts until we had a policy from the Congress. The February numbers were an estimate of how the economy would perform if our policies were implemented, not a projection of what the economy would do on its own. Lowering the growth projections would widen the deficit at an inopportune time—just at the point of congressional decision on the President's tax bill. Treasury did not think Congress would pass a tax bill if it seemed that the administration expected the deficit to grow rather than the economy.

Here was another problem caused by not having a base-line forecast. The administration's numbers showed expenditures, revenues, and deficits under the policy assumptions of the President's program. But the program was not in effect, and OMB and Treasury needed expenditure and revenue figures based on how the economy was functioning in the absence of the policy changes. The pressure for "real numbers" based on updated guesses of the economy's direction was turning our statement of what the program would achieve into a forecast of the economy's behavior under whatever policies happened to be in effect. By turning our scenario into a forecast, we would seem to be lowering our expectations of the President's program.

A base-line forecast would have provided operating budget numbers and allowed the administration to contrast the economy in its base-line state with its projected performance under the new policy. Without a base-line forecast it was only a matter of time before the pressure for operating numbers took over our scenario. The Treasury view, which prevailed at the mid-year review, was that we should not jeopardize the prospects for a significant change in economic policy by prematurely changing our scenario into a forecast. Congress was close to making a decision on our policy proposals. Once that decision was made, we would have a policy upon which to base a forecast.

OMB was critical of Treasury's position. Stockman wanted a smaller tax cut than the President had proposed, and he wanted to project larger deficits in order to convince Congress to scale down the tax package and accept larger spending cuts. At the time Stockman had no inkling of the deficits that monetary policy was about to produce, though he used them when they arrived to press for tax increases. In May when we were girding for the mid-year review, we were still reeling from the sharp upturn in M-1 money growth. The administration had no idea that the Federal Reserve was about to slam on the brakes and throw us all through the windshield.

Although critical of Treasury's position, OMB adopted it a year later in 1982 when Stockman wanted to get a tax increase passed. The mid-session review of the 1983 budget coincided with congressional deliberation of the administration's $100 billlion tax-increase bill.[1] As a result of the recession the economic-growth projections in the budget resolution were too high, but lowering the projections would balloon the deficit and offset the tax increase. The House was already hesitant to pass a large tax increase just before an election and was unlikely to do so if a new forecast showed a large deficit regardless of higher taxes. As *Business Week* reported on August 2, 1982:

OMB officials feel that this is not the time to change forecasts. "Our first priority is to get the budget resolution through Congress," says Lawrence A. Kudlow, the OMB's chief economist. "The last thing we want to do is throw a monkey wrench into the process by coming out with a huge new deficit forecast that starts a new debate on economic policy."

The year before, when the administration was trying to cut taxes, it was OMB that tried to throw the monkey wrench into the process.

The mid-year review in 1981 was complicated by more than Stockman's maneuverings with the deficit and the absence of a

1. The tax increase measured $100 billion over three years and $229 billion over five years.

base-line forecast. The monetarists wanted to use the occasion to correct the "velocity problem." Velocity is the ratio of GNP to the money supply. Monetarists believe that it is a stable number. When Stockman used the core-inflation argument to raise the GNP projections and show a balanced budget, he put the relationship out of whack. Given the assumptions about declining money growth, the GNP projections implied a higher velocity than monetarists believed possible. The administration's monetarists were determined to lower the velocity number, and there were two ways to do it. One was to raise the money-supply number, and the other was to lower the GNP numbers. To lower the GNP, either real economic growth or inflation had to be lowered.

The monetarists, of course, were adamantly opposed to raising the money-supply numbers. That, they said, would mean that we would lose our credibility as inflation fighters. To lower the GNP, however, would produce a deficit, and we would lose our credibility as budget balancers. (In addition, we would lose our credibility as inflation fighters with those who believed that inflation is caused by deficits.) If we lowered the inflation rates, we would lose our credibility with the outside forecasters who believed in core inflation. Lowering the real economic-growth rates would abolish the supply-side effects that were the rationale for the President's program.

At two high-level meetings in the White House on June 5 and June 10 in Jim Baker's office, Treasury had to be very forceful to protect the President's program. OMB argued that lowering the GNP projections would reduce interest rates. Supposedly, the bond market was upset by the high velocity and the GNP projections and regarded them as signs of inflation. Lower GNP projections—which would widen the deficits—would *reassure* the bond market, OMB argued, because the bond market associated high economic growth with high inflation.

The OMB official making this argument, Lawrence Kudlow, was a former newsletter writer for a New York brokerage firm. In his OMB position Kudlow continued his profession as newsletter writer, producing more or less regularly an "Economic and Financial Update." At the June 5 meeting he argued strongly for lowering the GNP projections. But in his "Economic and Financial Update" of June 1, he argued that there had been a "flood of high-powered liquidity injected since February," which "suggests the possibility of new erosion in the future purchasing power of money." How, Kudlow was asked, could a person expecting higher inflation argue for lowering the GNP projections?

The monetarists in the administration had a different explanation for the high interest rates: they reflected the frequent U-turns in monetary policy, and the recent upturn in interest rates reflected the "flood of high-powered liquidity injected since February," which "suggests the possibility of new erosions in the future purchasing power of money." Whether right or wrong, such an explanation was at least consistent with the administration's policy posture. But the argument that a tax-rate reduction—especially one that improved the profitability of saving and investment—would unsettle the financial markets was not consistent with the administration's policy posture. After these reminders of their own words, Treasury's opponents became heated. One of them blurted out that the markets would be reassured if we did not have the tax cut at all.

That was going too far. The obvious lack of support for the President's policy alarmed Edward Meese, who spoke and closed off any downward revision of the GNP numbers. But he did not specify whether he meant the absolute levels or rates of growth. This was important because the first-quarter GNP was far higher than expected, raising the GNP base. At the same growth rates, the higher base would mean higher levels of GNP. The higher GNP levels would mean higher tax revenues and less deficit. On the other hand, to maintain the same GNP levels, the higher first-quarter base would require lowering the growth rates. After the meeting OMB and CEA seized on the ambiguity, froze the GNP levels, and lowered the 1982 and 1983 real growth rates to show a weaker case for the tax cut. The battle continued.

After Meese had spoken and settled the issue in Treasury's favor, Edward Harper, Stockman's deputy, said that he had been instructed by Stockman to vote with Regan and the Treasury. Stockman, he said, thought that any downward revision in GNP would kill the tax bill. Then after protecting Stockman politically by lining him up with the winners, he reopened the issue that Meese had closed by saying that Kudlow nevertheless did have a very important point. The tactic became a favorite of the tax-increase advocates. By October it was being used to reopen the President's own decisions.

The Agenda Runs Amuck

Modern governments have little control over their own agendas. Small nations like Poland and Finland no doubt have an acute awareness of this fact. The so-called Third World countries complain loudly that they are buffeted by super-power politics and the movements of prices in international markets, from coffee to bank credit. But even a big-power government like the United States has little control over its agenda. It is an unusual president who comes to Washington with a definite agenda, but even one who does soon finds that he is preempted by the commitments of previous administrations, the agenda of the "permanent government," and a procession of domestic and international crises. In the summer of 1981, as the struggle to change the economic policy of the United States was coming to a head, the Reagan Administration found its agenda dictated by the latest Mideastern crisis, the Ottawa summit, and a push by the Internal Revenue Service to tax fringe benefits.

One morning at a Treasury staff meeting Roscoe Egger, the IRS commissioner, announced that the IRS was about to issue regulations that would result in the taxation of employee fringe benefits. In addition, the IRS was going to take away the tax exemption of some private schools in Mississippi. The Reagan Administration was trying to reduce people's taxes, and the IRS was about to raise them unilaterally. We could see the headlines: "Reagan Taxes Workers' Fringe Benefits in Order to Cut Taxes for the Rich," "Regan's Folly Sinks President's Tax Bill." Chapoton, the assistant secretary for tax policy, said earnestly that as an "administrative convenience" annual company picnics would not be counted as taxable income to the employee. Maybe the Christmas ham or turkey from the boss would also escape the tax net.

Dennis Thomas, assistant secretary of the Treasury for legislative affairs, was alarmed. As a former Senate staffer he did not expect to be surprised by government inconsistencies, but he was. His job was to get the tax cut passed, and now out of the blue he was about to be blind-sided by an inconsistent policy of cutting taxes with one hand

and raising them with the other. In addition, it was not a propitious time to go after private schools when the President was trying to win southern Democrats over to his cause. The bureaucracy was testing us to see if they could dominate policy. Fortunately, we did not have to risk finding out. Within a matter of hours Regan received a letter signed by sixty-four senators:

We are concerned about the proposals being made by the Commissioner of Internal Revenue and the Assistant Secretary for tax policy to issue regulations soon regarding the taxation of employee fringe benefits. We strongly urge you to halt the publication of such regulations because there is no possibility that the Congress will allow such regulations to ever take effect, and the only result will be to create totally unnecessary political problems for the Administration at a time when efforts on the tax cut have reached a critical stage.

To be sure the Secretary understood, the letter continued: "You should be reminded that the plan to tax fringe benefits is not new. It arose during the Ford Administration and again under President Carter. In each case, a storm of protest developed." Some of us had fought the battle both times before, and we were glad the senators had saved us from having to fight it again, especially at a time when even worse mischief was coming out of the State Department bureaucracy.

In July the vote on the President's tax bill was impending. If the President lost the vote, that would be the end of his new economic policy. Yet right at this time he had to uproot himself and go off to the Ottawa summit in Canada. Jimmy Carter had set this agenda by going to the Venice summit in 1980. One congress cannot bind another, but that does not hold for presidents. Ronald Reagan was bound, and so was the agenda. A main item was "North-South Issues." The North is the United States, Japan, Canada, and Western Europe; the South is the Third World. At Ottawa Reagan was supposed to be agreeable to global negotiations, a game in which income is redistributed from the North to the South. In addition, he was supposed to be agreeable to providing billions of dollars to pay the Third World's energy bills by financing a World Bank "energy affiliate."

Summitry had begun in 1975, but with the turnover in heads of state, foreign ministers, and finance ministers, it was now firmly in the hands of the international bureaucracy. Summits had become circuses in which bureaucrats put figureheads through their act. To be sure that Reagan followed his, a set of briefing papers and speeches were prepared for him, including a "scenario and schedule" telling him exactly when he would meet with whom and what he should say. To make certain that the President of the United States understood that he had little to say about the agenda, he was duly reminded by his briefing papers: "The Venice Summit in 1980 created the expectation that North-South issues and foreign aid would be major themes at Ottawa."

Normally when the United States is rolled, it is a little at a time. The artful bureaucracy puts subtle, equivocal language in the President's mouth to commit him each time to more than he realizes. The bureaucracy weaves the web year by year, president by president, until it is inextricable. This time, however, the bureaucracy was not very subtle. They had Reagan hailing Mitterand as a "man of vision," endorsing French socialism as "a new spirit in the air," and committing the United States to "an active and cooperative role in North-South affairs." In his speech at the summit, Reagan was supposed to declare that the election of a socialist government in France made him "stand in awe of the fundamental human vitality of our societies." Here was Reagan endorsing the nationalization of the French banks. And all of this was written by diplomats who were supposed to be considering its effect on British Prime Minister Margaret Thatcher.

The bureaucrats must have believed that Ronald Reagan was uninformed about the new French government's statements and policies. Mitterand, the man of vision, had appointed Regis Debray as one of his foreign policy advisers. Debray had spent three years in a Bolivian jail for helping Che Guevara try to overthrow the Bolivian government. Two weeks before the summit Debray had Mitterand forcefully declaring his opposition to U.S. policy in Central America: "The West would be better advised to help these people than to force them to remain under the jackboot. When they cry out for help I would like Castro not to be the only one to hear them."[2] It

---

2. "U.S. Foreign Policy Worries Mitterand," *Washington Post*, July 2, 1981.

was the man with the leftist language and perceptions, and not Margaret Thatcher, with whom Reagan was supposed to align himself at Ottawa.

The summit, with help from the State Department and the media, was headed toward placing the United States once again squarely on the defensive. The President would find himself in the dock, having to defend high U.S. interest rates, a strong dollar, and tax cuts that were alleged to be inflationary.[3] He would also be on the defensive about Third World demands and the Siberian pipeline, which would be financed by Western credit at subsidized interest rates and make Europe dependent on Soviet energy.

My office had been involved in the Ottawa summit preparations only in peripheral ways. It was something of a puzzle because one of the tasks at the summit was to explain U.S. domestic economic policy. On July 4 the *Washington Post* reported that French Foreign Minister Claude Cheysson was complaining that "no one has properly explained American economic policy to us yet." We seemed to be keeping it a secret. Supply-siders had not been included in the many rounds of summit preparation, and we wondered what kind of explanation was being given. The London *Times* was urging that the United States adopt an anti-inflationary fiscal policy of higher taxes in order to lower interest rates. "This necessary course," lectured the *Times,* demands that President Reagan "postpone his promise to reduce taxes." The Bank for International Settlements warned that Reagan's monetary policy was causing serious difficulties for other countries and could lead to a breakdown of international economic cooperation. The State Department, ever sensitive to the complaints of foreigners, had actually launched a campaign against the Presi-

3. Europeans are billed for their Middle Eastern oil in dollars. The higher the value of the dollar, the more they have to pay for oil in terms of their own currencies. They wanted the United States to intervene in the foreign exchange markets by using dollars to purchase their currencies, an action that would hold down the value of the dollar and support the value of other currencies. Beryl Sprinkel, Treasury undersecretary for monetary affairs, had stopped the Federal Reserve Bank of New York from intervening in the markets in order to support exchange rates. He believed that intervention would complicate and offset the Fed's ability to reduce the growth of the money supply. Our allies' complaints were basically inconsistent. They wanted lower U.S. interest rates and at the same time an inflated dollar (which would raise interest rates) in order to lower the dollar's value in the foreign exchange market. At the summit meeting two years previously, the United States was criticized for a weak dollar and a failure to master inflation.

dent's tax cuts on the grounds that international relations were at stake.

On July 10 Canadian Prime Minister Trudeau was to have lunch at the White House with Reagan, Haig, and Regan in a pre-summit meeting. The administration was trying to decide how to respond to discriminatory Canadian restraints on U.S. investment in Canada and was leaning toward a threat of retaliation. I welcomed the rare sign of any U.S. backbone but believed we were missing a leadership opportunity. In July 8 memos to Secretary Regan and Richard V. Allen, the national security adviser to the President, I recommended a different approach. Trudeau should be told that the Reagan Administration believes that income-redistribution policies have received too much emphasis, both in industrial and in Third World countries, to the detriment of policies of income growth. The economic fate of the Third World must be turned away from the international bureaucrat dispensing largess and toward productive private investment. For this reorientation to take place, private investment must be welcome and property rights secure. By restricting U.S. investment, Canada was serving as a bad example to the Third World and lending credence to Marxist theories of exploitation. "This approach to Trudeau," the memo added,

might also have the effect of discouraging him from supporting any ideological attack from Mitterand on "North-South issues." As a result of weak leadership in the past, much of the world expects the U.S. to accept the defensive role. The offensive must be taken early if we are to regain the real role of leadership as opposed to being merely the figurehead leader.

My memo must have crossed the desk of an embattled Reaganite who recognized an ally because a thick packet of Ottawa briefing material soon appeared on my desk. It was July 8, and the summit was only ten days away. The preparation had been going on for months—indeed, ever since the previous summit—and it looked like a fait accompli.

The briefing papers had been prepared through channels that bypassed the Reaganites. Vice-President George Bush was in charge of coordinating the summit preparations. Robert Hormats, the assistant secretary of state for economic affairs and a holdover from the Carter Administration, chaired the interdepartmental group that prepared the briefings and policy statements for the President. Richard Allen at the National Security Council had been more or less bypassed and left without major responsibility, as had other Reaganites.

For a summit everything is prepared in advance by the bureaucracy, including a draft of the final communique that is issued at the close of the meeting, supposedly by the heads of state reflecting their weighty deliberations. In other words, it is a preprogrammed show, with even the joint final statement prepared in advance of the meeting. The Ottawa materials left no doubt as to why Reaganites had been excluded from the process. The draft communique was full of open-ended commitments and contained language implying that the United States acknowledged an economic responsibility not just for our allies, regardless of their policies, but also for the Third World. In the communique the leaders of the West, all burdened by the growing deficits of their welfare states, were looking forward from Ottawa to the Cancun summit and the prospect of global negotiations with the Third World.

Ronald Reagan was being maneuvered into a conflict-avoidance posture. Bureaucratic diplomacy allows no principle except getting along with the world, regardless of the cost and reality of the demands. Reagan was to be no exception. On July 4, Independence Day, the *Washington Post* thundered with French warnings:

French Foreign Minister Claude Cheysson warned today that the Reagan Administration could provoke "major difficulty" with its European allies, especially France, if it fails to give high priority to improving relations between underdeveloped and industrialized countries.

Concerned, I sent memos on July 8, 9, and 10 to Secretary Regan, Undersecretary Sprinkel, National Security Adviser Richard Allen, Counsellor to the President Edward Meese, and Assistant Treasury Secretary for International Affairs Marc Leland. At Ottawa the President was in danger of sweet-talking his way into leadership of someone else's policies. A major weakness in our summit strategy was the absence of any constraint on Mitterand's behavior as the result of the excessively conciliatory and laudatory attitude taken toward him. This could make it easier for him (and Trudeau) to grandstand for the left and turn the summit into a defeat for Reagan. As an option Reagan had to be prepared to ask Mitterand how far he was prepared to go in creating instability in the Western alliance by pushing economic policies that destabilize the franc and by making ideological attacks on American foreign policy.

The President needed to go to Ottawa in an assertive and confident frame of mind rather than with defensive answers to every conceivable charge. He needed to push the manipulations aside and carry Reaganism to the summit. It was late in the game to overturn the momentum, but the bureaucracy had unwittingly provided conclusive evidence that the Ottawa briefing materials contained definite dangers to the President. "Please do note," I advised the White House, "that in the draft of the President's statement there is a repeat of President Ford's statement about Poland being a free country. The statement has the President saying that freedom is 'imperiled in Poland.' Is the same staffer in the same job?"

On Monday, July 13, the *Washington Post* reported that at the last minute the responsibility for preparing the President for Ottawa had been shifted to the White House. Judging from domestic and foreign press reports in the aftermath of the summit, the effort to reposition the United States from whipping boy to leader succeeded. The French newspaper *Le Monde* reported that, in spite of European intentions to the contrary, at Ottawa President Reagan regained three "components of power—the supremacy of the dollar, legitimacy of a tough liberalism, and a refusal of technological transfer."

Reaganites won one. But the "permanent government" step by step gradually reasserted its control over policy and eroded the victory at the Cancun summit with the Third World on October 22. The State Department bureaucracy, ever mindful of the foreigner's point of view, steadfastly refused to accommodate the philosophy, themes, and substance of Ronald Reagan. The State Department's draft of the President's opening remarks at Cancun was an astonishing departure from the positions embraced by the President in his Philadelphia speech before the World Affairs Council on October 15.

In Philadelphia the President said that we need to understand the real meaning of development. It does not result from massive transfer of wealth or from collectivism seeking to fulfill goals "no matter what the cost to individuals or historical tradition." The essence of development is free people who "build free markets that ignite dynamic development for everyone."

To be sure the message was heard, the President stated it again:

A mere handful of industrialized countries that have historically coupled
personal freedom with economic reward now produce more than one-
half the wealth of the world.

And again:

The developing countries now growing the fastest in Asia, Africa and
Latin America are the very ones providing more economic freedom for
their people—freedom to choose, to own property, to work at a job of
their choice, and to invest in a dream for the future.

And yet again:

Perhaps the best proof that development and economic freedom go
hand-in-hand can be found in a country which denies freedom to its people—the Soviet Union.

"For the record," said the President, "the Soviets will not attend the
conference at Cancun" because "they have nothing to offer." In fact,
"we have just one question for them: who's feeding whom?"

Reagan then proceeded to give short shrift to the "propaganda
campaign in wide circulation that would have the world believe the
capitalist U.S. is the cause of world hunger and poverty." The
United States leads "the way in helping to better the lives of citizens
in developing countries" by providing the two things that they need
the most: open markets for their manufactured goods and access to
U.S. capital markets.

After dispatching the propaganda designed to induce guilt and
elicit large sums of penance money, the President went on to define
the Cancun agenda. The first item was

the roadblocks which developing country policies pose to development,
and how they can best be removed. For example, is there an imbalance
between public and private sector activities? Are high tax rates smoth-
ering incentives and precluding growth in personal savings and investment capital?

The President's Philadelphia speech presented a clear-cut philosophical and policy framework as well as a program of action as a
practical alternative to global negotiations. The President stated his
policies clearly, but his government did not hear him. The State De-

partment's draft of what the President would say at Cancun closely resembled the essential themes and approaches of the Carter Administration. There was nothing to be gained by short-changing the President's philosophy and program when other heads of state would be listening. But time pressures forced me to abandon the fight for a Reaganite foreign policy in order to prevent a reversal of the President's domestic economic policy.

President Reagan was led to believe that he had a "special relationship" with Lopez Portillo, the president of Mexico. To protect this relationship the President had to drop the "harsh rhetoric" of the Philadelphia speech and move in the direction of accommodating Third World demands. This was the explanation given to Reaganites for the "pragmatic" posture that Reagan would assume at Cancun. Not long after Reagan was repositioned on North-South issues for the sake of his special relationship with Portillo, the Panamanian leader Torrijos died. Portillo joined Castro in expressing concern at the loss of a leader in the fight against colonialism. In the Latin American context, colonialism means the United States. The special relationship did not prevent Portillo from packaging Reagan as a colonialist to be fought against unless he buckled and agreed to support wealth transfers.

In September 1982, not yet a year after Cancun, Portillo nationalized the banks after his mistaken economic policies had damaged the Mexican economy. Although he conceded that government mismanagement of the economy might be part of the problem, he asserted that the fundamental cause of Mexico's problem was the income discrepancy between rich and poor nations. According to the *Washington Post* (September 2), Portillo used the occasion of his speech announcing the nationalization of the banks to

vehemently reaffirm his differences with the Reagan Administration over policy toward Central America. In some of the toughest language that he has used to date, he called on the Reagan Administration to leave Nicaragua alone, to stop U.S. attempts to isolate Cuba and to negotiate a solution in El Salvador.

When these friendly statements appeared, it was obvious that Reagan's special relationship with Portillo had been nothing but empty talk.

The press reports on Cancun were quite different from Ottawa. On October 23 the *Washington Post* reported: "In conciliatory words far different in tone from his speech on economic development in Philadelphia last week, the President said he takes seriously the commitment to move toward global negotiations." It had taken the bureaucracy just three months to erode the Ottawa victory and lead yet another president in the policy direction of the permanent government. As the *Wall Street Journal* noted on October 27, "by agreeing to global talks, even with conditions, Mr. Reagan held out hope for Third World mismanagers that someday there will be a bag of paper gold to bail them out." The *Journal* went on to draw the point for a befuddled administration, which now thought of victory as avoiding confrontation and which believed it had bought a cheap victory with mere words. The words would be used to draw the noose tighter in the next round. "As long as such a process of erosion of the U.S. position is allowed to continue, U.S. efforts to change the terms of the development debate will be postponed." The President's domestic economic policy was undergoing the same process of erosion even as victory on the tax bill approached.

6

Victory and Defeat

ON JUNE 4 PRESIDENT REAGAN ENDORSED THE STOCKMAN compromise, saying that it would "not do quite the job" of the more timely and full 30 percent reduction "but will have generally the same effect." He may have wondered with whom he was compromising and why. The House Democrats had already rejected the compromise a few days before when it was offered to them by Senator Dole, and they soon began drafting their own tax bill. In addition, the first budget resolution had just passed the Congress two weeks before by large margins—244–155 in the House and 76–20 in the Senate—and it provided for the full Reagan tax cut. Whoever the compromise was with, it did not prevent a two-month battle over the tax bill.

The administration's bill was an economic-policy bill rather than the usual melange of tax breaks and tax reforms without a clear policy direction. Its purpose was to increase the incentives to work, save, and invest in order to improve productivity, cash flow, and opportunities in the private sector. Considering the amount of renovation that the economy needed, the administration's tax package was not very large. In H. C. Wainwright's political update of June 18 it was called "The Lion That Mewed" and, based on the administration's inflation assumptions, the company reported that:

the net effective cut from 1980 to 1984 is still only 7.5 percent for the median taxpayer. That would be little more than one-third the proportionate cut obtained within two years by Kennedy-Johnson Democrats. For the median income, Reagan expects to achieve only a 1 percent net cut.

The Treasury was concerned that the tax bill would lose yet more of its punch by being scaled back to make room for a variety of special-interest provisions. It was this concern that prompted Treasury's advocacy of a clean tax bill first and a second tax bill later in which special concerns could be addressed after the new tax policy was established.

Initially the fight was to prevent the bill from becoming cluttered and to prevent income-redistribution measures from crowding out the emphasis on incentives. However, Rostenkowski's bill embraced the basic supply-side approach of Reagan's bill, and the real fight was over who would get the credit for the tax cut. Rostenkowski and O'Neill were no longer fighting against a supply-side tax cut, but for control over the bill and credit with the voters in the November 1982 election.

When Reagan scaled down the personal income tax cuts on June 4, he also reduced the size of the business tax cut. The new package allowed the administration to reduce its 1982 deficit projection from $45 billion to $30 billion. Officially the aim was to win over the conservative Democrats, who wanted to campaign in the 1982 elections on smaller deficits. In addition, the smaller package made it possible to add some new provisions designed to attract swing votes. Business groups, however, complained about the scaled-down depreciation proposal, and in order to prevent business support from going over to Rostenkowski, the administration restored the business tax cut. In the House Reagan's tax package was introduced by Republican Barber Conable from New York and Democrat Kent Hance from Texas. Kemp-Roth had become Conable-Hance and was moving toward victory as the "bipartisan bill."

In the Republican Senate on June 25, the Finance Committee adopted the President's tax package by a wide margin of 19–1. The dissenting vote was cast by freshman Senator and former basketball star Bill Bradley, a Democrat from New Jersey. He was opposed to the tax bill because it cut taxes in proportion to taxes paid, and he wanted to use the tax cuts to redistribute income to the middle and lower brackets. I had met Bradley when he asked me to pay him a courtesy call prior to my confirmation hearing before the Finance Committee. I found him intelligent and sincere, but influenced by left-wing ideology. What, I wondered, was happening to America when a star athlete was opposed to rewarding merit and achievement on the grounds that it was inequitable? The depreciation of merit in the name of justice has serious implications for our economy and society. I imagined Bill Bradley's argument: merit counts for little compared to connections; what one needs for financial success is a network, and networks are unfair.

The President's tax package grew in the Finance Committee, picking up some special-interest provisions, although Senator Dole was given credit for preventing the bill from becoming too cluttered. On July 5 the *New York Times* criticized the "graffiti" that had been written on the bill as it moved through the legislative process. But among the graffiti was one of the most important provisions of the final bill. Senator Armstrong succeeded in getting the Finance Committee to accept his amendment indexing the personal income tax to prevent inflation from pushing taxpayers into higher tax brackets. Initially the administration was opposed to including the indexing provision in the bill, although later the President used the provision in a dramatic way to secure passage of his tax bill in the House.

The Ways and Means Committee drew out the drama for another month. When the committee's bill appeared on July 23, we had a second supply-side bill, for that is what the Ways and Means Democrats had produced. It mirrored the administration bill in almost every respect, including size. The committee replaced the cumbersome system of depreciation allowances by allowing business to write off as expenses the entire cost of machinery and equipment in its year of purchase, although the provision would not be fully phased in until 1990. In addition, the corporate income tax would be reduced from 46 percent to 34 percent by 1987. This package was a different approach from the administration's, but it addressed the same problems, albeit with a great deal of delay. The two bills had many of the same provisions: a reduction in the marriage penalty, a reduction in the top rate on investment income from 70 to 50 percent, larger tax-exempt deductions for individual IRA and Keogh pension plans, lower estate and gift taxes. The main difference was the individual income tax cut. The Democrats dropped the third year, stopping with a 5–10 package that was skewed toward incomes under $50,000, and it was not indexed. In addition, the "earned income credit," which in spite of its name amounts to a tax refund for people who do not pay income tax, was expanded. Incentives had made some inroads, but on the personal side of the tax code, redistribution still held some sway over the Democrats.

Nevertheless, the Ways and Means bill was proof that supply-side economics had come a long way in a few years. The Treasury had four veterans of the congressional wars in policy positions: former Roth aides Dennis Thomas and Bruce Thompson, Steven Entin from the Joint Economic Committee, and myself. We all agreed that in 1976, 1977, 1978, 1979 and even in 1980, we would have considered the Ways and Means bill a supply-side victory.

At 2:00 a.m. on July 22 a tired and coffee-logged Ways and Means Committee adopted a provision by a one-vote margin allowing 500 barrels of oil a day to be exempted from the windfall profits tax at a cost to the Treasury of $7 billion over the next five years. This sweetener was designed to hold the votes of conservative Democrats from oil-producing states to the committee's bill. A bidding war over a handful of swing votes began.

It was nip and tuck and could have gone either way—except for the fact that on July 16 the Senate passed the Armstrong amendment to index the personal income tax. Treasury's Office of Economic Policy went to work to bring the Reagan Administration on board with the Armstrong indexing amendment and, that same day, sent a memo to Regan including tables showing that without indexing the individual tax cuts would soon be canceled by inflation, allowing the upward movement in the tax brackets to continue.

The administration was looking for a way to dramatize the President's tax proposals compared to the Ways and Means bill. Rostenkowski was clever, and his two-year tax cut provided a bigger reduction for most taxpayers until 1983, when it ran out and taxes resumed their upward trend. The President's bill provided a larger tax reduction over three years, but after 1984 it too showed an upward trend in taxes. The President had said that he would get tax rates down and keep them down. With indexing that would be true. Entin designed a chart showing that indexing provided the dramatic comparison that the administration was seeking, and we gave it to Regan on July 22, the day the bidding began (see Chart 9).

The President found the chart convincing and used a color version in his televised speech on July 27, two days before the vote, quipping that the Democrat's tax cut is larger "if you're only planning to live two more years." The chart helped the President gen-

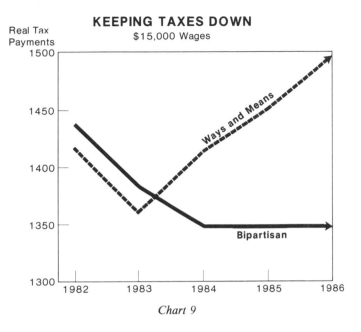

Chart 9

erate a tidal wave of public pressure for his tax package. On the morning of the vote Speaker of the House O'Neill said, "We are experiencing a telephone blitz like this nation has never seen." Forty-eight Democrats voted with the Republicans to give a supply-side President a 238–195 victory.

It was a victory in principle more than in substance. Six days before the vote a *Wall Street Journal* editorial, "Taxes and Recession," pointed out that "the impressive thing is how much of the tax cut has already been compromised away" as a result of delay. The tax cuts were in a "dead heat" with bracket creep over wide ranges of the tax schedule, and "if the current slowdown proves more severe than we now expect, surely the answer is to move marginal tax rates down faster, to give the economy not a nominal tax cut but a real one."

The Repeal of Victory

The President realized the role that the Treasury and, especially, the Office of Economic Policy had played in creating this victory. At the end of August he sent me a letter from Santa Barbara:

Dear Craig:

These first months in office have been an exhilarating experience, and your work in the adoption of major portions of our Program for Economic Recovery has been one of the high points. With Secretary Regan, you have helped immeasurably in providing the economic analyses to support this program and to generate and sustain the public confidence that has been so vital to our success.

As I signed the tax legislation, I could not help but think of the great role that you played in achieving this victory for the American people. I am grateful that I have your assistance as we continue our efforts at national renewal.

Sincerely,

Ronald Reagan [signed]

Orrin Hatch, who remembered all the difficult confrontations we had had to face together in the Senate, sent a congratulatory letter on August 4, the date of the final passage of the tax bill, to "memorialize its passage."

The White House staff was less generous. Richard Williamson, an assistant to the President, sent out a warm letter to the Treasury supply-siders. But others were of a different mind, and the supply-siders who had created the issue and fought the battles since 1975 were not toasted in the celebrations that followed the victory proclamation. The President was whisked off to California in order to avoid a White House bill-signing ceremony necessitating our participation along with Jack Kemp's.

At the end of September, two months after the tax bill had passed, there was a private reception at the White House at which President Reagan personally thanked congressional staffers who helped pass his economic recovery program. Reporters Evans and Novak remarked that the guest list showed that "White House lobbyists have trouble telling friends from enemies."

They invited Republican staffers from the Senate Budget Committee and House Ways and Means Committee who never concealed their contempt for the Reagan tax cut. Omitted from the list were conservative staffers from both houses who had fought for the Kemp-Roth tax bill before it became Reagan's and then went all out for the President's program.

Even more conspicuous by their absence from the guest list were those

Treasury officials who had done the most to get the tax bill enacted, even though many other administration officials were invited. Treasury lobbyists Dennis Thomas and Bruce Thompson were asked at the last minute. But Assistant Secretary Paul Craig Roberts and his deputy, Steve Entin, never did get to the reception.

I was in Atlanta that day explaining the President's economic program to the Rotary Club and could not have attended, but it is true that I learned about the reception only when someone sent me the Evans and Novak column. The White House staff went out of their way to send a loud and clear message: The Reagan Administration was not a supportive environment for a Reaganite.

The President was going to need help to hold on to his historic tax bill. Even before it was signed on August 13, the campaign had begun to raise taxes. On August 6 the Treasury staff alerted me to a sharp change in emphasis in OMB's view of the economic and financial situation. At that time, the problem with the economy was still considered to be inflation. Critics were alleging that the tax cuts and the deficit would worsen the inflation and that inflation fears, stemming from the President's fiscal policy, were responsible for the high interest rates. In contrast to this Keynesian view, the administration had a monetarist explanation of inflation and interest rates: both resulted from overly rapid money growth. Interest rates, especially long-term rates, can remain high even during a period of monetary restraint if people believe that the restraint is temporary. To reassure financial markets about inflation, the Federal Reserve Board needed to get off the roller-coaster and maintain a policy of moderate and predictable growth in the money supply.

In its "Economic and Financial Update" of August 4, OMB suddenly abandoned the monetarist explanation of inflation and interest rates and adopted the view that "fiscal policy is the cutting edge of monetary policy." The OMB memo absolved the board from any responsibility for the economy because "the Fed is caught between a rock and a hard place" and "placed in a near insoluble predicament." OMB was saying that the budget deficit was the source of inflation expectations and high interest rates. At a meeting of the board of governors of the Federal Reserve System on July 9, Alan Greenspan had expressed the same view. Monetary policy, he argued, is the junior partner. He seemed to expect that a restrictive monetary policy was going to be overwhelmed by inflationary tax cuts. Of course, exactly the opposite was occurring—a tax cut that was too small and too late was being overwhelmed by a restrictive monetary policy, and the economy was headed into a deep recession.

On August 10 another OMB document surfaced in the administration, this one an internal memo from Larry Kudlow to David Stockman. It mentioned an upcoming "September Offensive," which the Treasury knew nothing about. To get the offensive going, "a mini-budget document" was needed in order "to post significant revisions from the mid-session forecast." OMB wanted to lower the GNP forecasts in order to project much larger budget deficits. In pushing for these revisions, the memo maintained that OMB should not be inhibited by the facts: "As you know," Kudlow told Stockman, "I think we should go beyond a mere surgical incision based on available data." The memo gave no reason for projecting a gloomy outlook, other than to obtain large deficit projections. It was certainly not that Kudlow was worried about tight money causing a recession. "The recession (if there is one) should not be pinned on the Fed." Kudlow asserted that money growth was "unchanged from the inflationary growth path of the past four years," and "the Fed should be given no encouragement for additional ease." In the middle of one of the tightest monetary policies in the postwar period, Kudlow declared that "it is inconceivable to intelligent observers that monetary policy can be accused of excessive restraint." This was four days after Treasury Secretary Regan said in an interview published in the *New York Times* (August 6, 1981) that if money-supply growth continued to stay below target, we were "going to have a severe recession." Clearly Kudlow did not think that the secretary of the Treasury or his advisers were intelligent observers, but it was Treasury and not OMB that turned out to be right.

Coming as it did on top of his August 4 apology for the Federal Reserve, the memo caused speculation that Kudlow was campaigning for a seat on the board (Fred Schultz's term was about to expire) and was writing memos designed to make himself acceptable. But the memo revealed its true purpose. "High interest rates should not be blamed on the Fed. Instead, in order to dovetail into the September Offensive, high interest rates should be blamed on government deficits and borrowing."

OMB's plan was to use the high interest rates to argue down the administration's economic-growth projections and to project larger deficits. The deficits would then be blamed for the high interest rates. Never mind that the argument was circular and that the high interest rates preceded the deficits. Members of Congress would return from the August recess full of their constituents' concerns about high interest rates, and OMB intended to focus Congress on cutting spending and raising taxes as the way to lower interest rates.

Blaming fiscal rather than monetary policy for interest rates was inconsistent with the monetarist stance of Reaganomics. OMB's next step was to deride another principle of Reaganomics: the proposition that the tax cuts would increase private saving and help to finance the deficit. The campaign of derision was effective, signs of which began to appear in the press. By the end of the year senior White House staffers had shown many signs of the spreading mutiny against Reaganomics. On January 4, 1982, Steven Beckner reported in the Baltimore *Sun* that

White House communications director David Gergen expressed doubts about the fiscal and monetary course his boss is committed to . . .

Sounding like anything but a supply-sider, the communications director disdained hopes that increased savings will help ease the budget financing strain. "Have you seen any increase in the rate of saving?" he demanded.

The August 10 memo made it clear that OMB had abandoned Reaganomics, formed a team of its own, and was off and running with the bit in its teeth.

For the next couple of months it seemed that OMB could not be stopped. It was a frustrating period. Facts, economic analysis, and loyalty to the President's program carried no weight. The administration's economic policy was shoved aside by OMB's scare tactics on the deficit. It was a dangerous game because it focused responsibility for the deficit on the President's fiscal policy even as the Federal Reserve's recessionary monetary policy was producing large budget deficits. Ronald Reagan was going to be left holding the bag for Paul Volcker. Unless OMB could be stopped, the outcome would be higher taxes and the unraveling of Reaganomics.

In August OMB produced a four-page document, "Need for a Fiscal/ Political Game Plan." It was clearly a game plan designed to leave all policy initiative in OMB's hands. The deficit was declared to be "the paramount policy/political problem of the Administration." OMB argued that we could not wait to see if the President's economic program would work. Instead, the administration had to catch the House leadership by surprise with an unexpected September offensive, "a big package of downward revised budget requests, including defense," and "a crack at selective 'tax loopholes.' "

The plan was risky for many reasons. It would create the impression that the administration had hidden the deficit in order to get the tax cuts passed and was now pulling the deficit out from under the covers in order to bludgeon the Congress into more spending cuts than had been agreed. The Congress had just passed the budget resolution, and Del Latta, a Republican leader, had described it as "the largest package of spending cuts in the entire history of the Congress." With such praise, Congress might think it had done enough budget cutting for one year. By declaring the deficit to be the paramount problem, OMB was inviting Congress to reduce the deficit by reopening the President's tax bill. Indeed, OMB was reopening the tax issue itself by pushing for higher taxes.

There was just as big a risk that Congress would do nothing and refuse to reopen the month-old "historic" economic program—in which case the September offensive would fall on its face. The President would be handed a defeat one month after his big victory, and the political chemistry would be radically changed. The result would be to create hysteria over the deficits without making a dent in them and to send out the unmistakable signal that the administration had lost confidence in its economic policy. Treasury believed that OMB's September offensive was a high-risk strategy that was more likely to alarm than to reassure the financial markets in whose name it was being advocated.

Treasury also believed that a great deal of the apprehension that OMB was creating in the White House was smoke to cover up the true source of the deficits. The lower deficit projections were based on unspecified spending cuts, and OMB was not finding the cuts. In addition, Stockman had lost the cuts in social security by grabbing with both hands. The Senate had agreed to cut social security spending by nearly $6 billion by changing the formula for calculating the cost-of-living adjustment and delaying the benefit increase for three months in the 1982 fiscal year. But Stockman convinced the administration to propose more sweeping changes in the social security system, claiming 1982 savings of $9 billion. Treasury warned that the additional $3 billion did not warrant the risk. The public uproar that followed the announcement of Stockman's plan caused the House-Senate conference to drop altogether the social security cuts that the Senate had approved. Later Stockman was to repeat the mistake, forcing the President on the defensive for the first time in a nationally televised address in September. The outcome was that social security was removed from the budget process and turned over to a commission. Also, Stockman had only achieved $35 billion of the $49 billion in budget cuts that the administration proposed for 1982. One way for OMB to get off the hook was to blame the deficits on high interest rates, defense spending, optimistic assumptions about economic growth, and a tax cut that was too big.

In addition to the political risks there were policy risks. OMB's suggestion that high interest rates be blamed on government deficits was a bizarre and abrupt reversal of the administration's position. It would put us in a policy box, especially if we found ourselves in a recession. To understand the policy box, consider the logic of OMB's argument that deficits cause inflation and high interest rates. It means that inflation cannot be brought down with monetary policy, since lower inflation reduces the GNP (the tax base) and tax revenues fall, thereby enlarging the deficit. Since, according to OMB, higher deficits mean higher inflation, the result of an anti-inflationary monetary policy is a declining economy, higher inflation, and rising interest rates. There are only two ways out of the box: you must raise taxes in order to recover the revenues lost to lower inflation, or you must slash the budget more and more as inflation falls so that expenditures decline with revenues. In other words, the government finds itself cutting the budget and/or raising taxes as the economy goes into recession. That is austerity with a vengeance—a throwback to the policies of the 1930s and a far cry from the supply-side policy of balancing the budget through economic growth. As OMB led the government toward austere policies in a recession, Keynesians were untypically silent.[1]

1. See Paul Craig Roberts, "Where Did All the Keynesians Go?" *Wall Street Journal*, December 21, 1982.

It was not just supply-siders who were opposed to changing horses in midstream. Undersecretary Sprinkel's office advised Regan on August 11 that "blaming high interest rates on the deficit is a short-sighted ploy, which involves more than convincing Congressmen to reduce spending further." The Treasury staff in general could find no evidence for any of OMB's arguments. Indeed, they could not even find an argument that was consistent from one week to the next. On August 13 I received a staff memo:

The OMB Economic and Financial Update memoranda's analysis of the stance of monetary policy since March has been very erratic . . .

From late March to early April, the OMB opinion appears to have been that Fed policy was expansionary. Then, in mid-April, they thought they momentarily saw some tightening. In late April, they discerned some clear signs of restraint which seemed to persist in their analysis through May. Then, in June, their view switched to one that the Fed was once more on an expansionary course. Strangely enough, by mid-June they had decided that policy had probably been restrictive since mid-May after all. By late June, this view had become confirmed and they said, *"monetary policy is tight."* Late July seems to have witnessed another reversal in their view; and, pointing to the Fed's balance sheet, they began to conclude that policy was easing. This viewpoint seems to have taken firm hold in the latest memo.

As recently as June 16 OMB had said that monetary *"restraint means lower interest rates . . .* The model works. If only policymakers would use it." However, by August 4 OMB had abandoned this view, arguing instead that deficits determine interest rates—a switch in emphasis from monetary to fiscal policy. At a forecasting meeting on August 19, both CEA and OMB wanted to lower the GNP projections. However, they could not agree whether the growth of the money supply was contracting or expanding. Jerry Jordan (CEA) said it was contracting, and Larry Kudlow (OMB) claimed it was expanding. Treasury's position was that, in view of the monetarist stance of the administration, it would be difficult to revise the forecast if agreement could not be reached about the direction of monetary policy. Kudlow's position was peculiar. On Wall Street he had attracted attention to his newsletter by expressing a monetarist point of view, and this had been more or less his stance in the administration. By mid-August the evidence was clear that monetary policy had been tight for three months and would cause a recession if it continued. OMB wanted desperately to forecast lower GNP and higher deficits; yet Kudlow was shoving aside both the monetarism and the evidence that would support such a forecast. Obviously OMB wanted deficits, but not deficits that could be laid on the doorstep of monetary policy. OMB was determined to use the deficit to focus congressional attention on the budget.

OMB did not wait to see if the administration would agree with its policy and instead moved to preempt disagreement by giving the press the story that deficits were rising, that a balanced budget by 1984 might not be achievable, that defense spending would have to be cut and taxes increased. The press loved it. Here were all the signs of failure and a policy reversal, or a counterrevolution, before the ink on the historic tax bill was dry.

Treasury was dismayed to see OMB actually providing the leadership in spreading alarm and anxiety about the President's program. The impetus to turn victory into defeat was coming directly from OMB. Stockman succeeded in creating the impression that the administration was out on a limb with its economic policy and had to crawl back. But at the time only OMB was saying that. In July the Congressional Budget Office had released its own updated forecast for 1981 and 1982, and CBO's outlook for real economic growth, inflation, and unemployment was similar to the administration's. On September 9 Alice Rivlin testified before the Budget Committee. The striking feature of her testimony was its relative optimism. She projected a substantially improved economy: inflation would continue to decline, real economic growth would pick up late in 1981 and continue strong in 1982, and unemployment would fall.

This forecast represented a substantial change in outlook for CBO. They had accepted the supply-side view that a proper set of policies would reduce both inflation and unemployment. CBO forecast higher deficits than the administration's July projections, but not so much higher as to cause any panic or call the program into question. And even the higher deficits were projected to be falling to 1 percent of GNP by 1984. (The forecast, of course, meant that CBO did not see the Federal Reserve's recession coming and was slow to take the cue from OMB that it was time to unravel Reaganomics.)

Furthermore, OMB's deficit scare tactic was based on an alleged causal relationship between deficits and interest rates that no other part of the government, or outside economists, could verify. In early September the professional staff of the Treasury reported, again, that

Any linkage between budget deficits and interest rates appears to be rather remote and uncertain. Briefly stated, budget deficits are actually associated with low not high interest rates. This is a cyclical phenomenon, reflecting high revenues and a strong desire to invest during economic expansion, and low revenues and poor investment prospects during recessions.

Deficits could result in inflation only if they were covered by printing money, but "the Federal Reserve is not required to monetize deficits, and has often chosen not to do so in the past."

On October 13 a meeting of business economists warned the administration that it should stress the relative size of the deficit (in relation to the size of the economy), not its absolute size. The business economists also warned that the administration should give no appearance of backing away from its program.

Paul McCracken, a former chairman of the Council of Economic Advisers, made the point much more forcefully in an article in the *Wall Street Journal* (October 22, 1981). "Once again," he wrote, "we are seeing a tidal wave of panic threatening to sweep us into a reversal of policies . . . but the President's program is basically sound." While OMB was endeavoring to create panic over a rise in the 1982 deficit from $45 to $60 billion, McCracken moved to put the deficit into perspective:

On the average, budget deficits in 1971–80 were equal to 2.1% of GNP, which was about the figure for fiscal 1981. If the same ratio were to hold for fiscal 1981, the deficit would be $65 billion. If the average for the second half of the 1970s were to prevail this year, the deficit would be over $80 billion. And if this ratio were to be equal to the 1975–76 average, the current year's deficit would exceed $110 billion.

"Obviously," said McCracken, "the recent exceptionally high interest rates have deeper causes than the federal deficit, because the deficits we have had in 1980 and 1981 and confront this year are no larger, after allowing for the changing size of the economy, than those in several years during the last decade." The deficit was too large and needed to be worked down, "but we are hardly looking at a terrifying prospect out of context with history."

William A. Niskanen, a member of Reagan's Council of Economic Advisers, had studied the effects of deficits on inflation. His findings were published in the *Journal of Monetary Economics* (August 1978). Niskanen found that the rate of inflation was determined by the rate of money growth and that the rate of money growth was not related to the deficit:

Over the whole period (1948–1976), about 15–20 percent of the federal deficit appears to have been monetized. This effect, however, nearly disappears when one controls for the substantial shift in monetary policy in the last decade. In any given year, the federal deficit does not appear to have any significant effect on the rate of change of the money supply.

Since money supply growth determines inflation and the deficit does not determine the growth of the money supply, "federal deficits do not have any significant effects on the inflation rate operating either through or independent of the rate of money growth."

In a study published during Stockman's September offensive, the Joint Economic Committee of Congress came to the same conclusion: "Finally, and for this report, most important, neither changes in the deficit, nor changes in its roots—expenditures and revenue— had a statistically significant effect on the rate of inflation."

The evidence showed that in the United States deficits were a smaller percentage of the economy than in most other industrial democracies. OMB's deficit projections for 1982 and 1983 did not rival the 1976 deficit, which measured 4.5 pecent of GNP and did not prevent the real economy from growing at a 5.4 percent rate. OMB's claim that budget deficits determine, rather than reflect, the state of the economy was inconsistent with the fact that large deficits are the normal accompaniment of recession and that all recoveries take place in the face of the budget deficits that recessions leave in their aftermath.

The Treasury believed that the high interest rates came from an additional risk premium that had been added by uncertainty over the direction of economic policy. People holding long-term financial investments stand in risk of large capital losses owing to the changeability of monetary policy. This view was not unique. For example, on May 4 *Fortune* had written that the Federal Reserve "has so little credibility that short-run changes in monetary growth always raise questions about the direction of policy, and so devastate the financial markets." Treasury officials believed that the hysteria OMB was creating over the deficit would simply add to policy uncertainty by calling into question the President's whole program. It was clear enough from the start that the outcome of the September offensive would be: (1) to cast doubt on the supply-side tax cuts before they ever went into effect, and (2) to remove pressure for spending control by signaling Congress that the administration was so panicked by deficits that it would raise taxes.

The liberal press, the beneficiary of numerous OMB leaks, was quick to defend Stockman from Treasury's criticism. Treasury supply-siders were portrayed as "theological" voices crying out in defense of large budget deficits. There was, in other words, to be no debate. OMB had the ball, and the press was running interference. Suddenly I realized with a chill the dangerous position I was in from having been tight-lipped with the administration's secrets. The secrets all turned out to have short half-lives anyway, and the press was on the side of those officials who gave them away.

OMB claimed the support of the financial community, but many were objecting. For example, Leif Olsen, chairman of the economic policy committee of Citibank, spoke out forcefully. The counterattack on the Reagan administration's economic program disregards

the evidence of accepted theory to put the worst possible face on the outlook for fiscal policy. This of course, has helped to promote the general uproar in the credit markets which the critics then cite in support of their contentions.

But the facts are that changes in federal borrowing do not cause major increases in interest rates, nor do they cause increases in inflation. Tax reductions have never explained inflation. The indispensable ingredient of inflation is an overly expansionary monetary policy, and that has been ruled out—not just by the administration's strategy but by the financial markets' extreme reaction to it. Budget deficits are not desirable because they must necessarily borrow funds which would otherwise go to the private sector. But deficits should be understood, not blindly feared.[2]

2. "For the Record," *Wall Street Journal*, September 17, 1981.

The financial press, with a few exceptions, joined Stockman in attributing high interest rates to the budget deficits that were projected for the future. The Republican Senate and the senior White House staff were also quick to follow, and so were the House Democrats. It took Stockman a year to reverse the momentum of the President's program and raise taxes. His success is puzzling, because it is obvious that the financial markets were refuting Stockman's case for a tax increase even while he made it. Over the course of the year estimates of the deficit doubled and tripled (See Table 6), but interest rates fell substantially.

The 1983 deficit, for example, was estimated at $22.8 billion in March 1981. By September it had tripled, and by July 1982 it had doubled again to $115 billion, with unofficial estimates placing it in the $140 billion range. Yet from August 6, 1981, to August 6, 1982 (prior to the big financial market rally that began August 17, 1982), interest rates on Treasury bills had fallen 33 percent. The prime rate had declined 27 percent, federal funds were down 43 percent, and the rate on ninety-day commercial paper was down 35 percent (see Table 7). The interest rate on three-year Treasury notes had declined from 15.8 to 13.5, and ten-year bonds were down a full point. If deficits, or the fear of them, push up interest rates, how could interest rates fall so much while the deficits mushroomed? Clearly the financial markets did not believe Stockman's theory. The "theologian" turned out to be the former divinity student heading OMB and not the economists at the Treasury. But no one saw the evidence. Blind fear of the deficit, of which Leif Olsen had warned, prevailed. The blindness was so total that some stuck with the incorrect explanation of interest rates beyond the point of embarrassment. For example, on August 17, 1982, the day of one of the biggest bond market rallies on record, a *Washington Post* editorial lobbied for the Reagan-O'Neill tax-increase bill: "As it's working out, the

Table 6. Official Administration Estimates of the Deficit (billions of dollars)

	March '81	Sept. '81	Feb. '82	July '82
1981	45.0	59.1	98.6	108.9
1983	22.8	62.9	91.5	115.0
1984	+ 0.5	58.8	82.9	92.6

tax cuts have left the government with very large budget deficits that, in turn, keep interest rates intolerably high."

The final blow to OMB's theory that budget deficits would prevent a rise in stock prices and a fall in interest rates came on September 1, 1982. CBO revised its 1983 deficit projection upward from $118 billion to $150 billion, and the Wall Street firm of Saloman Brothers forecast a $178 billion deficit for 1983. Yet the strong rally in the financial markets continued. Jean Kirk in her T. Rowe Price communication sheet for August 30, 1982, reported that market analysts were attributing the rally in the financial markets to a change in monetary rather than fiscal policy. The Federal Reserve, worried by a weakening domestic economy and the near financial collapse of Mexico, realized it had drained too much liquidity from the econ-

Table 7. Interest Rates, August 6, 1981–August 6, 1982

	8/6/82	7/30/82	7/16/82	2/5/82	8/6/81
Treasury bills[a]					
13 weeks	10.31%	10.17%	12.62%	13.63%	15.36%
26 weeks	11.10	11.15	13.02	13.66	15.36
52 weeks	11.41	11.35	12.82	13.13	14.61
Treasury coupons[b]					
1 year	12.67	12.56	14.36	14.75	16.53
3 years	13.51	13.53	14.78	14.86	15.77
7 years	13.93	13.75	14.69	14.65	15.07
10 years	13.81	13.68	14.48	14.65	14.86
20 years	13.60	13.63	14.26	14.71	14.44
Federal funds[c]	10.73	11.45	14.63	15.43	18.84
Prime rate	15.00	15.50	16.50	16.50	20.50
Commercial paper					
90 days	11.27	11.75	14.46	14.92	17.44
6 months	11.69	12.24	14.26	14.57	16.76
New Aa corp. bonds[d]	15.43	15.37	16.20	16.60	16.07
Euro dollar (90 days)	12⅝	13¹/₁₆	15⁹/₁₆	15⁹/₁₆	19⅛

a. Bank discount rate on most recently auctioned bills.
b. Yields read from Treasury Yield Curve.
c. Average of past 5 days' effective rate.
d. Treasury weekly series based on reoffering yields of new corporate bonds rated Aa by Moody's.
Source: Office of Government Finance and Market Analysis, U.S. Treasury.

omy and eased monetary policy. "The bond and stock market rallies were directly related to the ease by the Fed," she reports analysts as saying, "not the tax [increase] bill or any statements by President Reagan. In fact, there are those who say it would have been very bullish if the tax [increase] bill had *not* been passed. Then Congress would be *forced* to cut spending."

The Press as a Battleground

OMB did not reply in-house to the Treasury's evidence refuting the unsubstantiated claim that deficits cause high interest rates. Instead, they took the battle to the press. OMB could rely on the fact that the higher-ups in the administration lacked the training to judge their case on the evidence. The press had no ability to weigh the evidence either, but they would be grateful to OMB for making a policy dispute public. On August 31 the *Wall Street Journal* quoted "a White House economist" who alleged that Treasury had taken monetarist reasoning for granted, thereby failing to see that deficits cause inflation and high interest rates.

Treasury had carefully examined the evidence, and OMB's decision to take refuge in the press confirmed our suspicion that Stockman had no evidence for his position that could survive the scrutiny of experts. We were dismayed that OMB was giving headlines to the press such as "The President Fights for Credibility" and publicly dramatizing policy disputes within the highest councils of the administration. The main effect, we thought, would be to shake the confidence of the public in the President's economic program. OMB had raised the stakes: they were responding to internal resistance by taking disputes to the press.

It was up to me to see if a mere assistant secretary could put his foot down before the President's program was unraveled. On September 3 I sent a memo to Regan, with copies to OMB, CEA, the senior White House staff, and two Treasury undersecretaries, expressing a concern that the press was beginning to perceive some administration officials bypassing the President and advocating a change of policy. If this continued, the administration might lose control over its policy to the press. The Treasury was as opposed to deficits as anyone else but thought that the deficits were being painted too darkly, "which itself may be negatively impacting on the market." It would be better if the government could first consider the evidence for a change of policy before one agency unilaterally announced a policy change based on unsubstantiated claims. Treasury was waiting to see the evidence that deficits cause high interest rates.

No evidence appeared, but stories about me did. Journalists I had never met or even talked with over the telephone suddenly reported that I was "strident," "inflexible," a "true believer," and "one of three Treasury Druids." In Washington no one is ever chastised for being a chameleon, since the town itself operates that way. The incentives are to be "pragmatic," "flexible," and manipulative. The liberal columnists are especially delighted with a conservative who foresakes his principles. He is then said to have grown and acquired new respect. On the other hand, being "principled" carries derogatory connotations of being hard to get along with. In Washington a principled person has two choices: give up the principles or make enemies. Years of rule by flexible pragmatists had produced the erosion in the U.S. economy and the country's international position that had brought Ronald Reagan, who campaigned on principles, to office. But, like others before them, Reaganites found that principles are inconsistent with the incentive structure, which is another way of saying that as soon as a President is elected he is captured by the past.

The September Offensive

During August 1981, while the President was on his California ranch and much of his government was on holiday, OMB prepared its big push for a change of policy. The day following the Labor Day weekend, OMB launched its offensive at a meeting of the Cabinet Council on Economic Affairs. The OMB memorandum began: "The latest rise in interest rates is yet another reminder of the continuous burden of government borrowing on financial market behavior." To be sure that the government was duly alarmed, OMB added to the 1982 projected budget deficit the Treasury borrowing requirements necessary to refund or roll over the public debt, and then for good measure threw in the sum of federal loan guarantees, direct loans, government-sponsored enterprises, and tax-exempt state and municipal financing to produce a 1982 federal credit-demand figure of $475 billion. OMB had found that the $60 billion deficit it was projecting for 1982 was not big enough to cause people to abandon the President's program, so it added in everything it could think of to produce a monstrous figure. Treasury staff produced their usual understated response and pointed out that, if Stockman was basing his interest rate argument on the magnitude of gross federal and federally assisted borrowing, eliminating a mere $60 billion deficit by balancing the budget would have little effect.

Eventually Washington did panic over federal borrowing, and ironically it was Washington's panic that was unsettling the financial markets. All sorts of harmful things were done in the name of reassuring Wall Street. For example, the "compromise" that reduced and delayed the personal income tax-rate reductions was supposed to have reassured Wall Street about the deficit and to have lowered interest rates. Instead, the compromise made Wall Street nervous, and interest rates went up. Investors saw the tax cuts sitting off in the future, where they were not firmly and safely in anyone's hands. If Congress failed to control spending, the tax cuts would fall victim to the budget deficits. OMB created the impression that the financial markets were afraid of the President's program, but the real fear was that the President would not be able to make his program stick. The economic policy flip-flops of the Carter Administration and the roller-coaster policies of the Federal Reserve Board had created expectations of continuous policy reversals. The hysteria that OMB was generating over the President's program was confirming the markets' expectations of further policy reversals. What was needed to calm the markets was a consistent policy, with administration officials showing confidence rather than doubt.

But confidence was inconsistent with Stockman's persistent aim to change policy. So he worked to undermine confidence from the "mid-course correction" that he wanted in June to the September offensive, and to the October, November, December, January, February, and March offensives, until he won. He began with the argument that deficits cause inflation. Then, when the inflation rate collapsed in spite of growing deficits, he argued that deficits cause high interest rates. When interest rates collapsed, he argued that deficits prevent economic recovery. Whatever was there—inflation, recession, trouble in the financial markets—he hooked his argument to it. Originally the Reagan Administration intended to balance the budget through economic growth. By gradually undermining the policies that would increase the rate of growth, Stockman turned policy around and steered it in the traditional Republican direction of balancing the budget by raising taxes.

On September 24, 1981, President Reagan went on national television and proposed additional 1982 spending cuts of $13 billion and tax increases of $3 billion (rising to $22 billion by 1984). Four things in particular stood out in the President's speech. The first was that he moved a long way away from Stockman's plan to save $5 billion by deferring the cost-of-living increases for social security recipients. Stockman's second run at social security had produced the predictable uproar, and to calm the political waters Reagan even gave back some of the savings that had been achieved: "I am asking the Congress to restore the minimum benefit for current beneficiaries with low incomes." Then to wash his hands of social security, he turned the matter over to a political commission. For the financial community concerned about ballooning social spending, the President's action removed all hope that social security payments would be brought in line with the economy's ability to pay. Far from reassuring the markets that the budget was going to be cut, the President's speech signaled that the largest item in the budget was exempt from the reductions—hardly a helpful sign to give to markets allegedly living in fear of deficits.

Second, only one month after he had signed the tax-cut bill, the President was asking for a $22 billion tax-increase package. It had all the earmarks of an administration running from its victory, retreating from its tax cut. For the previous month the news had been full of reports that administration officials thought the tax cuts too large. On September 6 sources inside OMB told the *Washington Post* that Stockman "never really expected Congress to pass a tax cut as big as the administration had requested." To make sure everyone knew that Stockman never had any faith in the tax cuts, the story appeared again in the *Post* a month later (October 5):

Stockman had long known that the tax cut was a potential problem for him. He had argued inside the administration that its implementation should be delayed, an argument he largely won. Then Stockman hoped that the Democratic-controlled House of Representatives would moderate the size of the tax cut—and thus the size of future deficits. "Don't worry, the House will bail us out"—this was a slogan at OMB and in the Senate Budget Committee, where many of Stockman's original tactics were first developed.

On September 7 Deputy Secretary of the Treasury McNamar told Peter Behr of the *Washington Post* that the administration was studying an array of controversial tax increases, including higher excise taxes on cigarettes and alcohol and limits on deductions for mortgage payments as ways of controlling the 1982 deficit. The story was duly reported the next day under the headline, "New Tax Increases Studied to Control Budget Deficit." The Treasury was rocked. Supposedly we were fighting tax increases, and here was the second in command supporting them. McNamar was forced to apologize for his faux pas in a staff meeting, but if we had had any doubts, we now knew that he and Chapoton, the assistant secretary for tax policy, would be pushing for tax increases from inside the Treasury. On September 15 Steven Weisman wrote in the *New York Times* that "the deficits are a product of Mr. Reagan's tax cuts" and quoted "a White House strategist": "In some respects we are a victim of our own success. Nobody really thought we'd end up with a tax cut as big as the one we got." Weisman reported that "suddenly, perhaps inevitably, White House aides have very quietly begun to trade criticism among themselves about the way the Reagan economic program was assembled and advertised in the first place, as if to acknowledge that some of the Administration's problems are of its own making." Treasury noted that the White House aides were not quiet enough to keep the *New York Times* and *Washington Post* from hearing them. "Growing concern in and out of the administration over the size of the deficit," said the *Post*, "compels the search for increased taxes."

Third, and most peculiar of all, the President went ahead with his televised proposals in spite of being warned by the Congress that they would not pass. For example, on September 22 Martin Tolchin reported in the *New York Times* that "Republican Congressional leaders warned President Reagan today that his $16 billion package of budget cuts would be defeated by Congress." Quoting "a Repub-

lican close to the White House," Tolchin reported that the worst
signal Reagan could send the financial community would be "to
send up something that's going to get killed in the Congress." On
the same day Murray Weidenbaum told the House Budget Committee that failure to approve the administration's new round of
budget cuts would have a serious effect on the financial markets: "I
think that would be a discouraging sign." The question is obvious:
Why was the President pushed by his advisers to undertake a course
of action when it was known in advance that it would have a negative outcome? Republican officials on Capitol Hill told the *Times*
that they hoped Reagan "would postpone the speech pending further study and consultation with the Republican leaders." House
Republican leader Bob Michel told Fred Barnes of the Baltimore
Sun (September 24, 1981) that the White House was making a fetish
of meeting the target of a $42.5 billion budget deficit in 1982.
"They've gotten hung up on a phony objective," Michel said. "The
objective is a healthy economy," not whether the deficit is $42.5 bil-
lion or $60 billion. "But they've set themselves up for a defeat when
it doesn't come in at $42.5 billion." Truer words were never spoken,
but in spite of all the warnings the President was pushed into the trap.

Fourth, the President did not mention monetary policy. It was as
if the Federal Reserve did not exist. In his speech the President
blamed the high interest rates on fiscal policy, that is, on his own
budget: "all of us know that interest rates will only come down and
stay down when government is no longer borrowing huge amounts
of money to cover its deficits." Reagan was now in Stockman's
hands and reluctantly agreed to scale back his defense spending proposals and to revise "the tax cuts to curtail certain tax abuses and
enhance tax revenues." As evasiveness crept into our program, "revenue enhancers" became the euphemism for tax increases.

Having locked the President onto the disastrous course of the
September 24 proposals that comprised the September offensive,
Stockman moved to disassociate himself from responsibility. The
day before the fateful speech, Evans and Novak wrote that Stockman "hoped to deflect" an "eager" Reagan from "an all-out battle
for his new budget cuts." Supposedly Stockman was worried that
Reagan would be "Carterized" by "repeating Jimmy Carter's ordeal
by Congress" and "having his domestic cuts rejected and his defense
budget savaged as the newly restored authority of the presidency

comes under assault." Again there is an obvious question: If Stockman was so fearful of the dangers in this course of action, why did he set the President on it?

As the Treasury had predicted, Stockman's September offensive fell on its face. Surveying the wreckage in its lead editorial on September 28, the *Wall Street Journal* said that it was time to shape up. Stockman, "the main malefactor in this misplayed game," had succeeded in making "the public and the Congress even more doubtful about the administration's confidence in its own program." The *Journal* found the President's $22 billion tax-increase proposals disquieting. "A few more flip-flops like that and Mr. Reagan will have himself a credibility problem." The President, the *Journal* thought, "would have been better advised to simply sit tight, try to make sure that the Congress delivered on the budget cuts it had promised in the summer and told his budget chief to lay off the heavy rhetoric." Nevertheless, the editorial thought that "the damage from the September panic is not overwhelming" and the President "on the whole withstood the assault," and it recommended that the administration review the process by which "it almost delivered itself back into the hands of its foes."

At this point it was too early for anyone to imagine Ronald Reagan and Tip O'Neill standing together smiling over a $229 billion tax-increase victory. However, the September Offensive had let the horse out of the stable. The Treasury saw it running away when we read Senator Domenici's statement a few days later in the *Washington Post* (October 8, 1981): "The most dramatic turnaround is the consensus that we have to raise some more revenues."

Stockman was already pushing for further delay in the tax cuts scheduled for July 1982 and 1983. In the second week of October none other than Kent Hance, who with Barber Conable had sponsored the President's historic tax cut in the House, proposed delaying the tax cuts. But Stockman had not yet generated enough panic over the deficit to succeed in reopening the tax bill. "I'm against it," said Conable. "I don't support raising taxes at this point. I don't want to create confusion about what the Reagan policy is." "It would make us look stupid," said an aide to Senator Dole.[3] However, Stockman kept pushing, and soon *Newsweek* (November 2) was

3. The quotes are from Edward Cowan, "Bids to Raise Revenues Expected in Congress," *New York Times,* October 19, 1981.

reporting that "what the Democrats really want is a retreat on the tax cuts, and last week budget director Stockman seemed to agree." "Stockman and his aides," said *Newsweek,* "were flooding the White House and Congress with a variety of revenue-raising suggestions."

By the end of October Stockman's September offensive had become "Reagan's fall offensive" and the *Washington Post* was reporting that the result was "casualties, not victories" (October 26). As Stockman watched the offensive crumble around him, he desperately pulled out of the OMB hat ever more pessimistic deficit projections in an effort to panic the Congress into enhancing revenues. The *Post* quoted "one of the Senate's most senior Republicans" and "a true Reagan loyalist" complaining that "every day we get new numbers, and every day the deficit projections grow higher." The Reagan loyalist "concedes privately," reported the *Post,* "that the recent proposals and performance of the President and his advisers have left him deeply troubled." According to the *Post,* Reagan officials themselves had come to see that by handing Congress "a second huge package of politically unpalatable domestic budget cuts, the President in effect surrendered the initiative in shaping the budget."

All of this damage had been done by Stockman; yet, mysteriously, the story went that "the White House at the highest levels" had lost confidence in the advice they were getting from Secretary Regan. The Treasury had opposed the September offensive and accurately predicted its results. Treasury marveled at the kid gloves with which the *Post* treated Stockman and the laudatory attitude taken toward him in story after story. It made no sense that a newspaper of the *Washington Post*'s bent would be so cosy with a man who wanted to cut "the social porkbarrel" out of the budget and throw the widows and orphans out on the streets. To save money, Stockman even proposed to close down St. Elizabeth's, the federal hospital for the mentally ill. Shortly the mystery would be explained by the appearance of the famous article in the *Atlantic Monthly* in which it was revealed that Stockman had been conducting clandestine interviews for the past ten months with *Washington Post* editor William Greider. The *Post* was clearly looking after the newspaper's best source of ammunition against Reaganomics.

By the autumn of 1981 press reports had made it clear that the fight over the President's program was not between the Reagan Administration and congressional Democrats, but among the Republicans themselves. The battle lines were drawn with OMB, the Senate Republicans, and the senior White House staff in favor of tax increases and the President, Treasury, and the House Republicans opposed. The press was interpreting the split in the government as a reflection of the "central dilemma of Reaganomics: monetary and fiscal policy are set on opposite courses" (*Washington Post*, September 20). The press believed that the tax cuts were inconsistent with monetary policy and that the administration was doomed to failure. In a sense the press was right. Where it went wrong was in describing our monetary policy as one of "tight money" when it was one of moderate, predictable, and steady *growth* in the supply of money. Among the liberal establishment there never seemed to be any doubt that the "dilemma" should be resolved by abandoning supply-side economics, rather than by pressuring the Federal Reserve to operate within its target range. It was an odd turn of events to find liberals on the side of tight money and against economic growth.

The alleged inconsistencies between monetarists and supply-siders was a new weapon in the arsenal against the President's program, and the allegations were strengthening Stockman's move for a change of policy. After all, why stick with an inconsistent policy? Key elements of the coalition that gave the President his tax-cut victory—Senate Republicans and conservative Democrats in the House—were passing out OMB's tables showing how to balance the budget by further delaying and reducing the tax cut. Jack Kemp, alarmed by the arguments that were being raised against supply-side economics while monetarism escaped criticism, began making a case for the gold standard as a way of allowing the money supply to grow without undermining confidence in the value of the dollar. The gold commission had begun its hearings, but the members were mainly opposed to gold. Watching a widening conflict, I made a last-ditch effort to get the President's men back on board with the President's policy.

During the last days of October, the November 16 issue of *Fortune* appeared. It contained an article, "Will Reaganomics Unravel?" that I had written first as a memo to White House Chief of

Staff Baker. The article warned against trying to balance the budget independent of the performance of the economy. For example, an economy sliding into recession produces less tax revenue, causing the deficit to widen. If the government responds to the deficit by raising taxes, it may contribute to the economy's decline, thereby further widening the deficit.

The main purpose of the article was to answer the charge that Reaganomics was at war with itself by demonstrating that the viewpoints of supply-siders, monetarists, and traditionalists were compatible. Supply-siders understood that inflation could cancel the tax-rate reductions by pushing people into higher tax brackets, thereby wiping out the supply-side effects that they counted on to raise the real growth rate. So they supported a policy of moderate and predictable growth in the money supply. Supply-siders also supported OMB's efforts to reduce the growth of spending because budget deficits draw down the pool of private saving, thus offsetting the supply-side effort to increase investment.

The monetarists for their part welcomed the help from a higher saving rate and a larger supply of goods and services in the war against inflation. It is easier to bring down the price level if better incentives and higher profitability are expanding productivity and the economy's output. More goods for the same amount of money mean lower prices. The monetarists also supported lower deficits in order to reduce the temptation for the Federal Reserve to monetize them.

As for the traditionalists, they understood that higher economic growth helps to bring the budget into balance by reducing expenditures for income-support programs and by bringing in more tax revenues. Neither were they at odds with monetarists, since lower inflation reduces big budget expenditures like social security and interest on the national debt.

The problem was not that the three viewpoints were incompatible but that one of the three might try to impose its own main concern—higher economic growth, lower inflation, or a balanced budget—as a single constraint on policy. The administration could not cure inflation all at once without worsening the deficit, and it could not balance the budget all at once without raising taxes—either legislatively or by inflating the money supply in order to push people into higher tax brackets. If the policymakers forgot the multiple constraints, my article predicted, they would unravel the President's program.

Recent administrations had been dominated by economic events. What plans they had were soon abandoned or revised beyond recognition. The Reagan Administration had come to town with a coherent view of what had gone wrong in the economic policy arena and what needed to be done about it. Much had been accomplished in a short period of time. Federal spending was being brought under control, and incentives to work, save, and invest were being restored. Inflation was falling, the dollar was riding high in the foreign exchange markets, and the price of gold was down from panic levels. The article concluded that the risk was not a veto from Wall Street, but that the administration might forget what it came to do in the first place. That was an idealistic way of putting it. The real risk was the blind ambition of some of the policymakers.

In addition to the economic justification for Reaganomics, there was a convincing political argument for holding the program together. "What we want to avoid," a House Republican aide told the *Wall Street Journal* (November 2), "is having some poor slob get a pink slip at the plant because of the recession. So he walks across the street to Joe's bar for a brew and finds he can't afford it because the Republicans have raised excise taxes on beer. He can't get a cigar because Republicans have raised excise taxes on tobacco, and he can't afford to drive home because the Republicans have raised the excise taxes on gasoline." That is what had happened in Great Britain. Margaret Thatcher had been turned from her program, and the result was prolonged recession with higher consumer taxes and tight money. By the end of October 1981 only the Treasury stood between the President and "Thatcherization."

The Treasury stood firm, but Stockman had no intention of playing on the President's team. On November 3 Stephen Nordlinger reported in the Baltimore *Sun* that "to the dismay of Secretary Regan Mr. Stockman has been meeting privately with the Senate's top fiscal officials, Senators Robert Dole (R.Kan.) and Pete V. Domenici (R.N.M.), to devise a tax package." "These senators, whose support Mr. Stockman has been assiduously cultivating, want to raise taxes to lower the deficit." In his *Washington Post* column the same day, Joseph Kraft saw a "broad consensus" developing around a new proposal to increase taxes and to cut defense spending that included OMB, the Senate Republicans, the senior White House staff, and the chairman of the Council of Economic Advisers. The only opposition, Kraft said, came from the supply-siders in the Treasury—"the voodoo fringe." (He conveniently left out the House Republicans and the President himself.) For trying to hold the President's program together, I was accused of making a "blatantly political appeal to ideological loyalties." Kraft declared that "far from being a catastrophe, the unraveling of Reaganomics would probably stimulate confidence," an OMB opinion that had been expressed unguardedly in Jim Baker's office in front of Ed Meese in early June. The only senior administration official still on the President's team was Don Regan, who Kraft declared to be "inhibited by the supply-siders in his own entourage." Kraft had just been seen at lunch with Larry Kudlow. So everyone knew that OMB was replying to the *Fortune* article through Kraft.[4]

On November 5 another liberal ally of OMB, Hobart Rowen, declared in his column in the *Washington Post* that "the time has come for the Reagan Administration to abandon supply-side economics." Rowen, a champion of the big spenders, was concerned that unless there was a sharp reversal of policy the deficit would be out of control. "What would such a reversal entail?" he asked. "Answer: a big tax increase, and giving Ture and Roberts their walking papers." He was calling for "Roberts and like-minded ideologues" to be fired because we supported the policies of the President who appointed us.

White House aides increased the pressure on President Reagan to accept tax increases. On November 4 Howell Raines reported in the *New York Times* that administration officials, "speaking with the guarantee of anonymity," acknowledged that "Mr. Reagan appears to be a victim of the success he had in ramming that tax cut through Congress," when he had acted on the basis of what one official called totally unrealistic economic forecasts. That, of course, was

4. Kraft's column was a personal attack on me and my professional reputation. Yet he had never met me or talked to me about my views, the President's program, or anything else, and he obviously was unfamiliar with my writings. It was a puzzle why Kraft was putting his own professional reputation on the line for OMB.

OMB's line, a curious one in view of the fact that OMB had always had more to say about the forecast than anyone else. By early November OMB had abandoned all pretense at interagency cooperation in working out a troika forecast. (The troika or forecasting team was comprised of OMB, CEA, and Treasury.) On November 9 I received a memo from the Treasury staff complaining that OMB was reaching directly into the Treasury's Office of Tax Analysis for revenue estimates corresponding to economic forecasts of which Treasury was not aware. OMB even had one forecast called "Modified Treasury Path," a surprise to the Treasury staff since "no one at Treasury was consulted on any details of the path."

On November 6 Jonathan Fuerbringer reported in the *New York Times* that by advocating tax increases, Stockman "is implicitly acknowledging that the original Reagan economic program cannot work." He described Stockman's conversion as "a victory for Paul A. Volcker, chairman of the Federal Reserve Board." Treasury was astonished that Stockman kept pushing. In high-level meetings the President had repeatedly rejected the tax-increase proposals that Stockman laid before him. On November 6 Reagan himself went public in a speech before a group of New York Republicans, declaring that "a balanced budget has never been an end in itself justifying any means" and that "we never agreed to balance the budget on the backs of the taxpayers." He repeated this theme many times. Yet, in spite of the President's signals, Stockman escalated his attack. He became quite frenetic. No one could understand why. A recession was taking shape, and it would remove from Stockman's shoulders any responsibility for balancing the budget. He was off the hook, but he was acting like a man whose entire future depended upon forcing a tax increase upon an unwilling President within the next twenty-four hours.

On November 11 the December issue of the *Atlantic Monthly* appeared bearing a cover article, "The Education of David Stockman," by William Greider. With it came the revelation that Stockman had been baring his soul to the assistant managing editor of the *Washington Post* in a series of taped interviews dating from the December before Reagan's inauguration. Stockman's purpose was a mystery. Greider cast some light on it when he wrote that the conversations "were not to be reported until later, after the season's battles were over, but a cynic familiar with how Washington works would understand that the arrangement had obvious symbiotic value." The meetings allowed Greider to know in advance "where the story was going." For Stockman, "who saw the news media as another useful tool in political combat," the meetings "were another channel—among many he used—to the press." Stockman and the *Post* had certainly done a job on the Treasury and the President's economic program, and Greider seemed to be suggesting that Stockman had had that in mind from the beginning. But since the season's battles were not over, the even greater puzzle was why Stockman had allowed the story to be published at the worst possible moment for himself, damaging his own credibility with quotes directly attacking policies he was supposed to be supporting. Among what the *New York Times* called many "quotations regarded as extremely damaging to the Administration" was Stockman's statement that "Kemp-Roth was always a Trojan horse to bring down the top rate . . . Supply-side is 'trickle-down' theory." Tip O'Neill said that Stockman had made devastating admissions that placed the credibility of the entire economic program in doubt.

At first people wondered if Greider had decided to do Stockman in, but it made no sense for a journalist to destroy his own source of inside information before the story was finished and, in the process, his own reputation for confidentiality. Then another bombshell hit that provided a clue to the mystery. Greider was quoted by NBC as saying that Stockman had agreed in September that it was time to publish the article.

In retrospect it looks as if Stockman intended from the beginning to replace the President's program, which he probably regarded as Kemp's, with a new one that had himself at the center. If that is what he had in mind, it makes little difference whether he was motivated by rivalry with Kemp, personal ambition, or deep conviction. He must have believed he would succeed in discrediting the supply-siders, and at the right time an article by a liberal journalist in a liberal national monthly would portray him as a far-seeing leader who had saved the country from "crackpot theories" that had found "their way into the legislative channels"—Stockman's own words, with which Greider had ended his article.

In September, when Stockman gave Greider the go-ahead, he

thought he had won. The Treasury had been rolled up in August, flattened in September, and discarded in October. H. C. Wainwright's political update of October 9 was titled "The Unmaking of a President," and it began: "September marked the month that Treasury Secretary Regan was eliminated as a player in the formulation of Administration policy. OMB Director David Stockman simply took the ball away." Stockman seemed to have suspected that his September offensive would fail to generate budget cuts but would succeed in focusing all eyes on the deficit, and he was ready to substitute tax increases for the unobtainable budget cuts. But at the last minute Treasury broke up Stockman's play. A White House memo on November 2 declared that Stockman's plan required the administration to reverse itself and to admit that "we did not know what we were doing last spring." Such a foolish move would "dramatically demonstrate that conservative Republicans cannot govern." In the week of November 2, the President overruled Stockman four times in succession. It was too late to stop the *Atlantic* article from appearing. Advance copies were already circulating, and Stockman came out a goat instead of a hero.

Stockman's disloyalty was extraordinary even for Washington, but White House officials immediately came to his aid. "We're all trying to rally around," one official told the *Washington Post*. "Stockman's carried so much water for the President it wouldn't be right not to stand with him now." "It undercuts us terribly," one official told the *New York Times* (November 12), but Stockman's job was not in jeopardy because he had become "too indispensable" to the administration's budget efforts. Senator Dole also wore his heart on his sleeve—on November 12 the *Los Angeles Times* reported his opinion: "I think he may have gained some credibility. I think people like candor in this town." As for House Speaker Tip O'Neill, he could not have been more pleased with his new ally. "The architect of the administration's economic program," O'Neill told the *New York Times* (November 12), "is admitting exactly what I and other critics have been saying for six months." President Reagan, after taking Stockman on a publicized "trip to the woodshed," retained him as budget director. In the following weeks the newspapers and magazines were filled with reports and analysis of the aftermath of the Stockman confessions. The opponents of the President's program defended Stockman. On November 17 the *Christian Science Monitor* wrote that "a good dose of honesty has been injected" into the administration's program.

It was at this time that the staunchest supporters of the President's program decided to leave the administration. They were not going to sacrifice their families and take risks with their careers to work for an administration in which loyalty to the President was penalized, but disloyalty and treachery paid no price.

Stockman's retention not only demoralized the President's supporters. It also raised doubts about the President's judgment and suspicions about the inner workings of the White House staff. As the word leaked out of the White House that Stockman had been saved by Jim Baker, these suspicions darkened. People even began wondering if Jim Baker, who had managed George Bush's unsuccessful campaign against Reagan for the nomination, had saved Stockman because he was doing such a good job of destroying the policies of Ronald Reagan and Jack Kemp, thereby paving the way for Bush to be the next Republican presidential candidate.[5] Stories about the political motives underlying the determined effort to discredit the tax cuts began appearing in the press. For example, on December 21 the *New York Times* reported that

the Presidential succession is a factor, with the economic decisions now before Mr. Reagan having a lot to do with whether Vice President Bush, the champion of the traditionalists, or Representative Jack F. Kemp, the supply-side evangelist, emerges as the stronger candidate to succeed Mr. Reagan as President.[6]

The *Times* went on to say that Reaganites were grumbling

that only one member of the Administration stands to gain if Reaganomics is abandoned or fails. That is Mr. Bush, who, back when Mr. Baker was running his Presidential campaign, denounced Mr. Reagan's tax-cutting proposals as "voodoo economics."

5. On June 30, 1982, Woodward reported in the *Washington Post* that Alexander Haig was fired as secretary of state as a result of a master plot directed by James Baker, Richard Darman, and Vice-President Bush, "who wants to be president and allegedly considers Haig a potential rival." A secretary of state is much more visible than a vice-president.

6. The story overlooked Senator Dole's presidential aspirations, but by September 5, 1982, Hobart Rowan was calling attention to Dole as a candidate based on his anti-supply-side credentials (*Washington Post*).

It looked to others as well that the supply-side effort to rejuvenate the economy was falling victim to a political counterrevolution by the establishment. On November 5, a *Wall Street Journal* editorial also found "a clue in the cast of characters." "The tax-boost drive," observed the *Journal,* was "cheered in the press by Joseph Kraft, David Broder and George Will, who are distinguished not by their grasp of economics but by their eminence in the Washington establishment." The attack on Reaganomics had little to do with deficits, "which have never previously caused any ripple of panic on the Potomac." Everyone understands that "what the current tax-boost drive is all about is protecting the power of Washington," which "has long understood the use of the balanced budget as a lever for increasing taxes and thus its own sway over the nation."

The *Journal* pointed out that government was an old hand at projecting a balanced budget by allowing taxes to rise. For example, Carter's recipe for a balanced budget was to allow taxes to rise from 20.3 percent of GNP in 1980 to 22.8 percent in 1984. Ronald Reagan had been elected to stop this game and had promised to balance the budget at lower levels of spending rather than at higher levels of taxation. Those in charge of spending control, Stockman and Domenici, "should be forbidden to ever mention revenues and be judged solely by how well they contain spending." For the President "to throw in the towel in this early round would be a capitulation not merely on the Reagan Administration's economic theories but on the view of government it was elected to pursue."

On November 12, 1981, Senate Budget Committee Republicans led by Stockman's ally, Senator Domenici, were reported to be considering a plan to balance the 1984 budget by raising $48 billion in new taxes. If a large part of Congress was eager to raise taxes just three months after lowering them, an even larger part was unwilling to stick to the 1982 spending targets. In a tie 199–199 vote in the House that day, a bipartisan group was unsuccessful at trying to block an Interior Department appropriations bill that was $1 billion above the President's request.

Five days later Murray Weidenbaum announced a gloomy recession forecast for 1982 and in the same breath proposed a tax increase, a prescription that had not been in anyone's textbook since the 1930s. Stockman was temporarily silenced because of the *Atlantic* article, but he was speaking through other voices. President

Reagan and Secretary Regan blamed the recession on the delay of the tax cut and on a monetary policy that was too tight, but Ed Cowan in the *New York Times* (November 22) reported that Weidenbaum "takes a different, more conventional view"[7] that the recession was the result of "unwinding decades of inflation." When asked if that was not the old Republican policy of fighting inflation with unemployment, Weidenbaum answered: "Recession was never a deliberate—a target—a desire." Stockman, however, was reportedly counting on the deficits that the recession would bring to vindicate him.[8]

On November 12 the President told Secretary Regan that "I believe in my program" and that "you are closer to my thinking than any other member of my administration." At 11:35 that morning Regan reported the President's words to me and declared confidently and enthusiastically: "We defend and advocate the President's program." That, of course, was what I had been doing, but I had begun to wonder if there was any point to it when the President had surrounded himself with people who did not believe in his program. I did not see how we could succeed when the budget director, the White House chief of staff, and the chairman of the Council of Economic Advisers refused to take their cue from the President.

As the unexpected recession quieted the ballyhoo about inflationary tax cuts, the President and a small group of advisers, including Jack Kemp, began talking about speeding up the second installment of the tax cut from July 1982 to January 1982 as a way to get the economy moving again. On November 27 Evans and Novak reported on the switch in emphasis back toward cutting taxes and away from raising them but saw an inherent problem. They called it "The Stockman Tax Trap." Stockman's retention as budget director, they reported, courts "divisiveness on economic policy" and increases the probability of another "bitter internal struggle over tax

7. Reagan's and Regan's statements that tight money and higher taxes are recessionary is the conventional view found in every textbook. Weidenbaum's view that you cause a recession in order to lower inflation and then raise taxes in order to balance the budget is so unconventional that it cannot be found in any textbook. The press, however, always attempted to portray the President's and the Treasury's views as very unconventional as a way of casting doubt on them.

8. See Evans and Novak, "The Stockman Tax Trap," *Washington Post,* November 27, 1981.

policy." A friend of Stockman's told the columnists that "Dave Stockman was by no means ready to follow the file of faceless budget directors into the dustbin of history." He was determined to prevail over the President. And he would.

The December Crisis

To recap the autumn's events: Just as panic over Reaganomics began fading in such quarters as Wall Street and the Congressional Budget Office, it appeared within the Reagan Administration. In September CBO Director Alice Rivlin surprised Congress with her projections of declining budget deficits over the course of the Reagan Administration, and the Wall Street firm of Drexel, Burnham, Lambert published its view that "the evidence is mounting that we are moving in the direction of a lower inflation rate." In the same month the Reagan Administration began backing away from its program.

First, Stockman rewrote the administration's explanation of inflation. Formerly, the cause was excessive money creation and the remedy was slower money growth. After the rewrite, the blame for inflation was on budget deficits, which were worsening under Volcker's regime of six months of zero money growth—a policy far below Federal Reserve targets and one unexpected by the administration. Next, Stockman claimed that the recessionary deficits would prevent economic recovery, an unconventional view that became the conventional wisdom. Then, in the face of congressional opposition (which included the Senate Republican leadership) to further reductions in spending, the administration backed away from its plan to control the deficit by a combination of economic growth and spending restraint and proposed tax increases instead. In September Reagan proposed a $22 billion package of "revenue enhancers" on national television. Before the end of autumn Stockman had ballooned the necessary tax increase to $80 billion. Tip O'Neill was reported to be dumbfounded by how quickly the train that had run over him came uncoupled. The Reagan strategy of balancing the budget through economic growth was being replaced with the Stockman strategy of balancing the budget with higher taxes. Stockman succeeded in panicking Congress and the White House staff but not the President, who resolved the issue by accepting higher deficits rather than higher taxes. Shortly afterward an article based on ten months of interviews with Stockman appeared in the *Atlantic* containing statements that seriously damaged the administration's credibility. The White House rallied around Stockman instead of around the President's economic program, and within a few days the push for a tax increase, which had just been defeated, revived and was again going strong.

The autumn of 1981 was a time of ungluing. The pointless and destructive "internal debate"[9] engineered by OMB had the effect of worsening the recession. The appearance of disarray within the administration and lack of confidence in its own economic program compounded the uncertainty of both the ordinary citizen and the financial markets over the future course of economic policy. In addition, OMB's use of the deficit to generate panic and force a reversal in policy generated media headlines proclaiming President Reagan's first economic failure. The failure belonged to monetary policy, which produced the deficits by producing a recession. But because of Stockman the headlines could proclaim Reagan's defeat on his balanced budget and his retreat from the "main goal" of his administration. The image of failure on top of the apparent disarray weakened the President's hand in dealing with Congress and the media. The situation was further worsened by the numerous statements from high officials that the President would be forced to raise taxes if Congress failed to cut spending. In effect, administration officials told Congress that it could count on more tax revenues if it was "unable" to cut spending. It was clear to the financial markets that the President's program was still up for grabs. The markets know that most presidents attempt and achieve very little in the arena of economic policy, and the September offensive showed the markets that Reagan's attempt to put economic policy on a new track was opposed by members of his own administration and his own party in the Senate. In addition, the recession strengthened the belief that economic policy was still on a stop-go course and that, after a period of fighting inflation with unemployment, the government would return to fighting unemployment with inflation, especially with elec-

9. Of course the debate was not internal. OMB and the White House staff conducted it in the press.

tions coming up. These signals and not the deficit were the main source of the administration's credibility problem.

These points were made to Treasury Secretary Regan in November 1981. In addition he was reminded that the economy would be under a regimen of tight money for a year to eighteen months before the tax cuts made much of an appearance on the scene. If the Federal Reserve let the money supply drop with the economy, which was its usual procedure, the monetary deflation would be too powerful for the limited fiscal stimulus, and the administration would find itself going into the 1982 elections in the middle of a recession.

It is impossible for an administration to bring about fundamental changes in economic policy unless its officials are behind it, and Stockman, Baker, and Weidenbaum were not. On November 13 Douglas Hallett wrote in the *Wall Street Journal* that "it is widely reported that the dominant White House policy figures now, along with Mr. Meese, are such veteran Nixon-Ford administrative and public-relations specialists as James Baker, David Gergen, Max Friedersdorf and Richard Darman, whose jobs—and maybe instincts—lead them to focus on the headline of the hour, the bill of the moment and the conventional wisdom of the day." Since Stockman controlled the headline of the hour—ever higher deficit projections—it was easy for him to turn these officials in his policy direction.

The many signs that the program was coming unstitched produced negative psychological effects that reinforced the expectations that no President can really achieve very much. Having witnessed the Republicans nearly destroy their own program, people entered the Christmas season wondering what was coming next. The President who had refused to give up his policy was now going to be sandbagged by his government. The President's men might tell themselves that it was for his own good, but they clearly were not going to let Reagan's policies prevail. December brought press stories about the "battle for Reagan's mind." The President's firm decision not to balance the budget on the backs of the taxpayers was simply overlooked by his chief aides as if he had never made it. They kept the press plied with stories on the progress of their battle for the President's mind, and the press duly reported that the outcome would be tax increases.

In speeches and interviews throughout November and December President Reagan blamed the recession on the delay and diminution of the first installment of the tax cut. Again, his government did not hear him. On December 5 Weidenbaum sent Reagan a memo disputing his explanation of the recession. The memo was promptly leaked to the press. Obviously, someone was anxious to undercut the President by having him contradicted in public by his chief economic adviser. The officials who had engineered the initial delay of the tax cuts and were arguing for additional delays could not have been pleased with the President's explanation of the recession.

The next day White House press spokesman Larry Speakes told reporters that high unemployment was "the price you have to pay for bringing down inflation," and the faux pas was duly reported in the press the next day. Whether Speakes knew it or not, he was describing the President's economic policy in terms of the traditional Republican solution of squeezing inflation out of the economy by squeezing workers out of employment. Here was the Phillips curve all over again, and to supply-siders it seemed that there was no escaping the dead hand of the past. It was like Nixon declaring "we are all Keynesians now." The irony was not lost on the *Washington Post* and the *New York Times* who snatched it up as proof that Reaganomics was finally coming to grips with Keynesian reality. The endorsement of the Phillips curve by administration officials could not have been reassuring to the financial markets. In the Phillips cycle a democracy facing elections soon stops fighting inflation with unemployment and begins fighting unemployment with inflation. Little wonder that interest rates remained high.

A copy of Weidenbaum's memorandum to the President was sent to me anonymously from the White House. Weidenbaum told the President that, had the full tax cut come earlier, the only probable effect would have been to put upward pressure on interest rates. I sent Weidenbaum a memo pointing out that he was not only contradicting the President and the Treasury secretary, but also the reasoning upon which Reaganomics was based. The way we planned to get off the Phillips curve and avoid fighting inflation with unemployment (and vice versa) was to increase incentives and cash flow through the tax system, while gradually curtailing the rate at which the Federal Reserve was increasing the money supply. When the tax cut was delayed for the sake of balancing the budget (only on paper as it turned out), we were left on the Phillips curve with tightening money and no supply-side offset. The novel feature of our policy was sacrificed to a vain attempt to balance the budget with higher taxes, and we ended up in a recession. The high interest rates inherited from the Carter Administration had played a part, but so had the critics of the President's program, who claimed that it would be very inflationary. The administration itself had overreacted to the inflation fears by delaying the tax cut, and the Federal Reserve had overreacted by bringing in money growth below target. This explanation was consistent with our program as well as with the facts and served the President's purpose far better than the statement that "unemployment is the price you have to pay for bringing down inflation."

My memo to Weidenbaum, along with my memo to Speakes complaining of his statement that we had thrown people out of work in order to lower inflation, were leaked to the press (Baltimore *Sun*, December 17, 1981). Next, Jim Baker wanted to know why Secretary Regan could not control his people and prevent them from taking disputes to the press. Treasury would not buckle, so the White House staff increased the pressure. It made it difficult for Treasury to send memos to the White House and reduced our ability to support the President.

While voices from the administration were explaining how unemployment was the price paid for lower inflation, kindred voices were saying that enormous deficits were the price paid for tax cuts, as if there were no connection between recession and deficits. New deficit projections appeared showing deficits of $109 billion in 1982, $152 billion in 1983, and $162 billion in 1984. On December 7–8 newspaper reports said the "whopping deficit projections" would play a role in forcing the President to abandon his opposition to higher taxes and cuts in the defense budget. The deficits were obviously exaggerated because at that time few expected a severe or lengthy recession. Indeed, Stockman would not even admit that money was tight.

Various ploys were used to get the President to accept tax increases. For example, on December 9 Steven Weisman, citing "knowledgeable aides at the White House," reported in the *New York Times* that

it is the strategy of Mr. Stockman and Mr. Baker to have the President review all of the proposed budget cuts before making a final decision. In this way, Mr. Reagan would presumably see for himself the political difficulty of enacting major new spending cuts and come around to the view that he must seek new military cuts or new taxes.

Another strategy was to supply senators with doomsday deficit projections and then schedule them in an array of meetings with the President. The aim was to present the President with a united front. The senators would come into the Oval Office waving the deficit projections and complain that there was no way they could possibly reduce spending any more than they had. On December 19 Howell Raines reported in the *New York Times* that "White House spokesmen have downplayed these meetings so as to avoid the appearance that Mr. Reagan's staff is trying to put pressure on him to accept tax increases."

On December 12 Weisman quoted a White House aide that "a full-scale battle" is underway "for the soul of the Reagan Administration and the mind of Ronald Reagan." This was a euphemistic way of acknowledging that the President's men were ignoring their chief's policy statements and forcing his policy into the traditional Republican mold. Weisman reported that the Treasury secretary was frustrated "by Mr. Baker's and Mr. Stockman's continuing push for an approach that the Treasury Secretary maintains has been rejected by the President." He was more than frustrated; he was amazed at the tenacity with which these two men fought their chief of state. Indeed, the impunity with which they undermined the President had a chilling effect on Reaganites in the government and alarmed the President's supporters on the outside.[10] The *Wall Street Journal* began pointing out that the President had a management problem.

On December 13 Joseph Kraft reported in the *Washington Post* on how the President's men were "ganging up on the President" to bring him out of his "dream world." And on December 14 Evans and Novak reported that the President "has to fight better than two-

10. See Evans and Novak, *Washington Post*, February 5, 1982.

thirds of his economic team to save his program." Soon Ronald Reagan would be complaining about it himself.

At a nationally televised press conference on December 17 the President of the United States declared: "I have no plans for increasing taxes in any way"—certainly an unequivocal policy statement. "You can balance the budget by robbing the people, by imposing a punitive tax system on the people," Reagan said, but "you will find you've torpedoed the economy." To underline his message to his staff he said: "The only proper way to balance the budget is through control of government spending and increasing prosperity and productivity for all. That's what our program is aimed to do, and I have every confidence it is going to do it."

Yet again the President's aides did not hear him. Within minutes of the President's words Jim Baker sent Larry Speakes out to take them back, prompting the *Wall Street Journal* in a lead editorial to ask "Who's in Charge Here?" Clearly not the President, the *Journal* observed.

At his press conference, you may recall, Mr. Reagan was quite categorical about tax policy—"I have no plans for increasing taxes in any way." A few minutes later he was overruled by Press Spokesman Speakes . . . The tempo is speeding up . . . It used to take about a week between the President's squashing the tax-boost movement and one of his aides proposing it all over again. Now it seems to be down to about 15 minutes.

Evans and Novak wrote that they now understand why President Reagan had only been allowed to hold six press conferences in his first year of office. A press conference let "the prisoner of Pennsylvania Avenue" briefly escape from "his cage." This last time out "the President had shattered the illusion nurtured by senior aides that he was moving irrevocably toward approval of higher taxes to balance the budget." The President's prison, the columnist wrote, "is partly self-made." In Washington, as when he was governor of California, he relies heavily on aides and allows them to exercise "so much control that his aides seem to forget who is President." The President's aides, the columnists reported, are "pragmatic staffers who would have been at home in the last three unimaginative Republican administrations." In contrast, Reagan is a president with convictions who wants change but who "has only a tiny window to receive and transmit information beyond the confines of his elite staff." The columnists went on to report that there were two economic policy teams, the President's small team and the team of the shoguns who surrounded him. Quoting "a senior White House staffer," the columnists said that Jim Baker was complaining to Secretary Regan "that anti-tax talk coming out of the Treasury hurt the administration. Indeed, officials fighting tax hikes as contrary to Reaganomics were told they were not 'team players.' " The President, the columnists reported, disagreed with the use of "revenue enhancement measures" as a euphemism for tax increases, but could not even stop that.

Surveying the situation for the *New York Times* on December 21, White House correspondent Howell Raines reported:

Privately, the President complained, according to aides, that his staff was not resisting the effort of the budget director, David A. Stockman, to maneuver him into calling for higher taxes. Publicly, he contradicted the senior advisors who back Mr. Stockman by saying on Friday that he was against "increasing taxes in any way." This led to an extraordinary spectacle. Minutes after Mr. Reagan's news conference, James A. Baker 3d, the chief of staff, dispatched the White House spokesmen, David R. Gergen and Larry Speakes, to tell reporters that the President had not really meant what he had said.

In case readers did not get the picture, Raines elevated the clarity:

Mr. Reagan has fought, sometimes with almost no support on his senior staff, against such efforts to dent his supply-side faith, and that has spurred the tax raisers to new maneuverings. For example, when Mr. Reagan did not respond to the Stockman deficit figures first presented to him on December 4, they were leaked to the press on the following weekend. Public and Congressional alarm over these figures was supposed to make Mr. Reagan see the inevitability of more taxes.

Instead, in a follow-up meeting on December 8, Mr. Reagan said he still believed, with Mr. Regan, that tax cuts, not increases, were the way to generate the long-range prosperity that would control the deficit.

It was after this meeting, which was dominated by Mr. Stockman and his talk for new taxes, that Mr. Reagan suggested that his other advisers were not standing up to the budget director.

On Christmas day Evans and Novak asked, "Is the Chief of Staff Out of Step?" The answer was yes. Not only were "Reaganites on

the White House staff" beginning "to finger Baker and his two lieu-
tenants, Richard Darman and David Gergen, as uncommitted to the
Reagan Administration," but there was an unbridgeable cultural
difference between the President, with his "small-town working-
class roots," and his chief of staff, "an Ivy League lawyer of inherited wealth." The former was committed to change, the latter to
the status quo. The case against the tax increase, the columnists
pointed out, was political as well as economic. The President could
not propose a tax increase without Democrats seizing it "as a con-
fession of failure for Reaganomics." Nevertheless, the President was
losing:

The culmination came Christmas week with front page stories on successive days in the *New York Times* and the *Washington Post* claiming
that all presidential aides had bought the Stockman-Baker tax increase.
The inescapable implication was that only the poor old president, bogged
down in ideology, opposed such a reasonable course.

It ruined my Christmas. Treasury was fighting a heavy battle, and
the White House staff was trying to demoralize us by planting story
after story that Regan was joining their camp. For example, Howell
Raines, reporting on the President's lonely battle (*New York Times*,
December 21), said that "the President may feel even lonelier by
midweek." An administration official had told Raines that "Mr.
Regan will join Mr. Baker, Mr. Stockman and White House economists in endorsing" tax increases. The Treasury subcabinet knew
that Secretary Regan was being worked over hard. When he would
not desert the President, Stockman and Baker began working on his
ego by leaving him out of policy meetings.

While Treasury was being lambasted in the press for supporting
the President, puff pieces were appearing on Jim Baker, who held
weekly meetings with the national news magazines—*Time, Newsweek,* and *Business Week*. On December 7 he was described in
Business Week as "Reagan's ace lobbyist" who was "filling a policy void" left by Stockman's public doubts about Reaganomics,
Regan's "lack of knowledge of federal programs and political fi-
nesse," and Martin Anderson's failure "to assert himself as a major
player in the economic policy hierarchy." The story had many
strange aspects. First, to speak of a policy void was to imply that the
President himself was not a major player in the economic hierarchy.

Despite the fact that Reagan had unequivocally stated the policy of
his administration time after time, *Business Week* was reporting that
it would be up to Baker to try to fill a policy void. Second, Baker
had no special knowledge of federal programs. Third, Anderson, a
long-time Reagan aide who was supporting the President's policy,
was described as having little influence—which could only mean
that the President had little influence. The picture was being drawn
of a conventional president with no mind of his own and whose policies would be set by whichever aides got his ear, the usual "palace
politics" maneuvering. It was a convenient image for the manipulators, since a president with no policies of his own cannot have them
sabotaged by policy players. Fourth, at a time when Reagan was
growing increasingly angry over being contradicted and pressured
into tax increases, Baker did not mind showing in a national magazine that he favored tax increases.

During the first days of December the President's men, tired of
the obstinate holdout against their policy, decided to strike. Stockman was trying to issue an official administration forecast that
would show large budget deficits—his main weapon in his fight to
change the economic policy of the Reagan Administration. He was
not trying to issue a forecast of a recession because that would make
it clear to all that the deficits were due to falling income and would
strengthen the case for tax cuts. The deficits were supposed to be the
result of too much tax cutting, and Stockman wanted to forecast deficits in advance of a recession. His argument was: deficits cause inflation and high interest rates; high interest rates cause recession; to
avoid recession we must raise taxes to lower the deficit. The question
he faced was how to forecast the deficits. Here Stockman put back
on the monetarist cap, which explains inflation rates in terms of the
growth of the money supply, and became a firm supporter of
Volcker's tight money. On the basis of monetarist reasoning about
tight money, he drastically lowered the inflation projections. The
lower inflation brought down the nominal GNP projections or tax
base, and large deficits appeared.[11]

11. According to a Congressional Budget Office estimate at the time, a one-per-
centage-point change in the annual rate of real economic growth can widen (or narrow) the deficit $66 billion by 1986. An equivalent change in the inflation estimate
would widen (or narrow) the 1986 deficit projection by $49 billion. Together, a one-
percentage-point change causes a $115 billion swing in the deficit projection.

Stockman now had his deficits, but he had obtained them in a way that was inconsistent with his argument. His forecast showed low and falling inflation and high and rising deficits (see Table 8). Obviously, OMB's argument that deficits cause inflation and high interest rates did not apply to OMB's forecast. OMB was having its cake and eating it too, since the whole forecast was designed with the predetermined view of producing large budget deficits.

The next step was to get the President to accept the forecast. Stockman came up with a scheme. The President would be shown the new forecast in comparison with the "Blue Chip" forecast (an average of 42 private forecasts). The administration's forecast would show higher real economic growth and far lower inflation than the Blue Chip forecast (see Table 9). The "rosy" administration forecast, the President would be told, put an optimistic light on the economy and was evidence that the administration believed in its program.

The plan was to get the President to accept the rosy projections *without telling him the deficit implications.* Then the following week the President would be presented with the deficit implications of the agreed-upon forecast. He would be in the bag. Even his rosy projections would result in large budget deficits unless taxes were raised.

Stockman sold the plan with the argument that the economic pro-

Table 8. OMB Projections, December 1981

	1982	1983	1984	1985	1986
Inflation rate	7.7%	5.5%	4.4%	3.7%	3.5%
Budget deficit (billions)	$109	$152	$162	$165	$182

Table 9. Administration and Blue Chip Forecasts

	1982	1983	1984	1985	1986
Real economic growth					
Administration	0.2	5.4	5.2	4.7	4.2
Blue Chip	1.2	3.7	3.9	2.9	2.8
Inflation					
Administration	7.7	5.5	4.4	3.7	3.5
Blue Chip	7.8	7.7	7.5	7.8	8.1

jections should be separated from the budget implications so as not
to confuse the President. Regan was uneasy about such blatant manipulation of the President, and in a quiet casual way on December
3 he tested out the plan on the Treasury subcabinet. He was advised
against showing the President economic projections without telling
him their deficit implications. Most of us felt sympathy for the situation Regan was in. He was loyal to the President, but the President's
failure to bring Stockman and Baker in line with his policies allowed them to force Regan into the role of the dissenter who was not
a team player. Coming from the business world where he was
trained to seek consensus and to avoid confrontation, it was a pain-
ful situation for Regan. It was hard to see where the rewards were
for being on the President's side.

The President was being told incessantly that the outlook for his
program was too optimistic. Somehow this was supposed to be all
the fault of the Treasury. But the Treasury had been opposed to
forecasting a balanced budget in the beginning and had lost the
fight to prevent Stockman from being "pragmatic" and using the
core-inflation argument to hide the deficit. In a sense we had lost the
war then because, by projecting a balanced budget, Stockman made
it an issue. In Treasury's view, the important consideration was not
the size of the deficit, but whether it was declining as a percentage of
GNP and private saving. Having failed to prevent Stockman from
forecasting deficits that were too small, we found ourselves trying to
prevent him from forecasting deficits that were too large.

Treasury prepared for the White House a comparison of the forecasts for the last eight years. Reagan's ranked seventh in terms of
optimism. Treasury then compared the projected Reagan recovery
with the other post war recoveries. It was by far the weakest,
projecting real growth rates substantially below the average for
postwar recoveries, despite the fact that the Reagan recovery was
adding the secular kick of the tax cut to the normal cyclical upturn
of the economy. Of course, none of these arguments made much
sense in the face of a recessionary monetary policy, but (strangely
enough) the battle was not being fought over monetary policy. The
tax cuts were at issue and nothing else.

In the attempt to exclude Treasury from policy influence, supply-
siders were pictured as biased in their advice because of their pro-

clivity to cut taxes. Yet supply-siders had made it clear that not just any tax cut was a supply-side tax cut. The important incentive effects come from reducing the rate of tax on additional earnings. It is the marginal and not the average tax rate that supply-side economics stresses. It is possible to lower marginal rates and to take offsetting actions to prevent revenue loss without canceling the incentive effects.

Supply-siders objected to tax increases for two reasons, one economic and one political. Raising taxes conflicted with the budget goal, which was to reduce government spending as a percentage of GNP. Treasury felt that proposing higher taxes would invite Congress to drag its feet on budget cutting. The administration, which had panicked the public, the financial markets, and itself with deficit fears, would then be forced to respond to the deficit by further raising taxes. Treasury warned that it was very easy to crowd out the private sector by raising taxes to balance the budget.

Politically, Treasury was concerned that a tax increase would look like a policy reversal and be interpreted as a major political defeat for the President. It would be taken as an admission that the President had gone too far or that Reaganomics was a failure. The Democrats were making it clear enough that this was how they were going to explain any tax increase. For example, Reagan had given a written pledge to Representative Glenn English, a Democrat from Oklahoma, that he would not impose a windfall profits tax on natural gas. In December there was talk about getting English to release Reagan from his pledge. On December 19 Howell Raines reported in the *New York Times* that English "said that if the Administration wanted new taxes, it must be prepared to say that supply-side economics had failed." Watching Stockman push so hard for tax increases in the face of such statements created the impression that Stockman wanted supply-side economics to be perceived as having failed.

Finally, there was the question of whether the administration was creating its own deficit problem by basing its forecast on unrealistic assumptions about a progressively tightening monetary policy for the next five years. The Federal Reserve had already overdone it the first year and thrown the economy into recession. The response was likely to be too much money, not further tightening.

On December 11 a story appeared in the *New York Times* reporting the previous day's confidential meeting between the President and his panel of economic advisers.[12] According to the reporter, Howell Raines, the meeting "was described by a White House official as 'contentious' and unproductive because of the dispute that broke out between the supply-side advocates and the traditional conservatives who serve on the 12-member board." The White House officials, "who spoke on the condition that they not be identified by name," told Raines that only Kemp and Laffer had urged the President to stick to his program. "On the other hand, the more traditional economists at the 40-minute meeting urged Mr. Reagan to adopt a 'more flexible' approach that could include" higher taxes. Someone high up in the White House had planted the story that none of the President's advisers supported sticking to the program except the supply-side extremists. Since Baker, Darman, and Gergen were the only senior White House officials present, it seemed obvious that the story came from Jim Baker's operation. Furthermore, the story was untrue. Several people present, disturbed by the story in the *Times,* gave an entirely different account: the majority advised the President to stick to his policy. The battle no longer depended on facts and analysis, if it ever did. The President was being maneuvered by his senior staff into the position of an isolated extremist. On December 14, the *Wall Street Journal*'s lead editorial, "Forces of Reaction," said: "What the President needs now is steadfastness. And much depends on his personal qualities, since his staff has become a means of the Washington establishment pressuring him rather than a means of his pressuring Washington to implement the policies for which he campaigned."

On December 15, while Jack Kemp was shepherding the President's foreign aid bill through Congress, Stockman met with the other members of the House Republican leadership and used the deficit forecasts that the President had rejected to terrify them about the budget. He was assaulting the President's program in its strongest stronghold. Four weeks later Stockman would have the House

12. The Economic Policy Advisory Board consisted of William Simon, Walter Wriston, George Shultz, Milton Friedman, Arthur Burns, Charls Walker, Alan Greenspan, Herbert Stein, Arthur Laffer, Peter Flanigan, James Lynn, and Paul McCracken.

Republican leaders pleading with the President to raise taxes. The *Wall Street Journal* called it "Voodoo Politics."

On December 17 the Treasury was gathered at a Christmas party in Undersecretary Ture's office when the President announced at his press conference that he had no plans to postpone or cancel any of the tax cuts or to increase taxes of any kind. When the reports were brought into the room, the assistant secretary for tax policy and his deputy lost their Christmas cheer and left the room with long disgusted faces. The Treasury was being chipped away. On December 23 Rich Jaroslovsky reported in the *Wall Street Journal* on the "persistent efforts" by Reagan's aides "to coax him to propose raising taxes." The President replied, in a "Dear Fellow Americans" letter published in the January issue of *Washingtonian* magazine, by promising to oppose tax increases in 1982. Noting that Americans were already "shouldering the highest tax burden in our history," Reagan said that "if the deficit continues to grow it will not be because your tax cut was too big, but because spending cuts were too small." The President's aides apparently had not told him that the deficit was growing because the Federal Reserve had thrown the economy into recession.

On December 21 Raines reported in the *New York Times* that a new economic forecast would be presented to the President by midweek. Treasury knew nothing about the forecast. On December 23 Secretary Regan announced that the President had firmly decided against any tax increase in 1982. He was willing to live with the deficit. Later when Treasury was shown the forecast underlying the President's January budget message, the staff found that OMB had taken every opportunity to exaggerate the size of the deficit. For example, the GNP deflator, one measure of inflation, was marked down from the mid-session review. This lowered revenues. However, the consumer price index, another measure of inflation, was marked up, and this boosted payments under entitlement programs. The result of marking down one measure of inflation (the deflator) while marking up another (the CPI) was simultaneously to lower revenue projections while raising outlay projections of inflation-adjusted spending programs— a double whammy for the deficit. In addition, Treasury found that Stockman's "unidentified spending cuts" in his original budget together with the botched social security reforms accounted for two-thirds of the $90 billion increase in the 1984 deficit projection. The budget was still out of control on the spending side, which is what the liberals wanted and why they all got on Stockman's bandwagon for a tax increase. It was just as the *Wall Street Journal* said: Washington was heading "happily back to business as usual."

Baker and Stockman were too far out in front of the President on the issue. If they lost they would end up with egg on their faces. In the middle of December Secretary Regan told me that the Office of Economic Policy had fought the issue hard and made itself a target. Despite this warning I was not prepared for how nasty things were going to get before the year was out. At a New Year's Eve party White House officials cracked jokes about whether I had Jim Baker's permission to come out and how the President, since he was out of step with Baker too, had been upbraided and sent home to California. The jokes puzzled me until it was explained that a long front-page story had appeared in the *Philadelphia Inquirer* about bitter rivalries that were developing between Jim Baker and Ed Meese. The Meese people were getting tired of all the stories that were being planted in the press to their disadvantage. A deputy to Meese was quoted as asking angrily, "Why do people talk about our side of the White House? We don't talk about their operations or their business." At the end of the story the reporter, Saul Friedman, reported that Paul Craig Roberts had been "upbraided and sent on vacation" for being out of step with Jim Baker. The story was untrue, but it had come from so high up in the White House staff that the reporter did not bother to check it with me or the Treasury. Things had gotten so bad that reporters could not even write stories about press plants without being used to plant more. On January 4 I complained to Secretary Regan about the planted story in the *Philadelphia Inquirer*. "I have suffered a number of personal attacks in the press without saying anything. Maybe that was a mistake, because it is getting out of hand." My note came back, and across the bottom Regan had written: "I won't let it get out of hand. If we have any more of this I'll personally go to bat for you. You have my word." I wondered what the secretary could do, when the President could not even get his staff to follow his lead.

The State of the Union

On January 6 the secretary gave up. On TV's Today Show he said, "I think there will be some new tax increases in '83 and '84." The next day Helen Thomas (UPI) reported that "there were indications Reagan was not pleased with daily leaks of tentative budget decisions and the public statements by Regan and others that tax increases might be needed, despite the President's stated determination to avoid them." I told Regan that he had made a mistake. He said no, that it had been explained to him that the President had seen the necessity for tax increases and was just putting on an act, holding out for maximum leverage on spending cuts. No doubt the White House staff insisted to Regan that they did not want him left out on a limb, but I did not think the President would want the image of intransigence unless he was serious. Besides, I also knew that I had been dodging real bullets: if the President were only acting, the power jockeys would have held their fire, content to have me out on the limb.

Continually rebuffed by the President, Stockman and Baker mounted a new stratagem. They seized on the President's "new federalism" program, still in its pilot stage, to turn federal programs over to the states along with revenues to pay for them. The President's men explained to him how his long-sought federalism program could more easily become a reality if it were financed by raising federal excise taxes. That, of course, would leave the federal budget with fewer expenditures and the same amount of revenues. Thinking they had him hooked, they spread the word that the President was going to raise excise taxes. It was not the worst idea that the tax-increase advocates had come up with, but it still ran the risk that once a tax-increase bill was introduced, the White House would have a hard time controlling it. Ways and Means Committee Chairman Rostenkowski declared that the "simplest avenue of approach" was to delay the third-year tax cut.

On January 21 the lead story in the *New York Times* declared that the President had decided to ask Congress for increases in federal excise taxes. The story stressed that the President's decision "was a rebuff for supply-side economists at the Treasury." Treasury came to the conclusion that, however sincerely Stockman and Baker believed in the tax increase, they now saw the issue primarily as a power struggle with Treasury. Treasury did not see it that way at all. We did not care who had the power as long as the President had his program. Treasury began to joke that we could have forestalled Stockman and Baker by having come out first for tax increases.

If someone thirsting for Treasury's blood had not been so anxious to have the *Times* declare that the Treasury had been rebuffed, the President might have accepted the excise tax increase. But he was tired of reading about closed-door discussions of his policy options in the next morning's newspaper. And he was angry over his aides' attempts to box him in and foreclose his options before he made his decisions. On the day the *Times* announced that Reagan was going to raise excise taxes, he met with the U.S. Chamber of Commerce and found out that he was not as lonely as his aides had led him to believe.[13]

That clinched it, and on January 26, 1982, in his nationally televised State of the Union Message before a joint session of Congress, the President delivered a stinging rebuff to David Stockman and James Baker. Strongly reaffirming his commitment to his economic program, the President declared:

The doubters would have us turn back the clock with tax increases that would offset the personal tax-rate reductions already passed by this Congress.

Raise present taxes to cut future deficits, they tell us. Well, I don't believe we should buy their argument . . .

Higher taxes would not mean lower deficits. If they did, how would we explain that tax revenues more than doubled just since 1976, yet in the same 6-year period we ran the largest series of deficits in our history. In 1980 tax revenues increased by $54 billion—and in 1980 we had one of our all-time biggest deficits.

Raising taxes won't balance the budget. It will encourage more government spending and less private investment. Raising taxes will slow economic growth, reduce production and destroy future jobs, making it more difficult for those without jobs to find them and more likely that those who now have jobs could lose them.

13. After the meeting Richard Rahn, the Chamber's vice-president and chief economist, received a telephone call from an OMB official who was furious that the Chamber had urged the President not to raise taxes. The official told Rahn: "We are going to get you; we are going to get the Chamber; and we are going to get your friends at the Treasury."

So I will not ask you to try to balance the budget on the backs of the American taxpayers. I will seek no tax increases this year and I have no intention of retreating from our basic program of tax relief. I promised the American people to bring their tax rates down and keep them down—to provide them incentives to rebuild our economy, to save, to invest in America's future. I will stand by my word.

Ronald Reagan had survived his first year in office as a leader dedicated to fundamental change. He had had to fight hard, but he had succeeded in preventing Stockman and Baker from shepherding him into the establishment's fold.

In his speech the President totally rejected Stockman's economic views. He acknowledged that "the budget deficit this year will exceed our earlier expectations," but "the recession did that"—not the tax cuts. The President spelled out "the three keys to reducing deficits: economic growth, lower interest rates, and spending control." He pointedly did not mention higher taxes. The President also rejected Stockman's explanation of interest rates and gave Treasury's instead:

In the last six months of 1980, as an example, the money supply increased at the fastest rate in postwar history—13 percent. Inflation remained in double digits and Government spending increased at a rate of 17 percent.

Despite all the money, "interest rates reached a staggering 21.5 percent." Despite all the inflation, "there were 8 million people unemployed." OMB and CEA had been circulating for months reports claiming that the President's program would not increase private saving. It was all part of their effort to dramatize the deficit, and the situation was worse the fewer the private savings with which to finance the deficit. The President answered this part of the campaign against his program as well. "I am confident the economic program we have put into operation will . . . result in increased savings."

The President also used the occasion to show that the state department's permanent government and his own vacillating policy officials had not escaped his eye. "At Ottawa and Cancun," he said, "some of those I met with were a little surprised that I didn't apologize for America's wealth. Instead I spoke of the strength of the free marketplace system and how it could help them realize their aspirations for economic development and political freedom."

Normally, people whose views and policies are so fully rejected after a bitter struggle with their boss have the dignity to resign. The White House press corps, which had been used and manipulated throughout the year and now knew how badly, was expecting high-level resignations. It was clear to the press that the President and his senior aides had little confidence in one another. The morning after the State of the Union address, deputy press secretary Larry Speakes met with the White House correspondents. The first question on the tax program was:

Q: Is Jim Baker still employed today?

Speakes: Yes.

Q: Well, I would think that he's in bad trouble, wouldn't you?

Speakes: I don't know, I haven't heard . . .

Q: He led the losing fight, and the general who gets beaten usually gets thrown out . . .

Q: . . . in his speech he [the President] rather chastised those doubters who would go back and who told him that raising taxes reduces deficits, raising taxes helps balance the budget. It seems, as I well recall, there were no Democrats asking him to do this. As a matter of fact, they [the advisers] were differing from him rather fundamentally on economic policy. Is that not correct?

Speakes: I wouldn't put it in those stark terms [laughter] . . .

Q: The President has said—he talked about doubters. Can you tell me who those doubters were? Whether they were people in the White House and the Administration as well as . . .

Speakes: Well, it's no secret that there was a fairly good agreement among key advisors that they would like to see some excise taxes imposed. And they went at the President over a matter of a couple of weeks, and the President made a decision on that.

Q: Do you know any senior advisor who did not recommend it?

Speakes: Jack Kemp.

Q: Are you saying, are you agreeing now, that he was chastising his own people? . . .

Speakes: He was chastising those doubters, whoever they are.

Q: Well, they're in the White House. Stockman? Baker? . . .

Speakes: I don't make a secret about them, but I just don't want to get drawn into making a . . .

Q: Yes, but when your advice isn't taken, you lose power. You understand that. You've been in Washington a long time. I would think this morning that the people who really pushed this on him . . . are now in the doghouse. It's not the woodshed.

For the proud power jockies who imagine themselves running the world by manipulating issues, personalities, and access to the White House, and by planting misinformation on reporters who sell their souls for stories, this public disavowal at the hands of the President was traumatic. On January 27 Evans and Novak wrote of "the shock wave that rolled over the White House." Had Regan not succumbed at the last minute to "water torture at the hands of the White House staff," he would "now be king of the mountain."

Reporters and columnists began telling the story of how senior aides had worked to undermine congressional and business support for the President's program. In a front-page story in the *Wall Street Journal* on February 2, 1982, reporters Rich Jaroslovsky, Ken Bacon, and Robert Merry told how Baker and Stockman operated against the President by building "momentum with leaks and pressure." Describing the "concerted campaign to get the President to change his known position," the reporters said: "Both the campaigners themselves and the supply-siders who fought them use the same word to describe it: 'orchestrated.' " On February 1 Evans and Novak told how, after being defeated internally, White House aides went "afield for allies in their campaign to break down the boss's resistance" and how "senior aides led by chief of staff James Baker III leaked premature 'decisions' that turned out to be inaccurate." A *Wall Street Journal* editorial examining "The State of the Presidency" (January 28, 1982) spoke of the "unholy coalition of putative friends and avowed enemies" that had tried to defeat the President's policy. How long, the *Journal* wondered, before the President's aides "once again joined forces with Congress to conduct some new assault on the President?" The *Journal* made it clear that the President did not have enough help and hoped that he could "find the managerial skills to patch up the weak spots in his line."

On February 1 at a meeting in the Blue Room of the White House, journalist John Lofton told the triumvirate of Baker, Meese, and Deaver that "if loyalty to the President was the test of your jobs, none of you would be here."[14] The *New York Post*'s editorials were dagger sharp, proclaiming "political treachery in the White House" and exposing "managed leaks," "figure fiddling," and "outright lies."

Some of the President's disloyal aides were penitent. For example, Michael K. Deaver confided in Lou Cannon who reported in the *Washington Post* on February 1, 1982:

"I learned something from the process," said longtime Reagan aide Michael K. Deaver, one of the many White House advocates of tax increases. "Never try to talk any man who holds deep convictions out of them for reasons of political expediency because it would destroy him. We almost destroyed Ronald Reagan, and I was one of the people arguing for this."[15]

Cannon said that the President's men had him "on the verge of coming out against his convictions" and that the episode "left even some of his advisors wondering why they had spent so much time on a proposal that Reagan did not want in the first place."

On January 27, the day after the President's State of the Union message, Regan was back on the President's team, regretful that he had believed the misinformation that had caused him to desert the President. At his testimony that day before the Joint Economic Committee, the secretary began the arduous task of clearing out the jumble of misconceptions that OMB had spread around Congress over the past five months. Stockman had created the impression of huge tax cuts that allegedly had set the deficit on a course to the moon, but Regan stated the facts: "We have prevented major tax increases. We have not had major tax cuts." Regan testified that "bracket creep and social security tax increases produced roughly a $15 billion tax increase for 1981 in spite of the 5 percent cut." The 10 percent tax cut in 1982 "will be roughly offset in dollar terms" by the same factors. Only in 1983 and 1984 would there be a real tax cut. The tax cut had been delayed, against supply-side warnings, to the second half of the President's term. Yet the nonexistent tax cut had been declared a failure by Stockman and the *Washington Post* only

14. Howell Raines, *New York Times,* February 3, 1982.
15. Deaver's remorse did not last very long. Soon he was back in the fray again pushing for tax increases.

seven months into the first half of the term. Regan reaffirmed the supply-side view that "economic growth is the single best means of narrowing deficits," and "without spending restraint and faster real economic growth, it is doubtful that we will ever see a balanced budget." The secretary also set the record straight on monetary policy. The administration, he said, had expected the Federal Reserve to gradually cut in half the rate of growth in money over a four- to six-year period, which was "the assumption that we built into our economic projections." However, the reduction that actually occurred was much more rapid with three-fourths of the planned reduction occurring in the first year. In addition, the money supply was far too volatile and erratic with the Federal Reserve either above or below its target range. The erratic monetary policy harmed the economy by keeping interest rates high, and together with the rapid deceleration in money supply produced a recession and higher budget deficits.

Regan answered the complaints that he had vacillated between calling for tight money and loose money:

At various times during the year, we at Treasury have hinted, sometimes in private, sometimes in public, that we would like either faster or slower money growth. Some have accused us of being unable to make up our minds.

Nothing could be further from the truth. We have consistently urged faster money growth when the money supply was flat or declining, and slower money growth when the money supply was rising at double digit rates. We supported the Federal Reserve's targets, and consistently urged them to keep money growth even and steady within the target range.

It was a complete rejection of Stockmanomics. Treasury was now speaking out again. During part of Stockman's autumn and winter offensive against the President's program, Treasury had been throttled. Stockman had stopped testimony both by Secretary Regan and Undersecretary Ture, and the White House had prevented Treasury from reviewing the President's televised speech on September 24, the first White House effort to show the President backing away from his program.

The behavior of the financial markets also refuted Stockmanomics. Stockman had been lecturing the administration, the Congress, and the markets themselves for six months about the

catastrophic effect of large deficits on bond and stock prices. Without tax increases that would let the administration show a balanced
budget, Wall Street would go into a tailspin, he claimed. Yet, on
January 28 with headlines proclaiming no tax increase, years of
large budget deficits, and record Treasury quarterly borrowings, interest rates on Treasury bills declined, long-term bond prices rose,
the Dow Jones Industrial Index jumped 22 points, and the volume
was the highest in ten months with advances leading declines by five
to one. After watching Reagan resist such enormous pressure, the
markets thought they had a President who would provide some policy stability.

The Counterrevolution Continues

Just after Reagan's State of the Union address, the *Wall Street
Journal* wondered how long it would be before his aides conducted
"some new assault on the President." Not long, as it turned out. The
President's men did not hear his State of the Union message either.
The campaign against the President did not have to resume because
it never stopped.

   During the January battles the President's aides were worried that
Reagan would not have an opportunity for a graceful retreat when
they finally prevailed over him. They set about constructing an escape hatch for him by playing the theme of Reagan as a man of
principle who held out longest against tax increases. On January 10
the theme appeared in the *New York Times:*

The cries of dismay about leaks seemed also accompanied by some croco-
dile tears. After all, what better way to portray a President than as a man
of principle battling hard against raising taxes? If Reagan accepts some
increases, he will at least be able to say that he did so after thinking long
and hard about it.

After the State of the Union address, the theme of "Reagan as a
man of principle" was no longer useful. The President had proved
too principled. The new theme became "Reagan as obstinate nut."
Hobart Rowen played it in the *Washington Post* on January 31:

One has to ask, in the end, how Reagan could toss out the advice of virtually all his economic and political advisors, risking a national calamity.

The answer, among those who know him best, like *Washington Post* reporter Lou Cannon, is that his close brush with death at the hands of an assassin last year convinced him to follow his own deeply-held beliefs and instincts, even when others suggest a more practical course. If Ronald Reagan won't cut government down to size, he is said to ask himself, who will? When a President has such a deep sense of mission, neither his advisors nor logic count for much. One can only cross fingers and hope for the best.

Lou Cannon, for his part, revealed that Reagan had not been alone in the White House in his fight against tax increases. Martin Anderson, director of policy development, had stood with the President. This was a strange turn of events from the stories planted in the press early in 1981 depicting Anderson as a man out to frustrate the supply-siders. Anderson was now in a dangerous position. He was the only senior official who remained loyal to the President. When the power jockeys perceived this, they did not see Anderson as a second obstinate nut; they saw a threat and decided to try to destroy his reputation. Instantly stories began appearing in the press citing "administration sources" who were running down Anderson's performance on the job. He was "ineffective" and a "disappointment." Since Anderson had not spent all year leaking stories to the press, he could not fight back.

People who fight for power have nothing when they lose, which explains their fury when they are defeated. Following the President's State of the Union address, I appeared on national television with Roger Mudd and agreed with him that the President's advisers had egg on their faces. I hoped they would wipe it off, I said, and rejoin the President's team. Within seconds my wife received a threatening telephone call. In the incoherent words choked with rage, she recognized the voice of a government official.

In trying to force a change of policy upon the President, his aides had overstepped the boundaries of appointed officials. The President had reaffirmed his commitment to his economic program, but he would still have to choose between his policies and his advisers. A President with subordinates who have a different agenda than his own has a management problem that an assistant secretary of the Treasury cannot fix.

*   *   *

As hard as we tried, in the autumn of 1981 Treasury was not able to shift the administration's attention from fighting deficits to fighting the on-rushing recession. On September 3, I alerted Secretary Regan to the fact that H. C. Wainwright, a firm identified with supply-side economics, was about to release a forecast of a 1982 recession. Neither the permanent staff of the Treasury nor the appointed policy officials were comfortable about going into a recession slashing away at the budget and raising taxes, but that was the course Stockman had set us on.

In retrospect it is possible that some policymakers wanted a recession in order to break the back of inflation. In spite of the mounting evidence to the contrary, OMB continued to pretend that the real problem was the inflationary impact of the deficits. Regan's warning in the first week of August that the Federal Reserve was leading the economy into a recession had no effect. By October the situation was desperate. Regan again called for loosening the tight monetary reins and for the Federal Reserve to honor its own targets. *Time* (October 19) quickly described the Treasury secretary as a "wanderer from the true faith" and gleefully told how Weidenbaum called Regan and asked him, "What's going on here? We've got to be talking with one voice." What was going on was that the economy was sinking into the black hole of recession and the "one voice" was pretending that the problem was inflationary deficits caused by the tax cuts. Weidenbaum, the magazine reported, "was opposed to the Fed pumping more money into the economy now"—a strange point of view considering that the Fed had been pumping money out of the economy for the past six months and was far below its target (see Chart 10). Stockman, *Time* reported, rushed off to a breakfast meeting with reporters the next day where he "contradicted Regan by arguing that the Fed should keep the brakes on the money supply."

By October Wall Street realized that OMB's talk about inflationary deficits was bunkum. Albert Wojnilower, chief economist and managing director of First Boston Corporation and an influential Wall Street economist, warned that the Federal Reserve was hurtling the economy into a severe recession. In an interview with the *Los Angeles Times* (October 16, 1981), he questioned whether the White House would allow a relaxation in Federal Reserve policy.

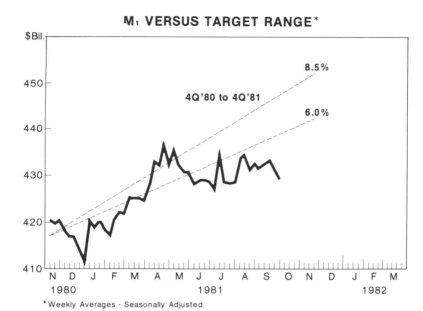

Chart 10

He said that key economic advisers close to President Reagan believe that "if we have to go through a depression to get inflation down, then so be it." As for Wall Street's alleged fears of deficits, he advised the Reagan Administration to abandon its efforts to balance the budget or even to reduce the 1982 deficit: "They should just leave the budget alone." The real problem, he said, was the prospect of a deep economic slump marked by widespread unemployment and "enormous threats of bankruptcies in industry and in state and local governments." OMB, which had struck the pose of being very concerned about Wall Street, did not hear a word of Wojnilower's warning. On December 4, in the middle of a deep recession, David Stockman gave the President an approving report on the Federal Reserve's monetary policy—a policy that threw the nation into a recession and crucified the President's economic program.

It is possible that CEA and OMB were incompetent and could not see that the Federal Reserve had the money supply far below its targets. On the other hand, the administration was influenced by the traditional belief that the economy had to be closed down in order to defeat inflation, and Stockman still wanted big deficits in order to justify a change of policy. The Federal Reserve was obliging by collapsing the economy. Not only was Regan branded an inflationist for warning about the collapsing money supply, but Volcker was absolved from any responsibility for the recession that ensued by blaming it on "high interest rates" caused by Ronald Reagan's budget deficits.

On Valentine's Day 1982 the President met with Volcker in a widely publicized "lovefest," and at a presidential press conference a few days later Reagan endorsed the board's policies. Evans and Novak wrote that "Ronald Reagan's embrace of Paul Volcker could have been a fateful decision with profound implications for this nation's political and economic future" (February 22, 1982). Indeed it was. Soon Reagan was offering Tip O'Neill $122 billion in new taxes. The Treasury could see all this coming in August 1981, which is why we fought tooth and nail against OMB's September offensive. The deficit was a stalking-horse for an offensive against the President's program.

Recalling the deletion of key supply-side explanations from important administration documents, recession may have been in the cards from the beginning. To delve deeper into the misselling of Reaganomics is to discover some fundamental inconsistencies in administration messages. For example, although White House officials were supposedly predicting noninflationary growth, their hollow-sounding words echoed doubt and their grave expressions indicated instead a classic Republican recession to squeeze inflation out of the economy. If the President's men believed that supply-side economics did what it claimed—bring about sustained growth with low inflation—why were they predicting rain? As early as May 8, 1981, little more than three months into the new administration, Ed Cowan had written in the *New York Times* that an administration that "deliberately talks down the economy must have a problem." Thinking back on my experiences in the administration, I cannot dismiss the possibility that a high-level decision was made without the President's knowledge to engineer a recession in order to reduce inflation. That would explain the intense pressure from within the administration to delay the personal income tax-rate reductions. With the economy in recession, the tax cuts would not have the proper environment in which to succeed and would simply expand the large budget deficits that accompany recession. It would also explain the otherwise inexplicable blindness of OMB, CEA, and the White House to the Federal Reserve's contractionary monetary policy from April to November of 1981 and the White House staff's extraordinary protectiveness of Volcker even to the detriment of the President's economic program. It is beside the point to suggest any conspiracy. The Republican establishment, which believes in fighting inflation with unemployment, was constrained by the powerful public case that Jack Kemp had made against such a policy. Therefore in principle the administration was supply-side, but in practice its faith still rested in the traditional pain-and-suffering approach to the economy.

As supply-siders left the Reagan Administration and as White House officials and the media created the impression that Reaganomics had failed, the constraint that Kemp had placed on the pain-and-suffering school faded, and they became bold and forthright. On March 4, 1982, David Stockman stood up in front of a Chamber of Commerce breakfast group and observed cooly that unemployment is "part of the cure, not the problem."

7

The Unraveling of Reaganomics

THE STATE OF THE UNION ADDRESS ON JANUARY 26, 1982, WAS
a victory for Reagan, but it was short-lived. Rebuffed by the President, his aides took their case for a tax increase to the Senate Republicans, who were encouraged to rewrite the President's budget in
order to produce the necessary tax increase that would whittle down
the deficit. Over the previous year the Office of Management and
Budget had created a link in the government's mind between budget
deficits and interest rates. According to OMB, the only way to get
interest rates down and permit a recovery from the recession was
to lower the budget deficit. Since neither party wished to vote for
budget cuts with the 1982 mid-term elections in front of them,
the Democrats waited patiently while the Republicans forced President Reagan to accept a large tax increase in the name of a smaller
deficit.

On February 6, 1982, President Reagan submitted his 1983 budget proposal to Congress. Spending was projected at $757.6 billion
(up 4.4 percent), receipts at $666.1 billion (up 6.3 percent), and the
deficit rested at $91.5 billion. Envisioning "the strengthening of the
minimum corporate income tax and the repeal of the business energy tax credits" as well as "improved tax collection and enforcement," the budget proposed $22 billion in higher taxes despite the
State of the Union message abjuring them not ten days before.

No sooner was the President's budget in the hands of the legislators than his own advisers and political allies were criticizing it. An
"influential Reagan adviser" was quoted in the *Wall Street Journal*
on February 8: "The way I read the American electorate, deficits are

such an issue politically that Congress and the President will be taking action to reduce them. It's going to be very tough for the Republican party to stay within those deficits forecast." Senate Finance Committee Chairman Dole echoed the administration official the same day in the *New York Times,* warning, "The Republicans I talk to are frightened about the deficits." Republican Senator Quayle of Indiana backed up Dole's view, predicting, "You'll see people starting to jump off the ship starting Monday."

The House Democratic leadership, which had been steamrolled in 1981 by a coalition of Republicans and conservative southern Democrats, was anxious for the Republicans to roll back the tax cuts, but Democrats did not want any responsibility for a tax increase. An aide to the House Democratic leadership told the *Washington Post* on February 9 that the Republicans "decided how large the tax cut would be last year; now they can decide how big the tax increase will be this year." Repealing or delaying any part of the Reagan tax cut would achieve two goals for the Democrats: it would lessen the pressure to cut spending, and it would put the Republicans themselves in the position of going back on their program. Nevertheless, when the initiative for a tax increase was passed to the Senate Republican leadership, Baker, Dole, and Domenici seemed to welcome the responsibility. On February 9 the *Washington Post* reported that Dole and Domenici were already considering "at least $5 billion more" in tax increases than the President's budget had proposed.

Compromising with His Aides

According to White House aides, the President's budget strategy was to wait for a viable proposal from Congress with which he could compromise. However, the strategy was a weak one because House Democrats were unwilling to undertake any major budget initiatives without the preannounced support of the President. *Business Week* summarized Congress' position in the February 22 issue: "faced with the unpalatable election-year alternatives—taking on the President in a bloody fight over tax increases and defense cutbacks, or somehow finding a way to cut domestic spending by even more than the $43 billion Reagan wants—Congress seems headed for legislative paralysis."

Howell Raines wrote in the *New York Times* on February 21 that a "new strategy of delay had been devised, White House officials say, because the decline in the economy has robbed Mr. Reagan of his ability to push his program through Congress as he did last year." Hedrick Smith expanded on the report of his colleague the following day: "Aides concede [Reagan] is stalling on big economic decisions in the hope that some improvement in the economy will rescue him by summer. Privately, though, top Administration officials acknowledge that the recession is deeper than they had thought a month ago and that recovery is not likely until the second half of the year." These were curious interpretations, since normally recession bolsters the case for deficits and tax cuts.

The strategy of the President's aides may have been based on another tactic—stalling would allow the deficit to swell as a result of the prolonged recession, and the big deficit could be used as leverage to force Reagan to accept a tax increase. The proponents of raising taxes would thus be able to put high-profile pressure on the President to increase taxes and, at the same time, escape responsibility for their actions. *Time* reported the indirect strategy of top administration officials: "They hope they can hold the Republican-controlled Senate in line and force the Democratic-dominated House to propose such popular alternatives as cancelling the tax cuts, freezing Social Security benefits or slowing the military-spending buildup."

The strategy of delay did not stop the OMB director from encouraging Congress to alter the President's budget. "Hints of Compromise" and "New Flexibility" dominated the headlines the day after Stockman's testimony before the House Budget Committee on February 17. When asked if the President would say that neither taxes nor the military budget was negotiable, the budget director answered, "I believe this administration, and I believe this President, will look very carefully at a good faith, sincere effort on the part of the responsible leadership of the Congress, particularly your party [the Democrats], to propose something different." With such encouragement from the budget director, it was not surprising that Congress answered the call to alter the President's program. In late February, Senate Budget Committee Chairman Domenici set forth a plan that included tax increases of $122 billion over three years, five times the tax increase the President had reluctantly accepted. Domenici reportedly had in mind eliminating the third year of the President's tax cut and repealing the new tax-leasing provision that allowed the sale of investment tax credits. Domenici's proposal ignored the President's commitment not to raise taxes. Nevertheless, on February 24 White House Spokesman Larry Speakes deemed the proposal "a good faith effort to come up with a comprehensive alternative," saying "we want to take a closer look at it before offering specific suggestions."

Addressing a small business group on Monday, March 1, President Reagan vowed not to retreat on the issues of the tax cut or the overhaul of the nation's defenses. "I think it's time for you and me and the American people to stand together and tell the Congress: 'No, you may not touch our tax cut.'" The President's advisers quickly modified his statement by explaining that the President was "playing a waiting game" with Congress in hope that the economy would begin to recover so Republicans could coalesce behind an alternative budget. An unnamed White House aide again painted the picture of an insincere President, telling the *Los Angeles Times* that it was the administration's strategy for the President to remain "relatively inflexible" while Congress tried to forge a compromise alone. If the President actually had such a strategy, it seems unlikely that his aides would have thought that trumpeting it to the press would help it to succeed.

On Tuesday the President defended his budget proposal in Albuquerque. The existing alternatives to his budget, he said, were "political documents designed for saving certain legislators' political hides rather than saving the economy." On Wednesday the Reagan message was to be even more powerful: in the text of his speech at the Los Angeles Music Center, Reagan was prepared to criticize the "ad hoc alternatives to the economic recovery program on both sides of the aisle" (Baltimore *Sun,* March 4, 1982). The appeal to both parties not to tamper with Reaganomics was quickly cut out of the speech the morning of March 3 after a phone call from Senate Majority Leader Howard Baker, who obviously had been alerted. Baker was sensitive to the President's criticism of the Senate Republican leadership for backsliding on the Reagan program. Although the speech was toned down, Reagan was still able to get his point across, saying that rescinding or deferring portions of the tax cut "might well stall recovery further, suppressing tax revenues and ensuring permanently high budget deficits."

Back in Washington, Reagan's aides were making it clear that they did not side with the President on the economic issues. On Wednesday, March 3, 1982, Stockman met with a group of House Republicans that included some "gypsy moths" from the Northeast, some members of the Budget Committee, and some members of the leadership. He told them that there was a severe financial crisis and that the President's policies would not solve it. He invited them to rewrite the President's budget, saying that it was up to them to change the President's mind. Subtly he drew the picture of the President as a stubborn old man who would not listen to his advisers and who was leading the country into disaster. He had done the same thing in the Senate, with the result that Senator Packwood publicly ridiculed the President as a man who responds to urgency with anecdotes.

On Friday, March 5, Steve Bell, staff director of the Senate Budget Committee, told a meeting of committee staff directors that the deficit might turn out to be only $80 billion; if that were known, there would not be enough panic over the two-digit figure to generate a tax increase in an election year. Bell said that it was necessary to act quickly on the alternative budget. He outlined a strategy of pitting defense advocates against tax cutters. He said that Senator Tower, chairman of the Armed Services Committee, would be told that the deficit would be reduced either with tax increases or by cutting defense.

The same day an economist at the Council of Economic Advisers reported that he had seen George Will coming out of Stockman's office twice in the past ten days. Will, an advocate of increased defense spending, began attacking the supply-side tax cuts in his column. On Sunday, March 7, newspaper articles quoted unidentified presidential aides as saying that, whatever the President's wishes, higher taxes were inevitable. Steven Weisman of the *New York Times* reported that White House Chief of Staff Baker was upset with President Reagan for criticizing Senate Republicans and provoking Senator Baker to complain that the President was "criticizing the very people who helped get his economic programs through

Congress last year." "It won't happen again," declared a White House official. Previously aides waited until the President finished speaking before they altered or retracted what he said. Now they were going to muzzle the great communicator himself.

On March 8 the *New York Post* accused *New York Times* reporters of working hand in glove with Jim Baker to scuttle Reaganomics and told how Baker had successfully planted in the *New York Times* the false story that the business community had turned against Reaganomics and wanted the third-year tax cut deferred. A few days later (March 11) in the *Times* Howell Raines quoted a participant in several congressional briefings as saying that he had not heard any of the President's men come up to the Hill at any time and actually try to sell the President's budget.

While the anonymous leaks reportedly irritated the President, there were plenty of open attacks on his program as well. The Chamber of Commerce had been a firm defender of the President's economic program. In order to show them that their stance left them on the wrong side of the Washington establishment, Senate Finance Committee Chairman Dole chose an appearance before the Chamber to tell a good-news, bad-news joke: "The good news is that a bus loaded with supply-siders went over a cliff. The bad news is that there were three empty seats," and "they are huddled with the President" (*Washington Post,* March 5, 1982).

The evidence was stronger every day that the President's aides were determined to force him to accept a tax increase. On March 11 Raines wrote in the *New York Times* that in the "second engagement of The Battle for Reagan's Mind," White House aides adopted a more "cautious strategy for maneuvering him into compromising on his 1983 budget." It was a more difficult task, the correspondent revealed, "now that the President and his staff have become so touchy about doing anything that would contribute to Mr. Reagan's image as an unbending ideologue who has to be manipulated by aides into accepting economic realities." White House aides, chastened when the President rejected their advice for excise tax increases, were reportedly "imploring Congress to shape their budget around the economic concerns that Mr. Reagan's aides cannot get him to consider." By March 10 Dole had a list of tax increases that would add $105 billion to the government's coffers by 1984. The list included a doubling of the federal excise tax on gasoline, an oil import fee, and a repeal of the 1983 installment of the tax cut—ideas that he was hearing from OMB and the office of tax policy in the Treasury.

Reagan on the Defensive

On March 24 White House aides reported that President Reagan "in a shift of strategy" authorized aides to begin discussions with Democratic leaders of Congress on how to break the budget stalemate. Steven Weisman of the *New York Times* reported that the change was due to public opinion polls showing that the voters viewed President Reagan as being intransigent in his budget stance. The fact that it was Jim Baker who was authorized to lead the discussions caught Weisman's eye, since he, along with David Stockman and Mike Deaver, were seen as being "the main advocates internally of making concessions on tax cuts and military spending." The President was under increasing attack for being intransigent and an unbending ideologue, yet it was his own administration and the Senate Republicans, not the Democrats, who had given him that image.

The *Wall Street Journal* editorial page again pointed out that the President's men were undermining the President. In "Reagan's Brain Drain" (March 25, 1982), the *Journal* suggested that President Reagan take matters in hand before it was too late:

Some conservative Congressmen have started to keep a tally on how often Chief White House Communicator David Gergen contradicts the President. Chief Economic Adviser Murray Weidenbaum recently delivered a paper that sounded more like a defense of Congressmen who want to raise taxes and expand spending than an argument for the President's announced policies.

Mr. Reagan needs committed advocates backing him in his crucial struggle to break the Washington pattern of the last two decades, to stop the inflationist, high-spending, high-tax policies that have undermined solid economic growth. It would seem to us time for a managerial review at the White House, with the goal of beefing up the administration with more people who understand what is afoot and who are committed to making the Reagan program happen. The President can set policy and communicate it to the people but he can't manage the difficult politics of translating that program into legislation all by himself.

The following day, the editors were back with a piece criticizing Congress for stalling on the budget: "To hear Congress tell it," the *Journal* began, "the only barrier to passing a balanced federal budget is President Reagan's intransigence." To the editors, Congress' refrain sounded "as phony as a campaign promise."

On April 3 the *New York Times* reported that the Office of Management and Budget was "quietly" projecting the 1983 deficit at $124 billion even if the President's budget were fully adopted. These forecasts were the "gloomiest official projections so far, even gloomier than Congressional Budget Office estimates the Senate Budget Committee formally adopted this week as its standard." The rising deficit resulted from a drop in expected revenues caused by the sharp decline in inflation and the continuation of the recession. Nevertheless, the leaked deficit figures circulated by Stockman and Baker seemed specifically designed to keep pressure on Congress to reduce deficits by raising taxes, and therefore raised much suspicion. On April 12 the Baltimore *Sun* reported that Stockman may have overestimated the 1982 deficit by as much as $30 billion in order to "maintain the momentum in Congress for an increase in taxes and a cut in military spending in 1983, both of which the President has resisted." One House Republican decided he had had enough of Stockman's budget games. In an open letter to the President published in the *Wall Street Journal* on April 19, Ohio Representative Bud Brown took issue with Stockman's budget predictions: "Mr. President," he wrote, "I can't help wondering whether your economic agenda is once again being undermined by doubts about your program within your own administration or by someone else's personal agenda."

The budget talks lasted the entire month of April, with the negotiators meeting in a variety of secret locations—George Bush's home at the Naval Observatory, Congressman Jim Jones's Capitol Hill townhouse, and the Blair House across the street from the White House. White House aides openly told the media that the purpose of secrecy was to avoid repeating the highly visible campaign of press leaks and pressures on the President that had botched the previous attempt to raise taxes. Senate Republicans, encouraged by the President's men, did everything in their power to draw the President into compromising on taxes. Senator Domenici, for example, said on

April 9, "We recognize that no agreement will pass both the Senate and House this year without the enthusiastic support of the President."

The secret budget negotiations crawled along in a tentative fashion, the negotiators reporting one day that they were "near compromise" and the next that the talks had stalled. On Tuesday, April 19, Senate Majority Leader Howard Baker increased the pressure on President Reagan by threatening that the Senate Finance Committee would scuttle the third year of the tax cut if the President did not agree to higher taxes in some other form. The next day, President Reagan telephoned House Speaker O'Neill to express hope that the two parties would move toward a budget resolution. At an impromptu press conference following his telephone conversation with the House speaker, the President revealed that he vowed to "go the extra mile" in working out a budget with the Democratic House leadership. Tip O'Neill had the President right where he wanted him—and the Senate Republicans had done all the work. In response to the President's phone call, O'Neill stalled for more substantial concessions: the President, he said, "has taken the first step . . . He has admitted the need for a change."

With Republicans making the case for a tax increase, Democrats decided to test the water. On April 26 the Democratic negotiators rebuffed an administration request for a guarantee that there would be no vote to repeal the third year of the tax cut. With Republicans endorsing what amounted to a $113 billion tax increase over three years, the Democrats, led by Ways and Means Chairman Rostenkowski, wanted a $165 billion tax increase that entailed canceling the 1983 tax cut.

On April 28 the President participated in a three-hour meeting at the Capitol with Democratic budget negotiators. Republicans reconstructed the debate for the press after the meeting. Reagan had accepted $122 billion in new tax increases over three years. Despite the President's enormous concession, the Democrats were still not satisfied. The April talks broke down, even though the President offered to consider a ninety-day delay in the third year of his tax cut if the Democrats would accept more spending cuts. Evans and Novak (*Washington Post,* April 30) thought "the final Reagan offer implies that the president agrees with O'Neill that something about his tax cut is what's really wrong with the economy. For Reagan to go so far means he has accepted Baker's iron conviction that failure to reach bipartisan agreement on the budget would further damage the economy."

The President was told by Baker, Stockman, and their Senate allies that unless he accepted a tax increase the Congress would not pass a budget resolution. Continued stalemate over the budget, Reagan was told, would worry the financial markets and keep interest rates high. A large tax increase was the ransom he would have to pay Congress for a budget resolution and Wall Street for lower interest rates. Once the President was forced to be "pragmatic" about his tax policy, the next step was to be political about who would bear the burden of higher taxes. A few months before, the plan had been to raise excise taxes. Now Senator Dole thought that it was the rich who should be made to pay. When *Fortune* (April 19, 1982) asked Dole why he wanted to take tax benefits away from sick companies in the midst of a recession, he replied matter-of-factly, "Even the rich ought to contribute to economic recovery." Dole told Cowan that the main reason he didn't support the income tax surcharge proposal that was floated in April was that it didn't dig deep enough into the pockets of high-income earners (*New York Times,* April 26, 1982).

Once the Democrats and the media saw the Republicans on the run, they chased them, shouting "Party of the rich, deaf to the cries of the poor!" CBS turned up the volume on Wednesday night, April 21, with a documentary, "People Like Us," narrated by Bill Moyers, former aide to Lyndon Johnson. The so-called documentary purported to show how the budget cuts were falling mainly on the poor and the disabled by presenting the stories of three victims of Reagan's economic policies. It worked, and once again Republicans were legislating in response to the other side's propaganda. Republicans began searching for "tax equity" and "fairness" issues in order to combat the charges that the administration was insensitive to the poor. Dole zeroed in on big business and talk spread of rolling back the business tax cut.

On May 4 the Senate Budget Committee chairman discarded the President's budget and proposed a new budget of his own that included a one-year freeze on social security benefits and a three-year tax increase of $125 billion. He indicated that Reagan might have to give up the third year of his tax cut: "I do not rule out a freeze on the third year of the scheduled tax cut, if that is the final element that a compromise of this magnitude hinges upon." When Domenici announced his new budget, Tip O'Neill made it clear that Reagan was having to compromise with his own party: "Howard Baker keeps thinking that the Democrats are key to all this, but they [the Republicans] control two-thirds of the Government."

The following day the President was brought to heel. The compromise budget consisted of a $95 billion tax increase and a defense cut of $22 billion. President Reagan surrendered by telephone during the committee meeting.

On Thursday, May 6, the President, flanked by House Minority Leader Bob Michel and Pete Domenici in the White House Rose Garden, announced his support for the new budget proposal, saying "it will continue to bring down the growth in federal spending" and "reassure financial markets by sharply reducing projected deficits next year and in the years beyond." Although Reagan had been forced to capitulate, his announcement was not treated as a presidential defeat by the press. The President was hailed a victor even in defeat—and not for the last time. In August Reagan was lauded in the media for the skill he used in shepherding "his" $100 billion tax increase through Congress. Weisman of the *New York Times* did manage to catch the irony of the situation. The President "showed how he could dominate the news and look as if he was in control of the national agenda even as control was actually being seized by others." White House aides were reportedly congratulating themselves "that the President had seemed to dominate the news events even as his frustrations continued on the economic issues."

On May 17 the myth so astutely spread by Stockman that Wall Street was insisting on tax increases as the price of lower interest rates was blown away when the *Wall Street Journal* quoted Moody's Investor Service, the bond-rating company, in their lead editorial, "Alice in Budgetland":

"Efforts to balance the budget via higher taxes could have a devastating effect throughout the economy . . . The expected drop in interest rates could well be meaningless in the long run if the economy's underpinnings continue to deteriorate—as we would expect them to under greater tax burdens ... The worst-case scenario might be that higher taxes would substantially deepen the recession and result in even greater budget deficits, thus leading to economic shambles."

Congress, however, paid no attention when Moody's said what politicians did not want to hear, and on June 10 the House by a vote of 219–206 adopted a Republian budget proposal requiring a $95 billion tax increase. During the many hours of budget debate, the extraordinary measure of raising taxes in a recession received little comment. According to the *New York Times* (June 11), the House Republican leadership made the vote a test of party loyalty. "We started bearing down on some of our members in a more militant fashion," House Minority Leader Michel was quoted as saying. Jack Kemp was notably one of only fifteen Republicans who voted against the Republican budget.

If the Wall Street bond traders were encouraged by the resolution of the budget crisis that had been dramatized by OMB and Senate Republicans, they showed it in a strange way. Interest rates jumped up sharply in the week that Congress came to an agreement. The Dow Jones industrial average hit its lowest point in two years, wiping out the spring run-up that some economists believed was a harbinger of economic recovery. Press reports blamed the fall in the stock and bond markets on larger than expected deficit projections for the 1983 budget, ignoring the massive tax increase and the reversal of economic policy.

Dole's Day in the Sun

As much as Democrats wanted Reaganomics to fail, they were careful to leave the initiative in the hands of the Republicans. On the last day of June 1982, Dole and the Finance Committee Republicans reported out a $100 billion tax increase that had all the earmarks of a liberal Democrat "tax reform" bill. Dole's bill imposed tax withholding on interest and dividends, imposed a new minimum tax on corporations and individuals, and repealed 85–95 percent of the incentives to invest in machinery and equipment in the 1981 business tax cut. It was a different bill from the one Russell Long had reported out in the fall of 1980, and it was a direct contradiction to the principles of the 1981 tax bill.

At 4:47 in the morning on July 23, the Republican Senate passed the Dole bill, 50–47. Not a single Democrat voted for the tax increase. Dole, who sounded euphoric at the prospect of a $100 billion tax increase on investment in the midst of a deepening recession, seemed confused that the Democrats had not jumped on his bandwagon. Anxious, perhaps, that the Dole bill would not become the historic law that reversed the Kemp revolution, Dole told the House Democrats that raising taxes in a recession was good politics and good economics: "If the Democrats fail to act in the House, we have got a campaign issue that won't stop. It's suddenly in the lap of Tip O'Neill. The future of this economy is now up to House Speaker Tip O'Neill" (*Washington Post*, July 24, 1982).

Speaker O'Neill saw it differently. The Republicans were destroying a popular President's economic program that had passed with a great deal of fanfare less than a year before. The Democrats would benefit only as long as the repudiation of Reaganomics came from Republicans themselves. Therefore, five days after the Senate passed the Dole bill, the House voted 208–197 to go directly to conference, thereby avoiding the responsibility for drafting a tax-increase bill. It was an unprecedented action. Normally, tax bills originate in the House and are then taken up by the Senate. This time the House abandoned its prerogative and left the responsibility in the lap of the Senate Republicans. Instead of fuming that the Senate Finance Committee chairman was encroaching, House Ways and Means Committee Chairman Rostenkowski told the *New York Times* (July 29): "I don't see why there should be any imprints on [the tax bill] by Democrats . . . It was a request by the Administration."

To underline their concern over deficits, some Republicans advocated a balanced-budget amendment along with the tax-increase bill. The amendment required Congress to adopt a balanced budget at the beginning of every fiscal year. It could be waived only in time of war, or by a 60 percent vote of both houses of Congress. In order to prevent Congress from balancing the budget by raising taxes, the level of taxation could rise only as fast as the growth in the economy. President Reagan pledged support for the amendment on July 12 in the rose garden and again on July 19 on the steps of the Capitol.

The balanced-budget amendment served to frame the deficit issue in terms of revenues and expenditures and thereby helped to prevent the deficit from being used as a political ploy to scuttle the tax cuts. Many liberals still see the tax-cut issue as a battle between private and public growth. The reason the tax cut was wrong in their eyes was that it hampered their vision of an ever-expanding public sector. The deficit issue was their only effective weapon to repeal the tax cuts and allow government to continue to grow.

Although it did not pass the House, the balanced-budget amendment helped to take pressure off the personal income tax reductions. Liberal Democrats had voiced so much concern over budget deficits in their battle against tax reductions that they could not easily oppose the balanced-budget amendment. It is noteworthy that the calls for repeal of the third year of the President's tax cut stopped at about the time the Senate passed the balanced-budget amendment.

Kemp Fights Back

With a tax increase looming, a group of House Republicans led by Jack Kemp circulated a letter to be sent to President Reagan to register dismay at the shift in policy from economic growth to austerity. The letter read:

Quietly, without debate, the Republican party is in danger of making a U-turn back to its familiar role of tax collector for Democratic spending programs. This is potentially an explosive scenario politically because the G.O.P. clearly will take the blame for any tax increase passed by Congress . . . Therefore, we find it impossible to support the Senate-passed tax increase.

Kemp summoned a group of Reaganites to Capitol Hill on the evening of August 4 with a telegram bearing this message:

All of us care deeply about making President Reagan's economic program a success. We plan to discuss the current and future economic outlook, including our opposition to the recently passed Senate tax increase.

Many of President Reagan's original supporters and closest advisers responded to the message. Two dozen Reaganites, including long-time aides Martin Anderson and Lyn Nofziger and former Treasury officials Norman Ture and myself, were present and agreed to resist the backsliding being forced on the President. Our joint statement read:

In the present weak economic climate and during a time in which the Congress refuses to support the spending cuts required by the budget resolution, we friends of Ronald Reagan oppose the tax increase now before the House-Senate conference. We believe that to restore the health of the economy and put Americans back to work, America should follow a course against high taxes and Federal spending.

These efforts were quickly countered. In the *Washington Post* unidentified "sources" went to work driving wedges between Congressman Kemp and President Reagan by planting the story that Kemp had clashed with the President and White House counselor Meese. The White House staff took to the newspapers again on August 6 to strike at Kemp. When Larry Speakes was asked if press reports were true that Kemp had "received a thorough scolding from colleagues and presidential aides," Speakes replied: "I generally do not quarrel with the press reports" (*Wall Street Journal*). The *New York Times* reported:

The White House went to great lengths to undermine the rebels, particularly Mr. Kemp. After the meeting between the President and Congressional leaders, Administration officials called reporters to relate how Mr. Kemp had been scolded for his opposition to the tax bill and warned to back the Administration position.

On August 13 Howell Raines reported in the *Times* that "key White House officials are convinced Mr. Kemp wants to build a Presidential campaign on the ashes of the Reagan economic program." Of course it was Kemp who was trying to prevent White House officials from turning the President's program into ashes.

When pushed to defend the tax increase, the President denied that it was an increase. In answer to columnist John Lofton's question in the *Washington Times*, "Why now a $228 billion tax increase through 1987?" the President responded with a letter on Friday August 6:

We found we could not put last year's coalition together unless we agreed to some increases in revenue. This was the price we had to pay to get reduction of outlays which amount to three dollars for every one dollar of increased revenue.

As for the tax increase itself:

> Over the next three years the increased revenue from the Senate bill will total roughly $99 billion. Of that amount, $31 billion is not additional tax. It is tax owed under the present laws but not now being collected. The remaining $68 billion is from shutting off unintended tax advantages . . . Personally, I had to swallow very hard. I believe in "supply-side," and that tax increases slow the recovery.

The President was misled by his aides into believing that the tax increase, which vitiated his 1981 tax cut for business, was a harmless compliance measure that would serve as a lever to pressure Congress into accepting deeper budget cuts. The *Washington Post* encouraged the President's misconception and in an editorial on August 9 took the supply-siders to task for opposing the "life-saving" tax bill.

"The Largest Tax Increase in History"

On August 15, 1982, the House-Senate conferees approved a $98.3 billion tax bill very similar to the Senate Finance Committee's bill. It was unclear how the House would vote. Although the administration had stepped up its intense lobbying for the tax increase, there was a strong sentiment in the House against it. The success of the tax bill in the House seemed to hang on Reagan's support. An administration official told the *Wall Street Journal* on August 16 that "left to their own devices, a lot of these Republicans would vote against this bill. And they'd vote against it even if asked not to—by anybody else but this guy Reagan."

On August 16, three days before the tax increase was scheduled for a vote in the House, the President took to the television cameras to support the increase. Reagan stressed that he was in no way going back on the achievements of the previous year or returning to business as usual. "Possibly it could be called the greatest tax reform in history, but it absolutely does not represent any reversal of policy or philosophy on the part of this Administration or this President." The Democrats used their time following the President's speech to endorse the new Reagan position. Representative Tom Foley told Americans that "weighing the benefits of passing this bill against the cost of not passing it, I have come to the conclusion that, despite our differences in the past, this is one occasion when the President's position is right."

Two days after the President's speech, an editorial in the *New York Times* congratulated him for coming around to the *Time*'s point of view: "Despite his reluctance, he can be proud of his ability to reverse field when he saw that it was the right thing to do." The *Washington Post* also graciously welcomed the President to their side of the argument, noting on August 17 that Reagan had made the "right case" for a tax increase.

If the President did not realize the scope of his defeat from the Democrats' endorsement of his speech or the *New York Times* and *Washington Post* editorial endorsements, he must have wondered when he was endorsed by the man whose policies he was elected to reverse. On Wednesday, August 18, amid reports that there were not enough votes to pass the tax increase in the House, Tip O'Neill joined forces with President Reagan, telling a group of Democratic congressmen:

the tax bill will not repeal Reaganomics, but it is a step in the right direction. I urge my fellow Democrats to support the bill because it is the only opportunity Congress has this year to restore sanity and fairness to national economic policy.

Despite the support of both the Republican and Democratic leadership in the House, it was still unclear how the House would vote on the tax increase. An aide to Congresssman Michel told the *Washington Post* on August 18 that it was the "most traumatic fight" since Reagan entered office. Although he endorsed the tax increase, Tip O'Neill warned that the bill would receive little Democratic support unless the White House could generate "about 100" Republican votes.

On Thursday, August 19, the Tax Equity and Fiscal Responsibility Act was debated on the floor of the House of Representatives. John Rousselot took the floor in a valiant effort to stem the retreat of the Republicans from the policy that had put them back in political competition five and a half years before. "There is no credible economic theory," Rousselot declared,

which argues that tax increases in the midst of a recession are proper economic medicine for the disease. Tax increases cannot produce lower interest rates. Additional taxes crowd productive dollars out of the economy in the same way that higher deficits do.

With the voice of experience, Rousselot told his fellow congressmen:

Reducing red ink in the budget does not take place because we raise taxes. The history of the last decade proves the point. Deficits can only be dealt with successfully in a climate of economic growth. Tax increases deter growth and only spending cuts are consistent with governmental actions which both promote growth and reduce deficits.

The ranks firmed. Congressman Myers wondered why Reagan wanted to raise taxes and provide Congress with more money to spend. Congressman Gregg, a new member from New Hampshire, recalled that the new Republicans "came here with a purpose," but the opportunity "to slay the colossus that is known as a Federal Government" was lost by this bill, and "we chose to compromise." Congressman Shumway declared that

what really lurks behind all the talk of tax reform and compliance by advocates of this bill is yet another attempt to finance unrestrained Federal spending. According to OMB Director Stockman, Federal spending, as a percentage of GNP, will reach its highest level since 1946 this year. The President's original program for economic recovery called for a reduction of this ratio to 19.3 percent in 1984. Current estimates are that Federal spending will consume 24 percent of GNP in fiscal 1984. During this fiscal year, the Federal budget will increase by 11.7 percent, a rate substantially greater than that of inflation.

Congressman Archer objected that Congress was voting on a tax bill on which no hearings had been held, an unusual procedure to say the least. Even in the unlikely event that raising taxes would close the deficit, Archer thought that there were other important considerations. One was a need for certainty in the tax law, but "it is not certainty when we pass a bill in 1981 urging capital investment and one year later we change all the rules."

Its political and economic faults aside, the tax-increase bill suffered a great deal from the irregular procedures by which it had come to a vote. No hearings had been held, and the Committee on Ways and Means, which is supposed to originate tax legislation, never marked up the bill. Several members complained that this made the bill unconstitutional. All things considered, it would have been an easy tax bill to defeat, but the White House succeeded in making a case for higher taxes. Somehow raising taxes was going to save the economy and the political leadership of Ronald Reagan.

In spite of the full-court press by the White House, some Republicans thought that the issue was one of keeping faith with the voters, not blind political support of whatever policy reversals came out of the White House. What did the voters want? Rousselot pointed to the latest *Washington Post* and ABC news poll which showed that 54 percent disapproved of the tax increase. Even worse for the Republicans, nearly half of those polled believed that the tax-increase bill meant that the President had lost faith in his economic program.

The White House had too weak a case to attract principled men to its banner. Edward Bethune, a supply-sider, rose "not in opposition to the President, but in support of the beliefs that led me to run for Congress in the first place." James Jeffries was even more forthright: "The American people have been betrayed." Prophetically, he left his Republican colleagues with a warning: "If you think that the voters are going to overlook this tax raise, you are sadly mistaken. Their response to the President's call for this tax bill has been negative. And it will be negative in November." (The Republicans lost 26 House seats in November 1982.)

Just before the vote, Kemp rose to put the tax increase into historical perspective:

Fifty years ago a Congress faced a similar choice. There was high unemployment, a huge deficit, the President wanted a tax increase, and the Congress went along blindly with it. Interestingly enough, interest rates did not go down, they went up; unemployment did not go down, it went up; and the deficit grew and the recession deepened into the Great Depression.

Kemp warned his party against backtracking on the achievements of the past five years in the vain hope that higher taxes would lower interest rates. Interest rates, he said, belong to monetary policy. They were already falling, and the Federal Reserve had lowered the discount rate. Congress should not offset the positive effects of lower interest rates by raising taxes on investment.

It was time to vote, and still the outcome was up in the air. About 40 undecided congressmen, both Republican and Democrat, milled around on the floor of the House. They were tense and would go with the tide, tipping the balance for or against the tax increase. In the House cloakroom, Tip O'Neill commented on the indecision, "We could win by a dozen, or we could lose by a hundred." Small groups of congressmen gathered together, and all heads turned to watch the large scoreboard behind the Speaker's chair light up as the vote was registered. Gradually it began to weigh more heavily in favor of the increase, and in the final few seconds the tax increase was adopted, 226–207. The final Republican tally was 103–89 for the increase. The Democrats voted 123 yeas to 118 nays.

The tax increase pitted what Representative Newton Gingrich called "the strange, unexplainable alliance of powerful political opponents who, together, form an establishment in Washington" against the forces of change. The President, who resisted higher taxes, finally succumbed to pressures from his aides and political rivals in the Senate.

The President was not the only supply-side casualty. Marjorie Holt, who had routed the Democrats with her amendment in 1978, was persuaded by Paul Volcker to vote for the tax increase. Bud Brown, a pioneer supply-sider on the Joint Economic Committee, also voted for the increase. However, eighty-nine Republicans stood firm with Kemp and Rousselot.

8

Assessing Reagan

BY THE AUTUMN OF 1981 THE *WALL STREET JOURNAL* WAS AL-
ready observing that President Reagan had a management problem.
By January 20, 1982, it was apparent to anyone who was keeping up
with events that the problem was "mammoth." In its lead editorial,
"Reagan's Management Problem," the *Journal* pointed out:

As chief executive officer he has failed in the task of creating a management structure to make the organization execute the policies he prefers.
Instead, the traditional concerns and policies of the incumbent bureaucracy are constantly thrust upon him, and it falls to him alone to accept,
reject or deflect ideas and proposals that originate elsewhere. No corporate chief executive, let alone one put in charge of a turnaround situation,
would be content with this passive role.

The editorial may have overemphasized the President's isolation;
the Treasury (some part at least) tried to help him. But on the main
point the *Journal* was correct. Furthermore, the President's accom-
plishments—the tax and budget cuts and the beginning of military
rearmament that had been achieved the previous summer—were
"threatened by Mr. Reagan's failure to take hold of the enterprise he
heads."

It was obvious that the President's senior aides did not support his
policies, but he did nothing about it. It was equally obvious that the
President declared publicly over and over that he would never raise
taxes—and yet he did. There was no public clamor for the President
to reverse himself and raise taxes. Indeed, in April 1982, the very
month he gave in and accepted higher taxes, the investment community, in whose name taxes were raised, exclaimed that the deficit was

a red herring, and that the real problem was "government spending as a percent of GNP."[1] Some 87 percent of the decision makers in the major institutional investment firms, controlling $540 billion of investment funds, were opposed to tax increases. No one wanted higher taxes except Stockman, Baker, Domenici, Dole, O'Neill, and Rostenkowski. In fact, when the Senate Republicans passed the tax increase, not a single Democrat in the Senate voted in favor of the bill. Why, then, did the President retain his advisers rather than his policies when he was finally forced to choose between them?

Intelligent people have different explanations. Edward Crane, president of the libertarian Cato Institute, wrote in the *Washington Post* that Reagan was never committed to his program in the first place: "Reaganomics is simply a fiction," one that Reagan used as a vehicle for putting himself on center stage.[2] Crane emphasized the "mass exodus" of principled people from the administration even before midterm as evidence that Reagan had no real political principles. He went on to argue that people were taken in by the President's rhetoric. Crane pointed to Reagan's record as governor of California where "his stirring campaign speeches called for reducing the burden on California taxpayers, but were matched by eight years of the most rapid growth (in real terms) of government spending and taxes in the state's history." Conservatives made similar points, claiming that when Reagan left the governor's mansion he left the state bare of any foundations for the conservative movement, bequeathing nothing to the conservatives who had responded to his rhetoric.

Douglas Hallett, a Los Angeles attorney, made a similar argument.[3] Maintaining that the problem was not Jim Baker, although "he probably shouldn't have been appointed to his current job," but Reagan himself, he wrote: "The one person who is scuttling Reaganism is Dutch Reagan." In Hallett's view, Reagan simply didn't give a damn:

The problem is a president who refuses to take the time to understand policy and is therefore unable to take command himself ... Not in this

---

1. *The Oppenheimer Report: Institutional Investor Attitudes towards Current Fiscal and Monetary Issues* (New York: Oppenheimer and Co., April 1982).
2. "Reagan Never Meant What He Said," *Washington Post,* August 19, 1982.
3. "The Problem with Reagan," *Wall Street Journal,* September 8, 1982.

century has there been a chief executive so uninformed about his administration's policies and so unconcerned about that lack of information.

The reason Hallett thought Reaganites always found their man, whether in the White House or in the governor's mansion, undermined by pragmatists was that Reagan "does not mean for his rhetoric to be taken literally and does not want to be challenged to act on it." Hallett painted a picture of Reagan as "a direction-pointer" rather than "an implementer" and concluded that his advisers didn't matter. But his argument would seem to support the opposite conclusion: if Reagan himself tends to remain uninvolved, it is important that his advisers are people who follow his pointers. Whether the President believes his speeches or not, the people who elected him do and that, after all, is what the government is supposed to act upon.

The *Wall Street Journal* editorial page (August 13, 1982) saw Reagan being led into a reversal by advisers who convinced him that no such about-face was really happening. In his televised speech on August 16, 1982, the President declared that the tax increase "absolutely [did] not represent any reversal of policy or philosophy on the part of this administration, or this president," and Reagan might well have believed this to be true. But he should have wondered when he saw Tip O'Neill in favor of the bill while Kemp and the Reaganites were opposed.

The *Journal* was unimpressed with the President's argument that the bill was a reform measure rather than a tax increase. It implied that the President did not know what he was doing, and in fact an anonymous White House official told *Time* that Reagan "didn't understand the bill." When the President declared in his news conference on August 13 that the tax bill was a compliance measure with 80 percent of the additional revenues coming from "collecting money that is already owed to the government and is not being reported," it certainly appeared as if Reagan did not understand that the measure repealed most of his business tax cut.

However the President saw it, the ABC poll conducted the evening after his televised speech (reported in the *Washington Post* on August 19, 1982) found that the public saw it as a tax increase of which a majority disapproved. "More significant politically," the

Post reported, was the "poll's finding that many Americans see Reagan's call for a tax increase as a major flip-flop," despite his statement to the contrary. The poll found that 48 percent believed that Reagan's call for new taxes meant that he had lost faith in his economic program; 41 percent thought he had not lost faith, and 11 percent had no opinion.

Hallet argued that the image of an uninformed President was hardly reassuring at a time when "the economy is in collapse and America's strategic position is declining." But chief exeutives have to rely on their managers, and Reagan's were not doing their job. Another example soon appeared. This time it was an override by the House and Senate of Reagan's veto of a $14.1 billion appropriations bill. Reagan called it a "budget-buster," but it was actually $2 billion under the mark. Congress accused Stockman of giving the President bad advice. Tip O'Neill called on Stockman to resign for failing to inform the President about the contents of the bill. The Republican chairman of the Senate Appropriations Committee, Mark Hatfield, said:

Frankly I'm getting sick and tired of David Stockman and his mirror act ... He's not serving the nation well, he's not serving the President well, he's not serving his party well.[4]

Others who watch the Washington scene closely, such as Evans and Novak, saw the tax increase as James Baker's attempt to portray supply-side economics as a failure and thus to remove Jack Kemp as a contender for the presidential succession.[5] Conservatives were puzzled that a pragmatist like Baker, who proudly declared his non-philosophical approach to governing,[6] fought so hard for a tax increase in the name of budget-balance ideology.

The Democrats and liberal journalists had a field day with the Reagan–O'Neill tax increase. Mary McGrory had a marvelous time with two long columns, "Reagan Takes Two Right Steps into the Camp of Left-Wingers" and "The President and Tip O'Neill Play Ball—as Switch Hitters."[7] McGrory reported that Democrats had made "the intoxicating discovery that bipartisanship can be fun,

4. *Washington Post,* September 11, 1982.
5. Evans and Novak, *Washington Post,* August 13, 1982.
6. *Business Week,* December 7, 1981.
7. *Washington Post,* August 19 and August 24, 1982.

when it means underlining the fact that Reaganomics doesn't work." Democrats were crowing, she reported, that the campaign issue "is not the Democratic leadership; it's the failure of Ronald Reagan's economics." "Reagan's theories have brought us to near depression," she declared, and "Reagan tried to gloss over the chasm that opened between him and the right by attributing the rebellion led by conservative Jack Kemp to Kemp's lust for the presidency."

Kemp believed that Stockman, Baker, and Greenspan had reopened the fight over economic policy that had been settled by the election of Ronald Reagan. Kemp objected to Baker's attempt to brand his opposition to the tax increase as stemming from dark and selfish political motives and declared that it was not "a revolt against the President to keep the same position you have always had."[8]

On August 18 the *New York Times* lead editorial declared the tax increase "a fitting flip-flop climax to the Great Tax Debate of 1982." Normally, liberal economics calls for big deficits in a recession in order to stimulate the economy and to reduce the horror of unemployment. What had happened to liberal economics? Why was the *Times* in favor of reducing the deficit in a time of recession, a Hoover policy that the *Times* had ridiculed for years? Perhaps the *Times* saw an opportunity to let a conservative President destroy both himself and the economic policies geared toward rejuvenating a market economy. Once Reagan and supply-side economics were in the trash can, the *Times* could resurrect the liberal agenda and get on with the moral business of building the welfare state, this time for big business as well with a resurrected Reconstruction Finance Corporation. Many of Reagan's supporters felt that the liberal media praised Baker as a good pragmatic politician because he let the President fall into one trap after another. The Federal Reserve produced a recession, and the President retracted part of his historic tax cut. What could a public unschooled in economics conclude other than that Reaganomics had failed?

In his State of the Union message in January 1982, Reagan said that "raising taxes won't balance the budget" but would worsen un-

8. *Washington Post,* August 12, 1982.

employment problems. Seven months later, when he made his pitch for a tax increase, he had a different view: "Do we reduce deficits and interest rates by raising revenue . . . or do we accept bigger budget deficits, higher interest rates and higher unemployment?" Whether the President believed he had changed policy or not, he had certainly changed explanations. Were Crane and Hallett right that Reagan was too uninvolved and never meant his campaign program to be taken literally? Was he a President with a management problem who was misled by advisers hoping to discredit Kemp or protect the status quo? Or was he a hero for having changed his mind, as others claimed?

Crane and Hallett can point to other developments in support of their conclusion that Reagan is more rhetoric than belief. The same month that brought the reversal on taxes brought the Taiwan communique, a weakening of the pipeline sanctions, and the beginning of what looked to some like the isolation of the Begin government and the sellout of Israel. Ronald Reagan had promised to upgrade our relationship with Taiwan after the downgrading it received at the hands of Carter, and the Republican platform promised "priority consideration to Taiwan's defense requirements." The morning after Reagan's tax-increase speech, however, his government downgraded Taiwan's defense requirements and announced limitations on arms sales to Taiwan. The State Department's Taiwan communique of mid-August seemed to suggest that Reagan was allowing communist China to determine our policy toward Taiwan. The embarrassing backdown on the sanctions imposed on foreign firms for shipping embargoed American technology to the Soviet Union and the stance taken against Israel for pushing the PLO out of Lebanon were further indications that the President's principles were not translated into policy. The question is why.

Economists and politial scientists (unless they have worked in a recent administration) tend to have an exaggerated idea of the power of a president.[9] They view the presidency as a position from which the occupant can organize to get what he wants. In this view, the power of the presidency does not prevent its occupant from

9. They also have an exaggerated idea of the "public interest" content of government policy. For a different view see my "Idealism in Public Choice Theory," *Journal of Monetary Economics,* August 1978, pp. 603–615.

making mistakes of judgment, but it does protect him from being the one who is acted upon instead of the one who acts.

When this view of the presidency is applied to Ronald Reagan, the picture is one of a man who decided to tie himself in knots. He carefully structured a policy advisory apparatus in order to play it off against his own views, thereby leavening his convictions with pragmatists who are accustomed to dumping agendas. Some political scientists believe that this is the way presidents protect policy from being dominated by their own convictions and make it subject to broad agreement. A president faced with a turnaround situation—as Reagan believes he is—who adopted such a method of governing would preclude the necessary changes. He would not only have to be insincere about his causes, but also a bad politician to contrive to defeat himself on his own issues.

To an insider's eye, none of the explanations that have been offered fully account for what happened. Ronald Reagan fought too long and hard against his senior advisers' pressure to raise taxes, from the autumn of 1981 through the spring of 1982, not to have been serious about his policies in the first place. Yet, in spite of all the determination that he displayed—overruling almost his entire government in his State of the Union message—the President could not find the determination, or what the *Wall Street Journal* called "management skills," to replace advisers who had formed their own policy team with people who would support his original policies. A clue to the real problem can be found in the fact that President Reagan did not see a disloyal David Stockman when the *Atlantic* article appeared but, instead, a man victimized by the press.[10] The President's management style seems to suffer from an excess of trust and generosity.

The President himself did not agree that he had given up on supply-side economics. There is little doubt that Reagan was boxed in by Stockman who, instead of making efforts on behalf of the President's 1983 budget, encouraged Congress to vote it down and produce an alternative budget that contained tax increases. The President was told that, without a budget resolution, interest rates would not fall and the economy would remain in recession, and that

10. See Reagan's interview in *Human Events*, February 26, 1983, p. 19.

the only way to get a resolution was to compromise and accept higher taxes. By that time it was probably true that he had lost control over budget policy, but it was a situation produced by aides who could have fought for the President's budget instead of against it. The President still had one other choice: replace the aides who had undermined his own budget with people who would fight for him. It is possible that Reagan was not sufficiently involved in the process to know that he had been sandbagged or that he was not committed enough to his policies to take the heat for firing senior officials like Stockman and Baker. But it is also possible that he does not realize his staffing problem since both Congress and the media are obvious candidates for the sources of his troubles.

The interpretation of the policy reversal as an attempt to discredit Kemp and supply-side economics has some validity, although this does not mean that it was an organized plot. There would have been nothing unusual about Baker, Bush, Stockman, and Dole using an opportunity that they themselves had helped create to eclipse a star like Kemp. Similarly, mainstream economists like Stein and Greenspan had many resentments against supply-side economics and found much to criticize. As people jockey for position, the activities that look like plots are no doubt taking place, but they seldom are the result of formal conspiracies.

Obstacles to Leadership

The explanations offered for Reagan's reversal focus on his personality rather than on the obstacles to his leadership. When these obstacles are examined, a different picture emerges. Because Ronald Reagan's management style is to delegate extensively and to rely heavily on staff, it makes a great deal of difference who the staff is. After winning the nomination, he was advised to pull the party together by bringing on board Republicans who had opposed him in order to defeat the Democrats in the general election. The numerous non-Reaganites invariably ended up with important positions in a government whose ideology they do not share, and the campaign manager of the President's opponent became his chief of staff.

In such an environment, it is hard for a President to avoid being captured. Once he appoints compromisers to office in order to give the necessary reassurances to the establishment, he achieves accommodation and not change. The first year of the Reagan Administration was a struggle between a few people in government who wanted change and a government full of people who did not. Eventually a rule developed for dealing with the forces of change—they were not invited to the decision meetings. As *Time* reported on August 23, 1982, when Reagan was told by his advisers that he had to accept a $100 billion tax increase or his economic program would be doomed and his popularity jeopardized, "the Baker-Darman group excluded from the meeting those who opposed" the tax increase, "including Presidential Assistant Richard Williamson and key congressional conservatives."

In the same story *Time* went on to reassure its readers that Reagan was now firmly under the establishment's control. The driving force in the White House was the "Legislative Strategy Group (L.S.G.), the brain trust that has coalesced around Chief of Staff James Baker," who "is guided by a belief that politics is the art of the possible." *Time* praised Baker's "Tolkien ring of power" for "its success in moderating Reagan's policies." Ed Meese had thought that there was a great difference between formulating policy (Meese's job) and implementing it (Baker's job), but *Time* quoted "a key member of Baker's group" as saying "that is a preposterous notion." Policy *is* implementation, so Meese lost out.

Once in government, aides and appointed officials always become involved in competing for access to policy levers, status, exposure in the media, and controlling power. The competition for power becomes much more important to the "players" than the substance of the policy, and policy concerns become subsidiary as players try to prevail over one another. Indeed, the widely used term "player" itself indicates that the policy process is viewed as a game. No doubt this sounds cynical, but it is merely the report of many who have observed and experienced political life in Washington. Meg Greenfield, the editorial editor of the *Washington Post,* has herself written about the corruptive nature of Washington (September 15, 1982). Americans think of corruption in their capital in terms of old-fashioned graft and sex scandals. Greenfield wishes that the problem did amount to nothing more than a case of temptations out of hand and a taste for high living. However, "ambition is the raving and insatiable beast that most often demands to be fed in this town," and in pursuit of this ambition people "will sell or sell out almost anything, including their own self-respect, if any, and the well-being of thousands of others." A president has little chance in such an environment. He has to rely on people he does not know and whose loyalties are to their own careers.

American culture no longer imbues people with a sense of fellowship, and the individualism we have always cherished has become shallow and egocentric. We have become extraordinarily tolerant of what once was considered undisciplined behavior. The end result is an environment of self-seeking instead of an environment of stewardship and individual excellence. Many feel justified in striving to obtain power over other people. They have lost the realization that the compulsive desire for power over others is an indication of great personal inadequacy. Those desperate for power define themselves in terms of their position of power over other people, not in terms of what they are or accomplish themselves. They measure themselves daily in terms of their success in putting other people down. Unfortunately, Washington attracts such people; they come in search of a stage, and then fight to push everyone else off even when they themselves have nothing to offer. This is the heart of the problem.

Vice-Admiral James Bond Stockdale has written on "The Principles of Leadership."[11] The first principle is: "you are your brother's keeper." Few in Washington observe this rule. Without it there can be no fellowship. Without fellowship there can be no leadership. An individual who attempts to lead will be attacked from every direction.

The Denunciatory Ethic

The obstacles to presidential leadership are formidable, but there is yet a more fundamental problem. Over the years the United States has moved from an affirmatory view of itself to a denunciatory view. Vietnam and Watergate played a role, but it is basically a problem of the American outlook, which is generous toward foreigners but very self-critical. Eugene Rostow has expressed it as follows:

We tend to blame ourselves for everything that goes wrong in the world, and to assume that other nations share our good intentions and will fol-

11. *American Educator,* Winter 1981.

low our good example. We take pride in self-flagellation, and seize every opportunity for excusing or ignoring the faults and shortcomings of others.[12]

What it comes down to is that the United States employs self-shame as a useful tool to achieve progress or change. From this perspective, leadership consists of stressing shortcomings in order to correct them rather than building on past achievements and successes. American reform movements, from civil rights to foreign policy, have stressed correcting past failures and righting past wrongs. A nation that relies on a self-critical posture as its means of achieving progress is forced to underplay its achievements. Inevitably it is at war with itself. When the indictments of economists, political scientists, sociologists, historians, theologians, ecologists, and arms controllers are added together, the result is a total indictment of America. One of the most successful nations in history, the United States projects abroad the image of a country totally dissatisfied with itself.

Consider a typical member of our intellectual elite. His commitment to society is conditional upon pushing through the changes in institutions and policies that he thinks are necessary to bring about the desired improvements. Therefore, his allegiance at any point in time is weak; to satisfy his desire for progress, he feels he must remain an opponent of existing society. He does not see his country's gifts of foreign aid as attesting to its moral sense, but the insufficient amount is evidence to him of an immoral foreign policy. He justifies foreign nationalization of his fellow citizens' property as a necessary remedy for neocolonial exploitation. He does not see lack of progress in arms limitations as a reflection on the opponent's intentions but, instead, on his own country's lack of good faith. A strong defense posture is not a justifiable response to an external threat, but is provocative and the cause of an arms race. He responds to warnings about a Soviet threat with stiff and strident protests against jingoism and, invariably, with that lead letter in the *New York Times* explaining the Soviet point of view. He reminds the alarmist of America's own sins and chides him for indifference. On the domestic

12. Eugene Rostow, "The Safety of the Republic," *Strategic Review*, Spring 1976.

scene he champions the failures as victims of society, and he explains the successful in terms of ill-gotten gains.

Commentators and political leaders who try to focus on American achievements and successes run afoul of the denunciatory ethic, which demands ever more corrections of past wrongs. A leader who adopts an affirmatory stance toward the nation provokes skepticism and indignation. Compare, for example, the morally indignant response from "informed opinion" to Ronald Reagan's statement that our purpose in Vietnam was noble with the approval granted critics who called the United States immoral. Politicians and opinion leaders learn that the way to avoid being criticized for being dangerously patriotic and unconcerned is to be constantly leading campaigns against American shortcomings—thus the denunciatory ethic.

Adversaries of the United States are spared the searing criticism that is applied to our own country. To denounce opponents is regarded as "cultural imperialism." Even worse, it would be using an external bogy to focus our attention away from our own shortcomings. That is why President Carter, in the midst of a serious crisis with revolutionary Iran over the hostages, felt it necessary to declare that "we won't abandon our struggle for a decent and fair society here at home." With our moral outrage momentarily directed toward Iran, we were starting to feel good about ourselves and to pull together. To preempt the inevitable accusations that he was leading a jingoistic campaign, Carter had to reaffirm that, the Iranians' bad behavior notwithstanding, we were not decent and fair either.

Patriotism has come to imply a lack of objectivity, whereas "anti-American" has taken on certain positive connotations. At times the designation is almost a badge of honor. To be anti-American is to be against imperialism, neocolonialism, racism, sexism, commercial exploitation (particularly of the environment and the Third World), pollution, poverty, inequality, and war. In short, anti-American implies broadmindedness, a person who can transcend the anachronism of narrow national interest to represent the world, humanity, and history's best impulses. Unlike patriots, anti-Americans seem to have the quality of objectivity because they can apply skepticism to their own country, without restraint, without holding something back for the good of their country.

Judging from the 1980 election, the mass of the people decided that an overemphasis on the negative had led the country into decline, and they chose as President a man whose emphasis is that America is good. Ronald Reagan's attitude toward America cuts across the grain of the denunciatory ethic. Perhaps the "America is wrong" theme has played out, but just as likely real change will require a reorientation of our intellectual frame of mind.

9

Principle versus Pragmatism in Economic Policy

THE EFFORT TO MAKE THE BUDGET DEFICIT THE FOCUS OF economic policy not only deflected attention from the failure of monetary policy and endangered the President's tax program, but also had adverse consequences for other important policy areas. In the case of social security, the opportunity to address the long-run problem was sacrificed to a shortsighted effort to balance the near-term budget. In the case of the world debt crisis precipitated by the rapid deceleration of inflation, it led to United States acceptance of the International Monetary Fund as an aid-giving agency.

Problems that are not confronted impose their own costly solutions. By evading a principled approach to problems, policymakers imbue them with a power of their own to build failure into the economy. The "pragmatic" responses to social security and international debt are two important cases in point.

The Social Security Crisis

Shortly after the inauguration, the Reagan Administration faced a crisis in social security despite the 1977 amendments that President Carter promised would make social security sound through the turn of the century. The largest of the system's three programs, Old Age and Survivors Insurance (OASI), was likely to run out of money during Reagan's term of office unless economic growth was robust. Even with the scheduled payroll tax-rate increases in 1981 and 1982, the combined assets of the Old Age, Survivors, Disability, and Hospital Insurance (OASDHI) trust funds might not have allowed the system to escape the cash-flow problem until scheduled tax-rate increases in 1985, 1986, and 1990 could take place. Moreover, these tax increases would only restore annual surpluses to the system for a decade or two before the system's fundamental imbalance reasserted itself. The long-term prospects of the system included large perpetual deficits and were dismal indeed.

Obviously, any changes to the social security system were going to be politically sensitive, even those designed to cover a temporary financing problem. Nonetheless, the short-term crisis was an opportunity to reexamine the system as a whole. The administration had available a wealth of scholarly research from the academic community on what needed to be done to reform the system and a number of talented people who were familiar both with that research and with the system's operations. Most important, we had a President who had often expressed concern about the consequences for private savings, economic growth, and job creation of an ever-expanding social security system. We could have done a thoroughly professional job of reforming social security and promoting economic growth for generations to come.

Instead, the opportunity was lost in a mad scramble for budget savings for fiscal years 1982–1984, with no thought to the long-term requirements. In their frantic effort to reduce the overall federal budget deficit with short-run surpluses in OASDI, the President's senior advisers presented him with his first major political and legislative embarrassment, which caused the President to lose control of the problem and led to the creation of the National Commission on Social Security Reform. The commission, in turn, led to a deplorable piece of legislation that violates most of the major goals of the President, and will do considerable economic and political damage.

The 1972 Amendments

There are two major areas of social security that involve indexes. The most familiar index is the annual cost-of-living increase, which occurred each July 1 until the 1983 Social Security Amendments moved the date to January 1. This adjustment increases benefits going to current retirees by the amount of inflation each year, as measured by the consumer price index. Thus, whatever benefit people receive upon first retiring is preserved in real terms and protected from inflation. This cost-of-living adjustment is often blamed for the deficits in the social security accounts and the overall federal budget, but it is not the real culprit.

The other area of indexing is the real source of the system's long-run troubles. When people retire, the amount of their first social security check, or initial benefit, is computed by a formula that involves wage indexes. These indexes cause the real value of each retiring generation's initial benefits to rise over time. The cost-of-living adjustment merely preserves the real value of these benefits over the individual's retirement period. It is the buildup of the real levels of the initial benefits, generation after generation, that is leading to the system's ruin.

Prior to the 1972 amendments, Congress had raised social security benefits over the years on an *ad hoc* basis. However, a 15 percent benefit increase in 1970, a 10 percent benefit increase in 1971, and a 20 percent increase in 1972 represented quantum jumps in benefit levels. These were reinforced by the 1972 Social Security Amendments, which were supposed to preserve these increases with automatic inflation adjustments each year beginning in 1975.

Unfortunately, the 1972 amendments contained a major formula error, which has become known as the "double indexing" or "decoupling" problem. It resulted in sharp increases in benefits for new retirees just entering the system and caused benefits to rise faster than wages. An average worker retiring in 1969 could expect to receive a tax-exempt social security benefit equal to 31 percent of the last working year's income. By 1972, *ad hoc* increases by Congress raised this so-called replacement rate to 38 percent. As a result of the automatic adjustments in the 1972 amendments, it rose to 41 percent in 1974, 44 percent in 1976, and 55 percent in 1981.

The source of the problem was fairly straightforward. The initial social security benefit a worker received upon retiring was computed in two steps. First, the worker's wages from 1951 until the date of retirement were added up and averaged over the number of months worked in order to determine an average monthly wage. This wage, split into several brackets, was then multiplied by an array of percentages called the "marginal benefit rates," which were set by law. The product was the worker's initial social security check. For example, if the benefit rates averaged 0.40, then the worker's first retirement check would equal 40 percent of his or her average wage. The 1972 amendments provided for the annual adjustment of the marginal benefit rates for each year's population of retirees by the amount of inflation over the year. If inflation had been 10 percent and the old benefit rates had averaged 0.40, the new benefit rates would average 0.44. Unfortunately, complete adjustment of the benefit rates for inflation overadjusted benefits. Over time, wages tend to rise with inflation. While wages earned in the distant past were, of course, not adjusted for recent inflation, wages earned in the years immediately preceding retirement would have been largely adjusted for inflation. Consequently, one part of the benefit computation, the average monthly wage, was already partially adjusted for inflation by the marketplace.

The correct way to increase the product of two numbers by, for example, 10 percent is to increase one number or the other number by 10 percent, but not both. By adjusting the benefit rates completely when the average monthly wage had already received partial adjustment for inflation, the formula made the resulting benefit grow faster than inflation.

We will probably never know the origin of the error. Perhaps it was because of carelessness by the Social Security Administration (SSA) staff or confusion over the correct way to index the product of two numbers. On the other hand, the staff of the Office of the Actuary has limited economic expertise. Perhaps they were unaware that wages are generally adjusted for inflation in the private sector, and that fully indexing the replacement percentage as well would overindex benefits. Alternatively, the actuaries may have assumed that inflation would be too low to make much difference. Possibly, the paternalistic SSA bureaucracy saw an opportunity to make benefits more generous and to make social security a larger factor relative to private pensions and personal saving in the provision of retirement income. In any event, the congressional staffs that worked on the legislation either failed to catch the error in the SSA proposal or went along with it for their own reasons.

The 1977 Amendments

By 1975, it was obvious that corrective measures would have to be taken. Projected benefits were outstripping tax revenues and would soon exhaust the social security trust funds. Two major panels looked into the matter. One was the Quadrennial Advisory Council on Social Security, convened in 1974, which issued a report in March 1975. The other was the distinguished panel headed by Professor William C. Hsiao of Harvard, which prepared the *Report of the Consultant Panel on Social Security to the Congressional Research Service for the Use of the Committee on Finance of the U.S. Senate and the Committee on Ways and Means of the U.S. House of Representatives* (94th Congress, August 1976).

There are two major views of the role of social security. One view is that social security's role is to provide a basic floor of retirement income to forestall poverty and promote financial independence of the elderly. Benefits should thus be at an adequate real level, providing a decent minimum amount of purchasing power. However, retirement income in excess of some basic level would be the responsibility of individuals, who would be expected to save over their working lives either as individuals or through a private pension plan. This was the original intent of the system. Others view social security as a pension system—indeed, the nation's main pension system—with benefits rising in real terms. Which of these two views is chosen is far more than a philosophical decision. It makes a great deal of difference in terms of cost and impact on the economy.

The two panels diverged in their views of what the system should become over time. The Advisory Council's view carried the day, and the 1977 amendments followed the concept of social security as an ever-expanding pension system. This was a major mistake, setting the system on an unaffordable path and guaranteeing repeated crises.

People retiring in the years ahead, particularly after the year 2000, are scheduled to receive substantially higher benefits in real terms than people who retired in earlier years. This does not mean that the system will be a good thing for today's young workers, however. Benefits will rise, but tax rates will rise even faster. In addition, the high tax rates will make contributions to personal saving and private pensions difficult, if not impossible. Many Americans will be denied the prospect of financial independence, which has ominous implications for economic growth.

Private savings are needed to generate private capital for investment, which in turn leads to economic growth. Retirees under fully funded private pensions receive a share of the added GNP that their savings have created. Because their savings caused GNP to rise, retirees are only taking back what they have created. They do not take a portion of the output or reduce the living standards of current workers.

Social security, on the other hand, is not a pension or a form of national saving. To call it a saving or pension plan is a major conceptual error. Social security is an unfunded system of taxes and transfer payments. Taxes paid by current workers are used to finance the benefits paid out to current beneficiaries. No capital formation or added GNP results. Current beneficiaries take a share of the production and reduce the income of current workers.

As social security grows at the expense of private saving, the nation does less investing and economic growth suffers. Lower economic growth reduces wages and employment, further reducing the income of current workers and thereby lowering the revenues of the social security system. This requires higher tax rates to finance social security benefits. A higher tax burden further stifles the economy, and so on, in a vicious circle. Practically speaking, social security as currently designed is unaffordable.

In the 1977 amendments, a new benefit formula was instituted that partially corrected the error in the 1972 formula. The new formula lowered replacement rates immediately on the order of 5 to 10 percent depending on a worker's lifetime earnings. Further adjustments were made to place the 1985 and later replacement rates for the average worker at about 42 percent. This partially rolled back the replacement rate from 55 percent under the 1972 amendments.

In addition, the automatic adjustment mechanism was overhauled to prevent the initial social security benefits from rising faster than wages. A method of indexing was selected that allows the initial benefit to rise along with wages, replacing the same percent of pre-retirement income for successive retiring generations. In other words, the benefits of workers in some future year, say 2025, will be the same percentage of earnings and the standard of living in 2025 as 1982 benefits are of 1982 earnings. This replaced the 1972 formula, under which the initial benefits of each new group of retirees grew faster than wages and rose as a percent of pre-retirement income. But it was still not enough of a correction to forestall huge long-run deficits.

The 1977 amendments also provided for increases in payroll tax rates for all three trust funds over the next thirteen years, with increases in 1981, 1982, 1985, 1986, and 1990. The cuts in the initial benefits for retirees and the five tax-rate increases were supposed to keep the system sound until the postwar baby boom retired after the turn of the century.

There were two problems with this solution, one in the short run, one in the long run. In the short run, the economy performed poorly between 1977 and 1980 in terms of inflation and wages. Inflation was very high, driving up social security payments as retirees received cost-of-living increases on their benefits. Wages failed to keep up with inflation, which meant that payroll taxes failed to keep up with benefit payments. The two recessions in 1980 and 1981–82 also hurt by increasing unemployment and reducing the social security tax base, driving down revenues (although in 1982 wages did start running ahead of inflation). By 1980, it appeared that near-term deficits would exhaust the OASI trust fund by 1983. After the 1985 tax increase, there would be annual surpluses for a period of time, letting the trust funds build up again. Some way had to be found to bridge the gap between 1982 and 1985.

In the long run, there is a far greater problem involving the health of the system starting in the 1990s. It was caused by the decision to let the initial benefit of each new retiring generation keep pace with real wages over time. While less rapid than the benefit growth in the 1972 formula, this is still much too fast for the economy to handle. The system faces perpetual deficits of huge proportions.

The modifications made in 1977 left the system on a path of expansion which will carry outlays significantly beyond currently scheduled tax rates. Under the economic assumptions (Alternative II-B) in the 1982 *Trustees Report,* OASDI benefits were scheduled to rise as a percent of payroll from between 10 percent and 12 percent near-term to between 17 percent and 18 percent long-term. This compares with a scheduled OASDI long-term tax rate of 12.4 percent of payroll after 1990. After a few years of surplus, beginning in the 1990s, a deficit was projected shortly after the year 2010, widening to a permanent gap of roughly 5 percent of payroll between out-lays and receipts in OASDI after the year 2025.

Adding in hospital insurance makes the deficit worse. The combined OASDHI outlays are projected to rise as a percent of payroll from 15 percent near-term to between 27 percent and 30 percent long-term. This compared with the scheduled OASDHI long-term tax rate of 15.3 percent after 1990. A deficit appeared shortly after 1995, widening to a permanent gap of roughly 12 to 15 percent of payroll between outlays and receipts in OASDHI after the year 2025. This translated into an annual deficit in excess of $300 billion by 2025 and in excess of $600 billion by 2060, measured in real 1983 dollars.

The source of the long-run deficits is twofold. First, as the population grows more slowly over time, the population ages and there are more retirees per worker. Second, the indexing formula allows initial benefits to grow indefinitely in real terms at the same pace as wages. With real benefits per retiree rising along with real wages, but with the number of retirees rising faster than the number of wage earners, the cost of the system must rise as a portion of payroll. Consequently, either payroll tax rates must rise sharply, taking more out of each dollar of wages, or the growth of real benefit levels must be reexamined.

The social security system is in crisis because it is scheduled to pay rising real benefits to successive generations. One way to deal with the problem is to reduce the scheduled rise in benefits. A switch from wage indexing (under which real benefits per retiree would triple in three generations) to price indexing (under which real benefits per retiree would roughly double) would essentially eliminate the long-run OASDI problem.

Price indexing was recommended in the 1976 Hsiao report. The Finance Committee under Senator Long was receptive to the proposal. The Treasury, led by Secretary William Simon, was also eager to take the more responsible course. But an election was approaching. President Ford, at the apparent urging of his political advisers and with the apparent blessing of his chairman of economic advisers, Alan Greenspan, wished to appear more generous. Ford opted for the much more expensive wage-indexing procedure. *This single mistake added well over $2 trillion in unfunded liability in pres-*

ent value terms to the system's long-run deficit. It accounts for over 100
percent of OASDI's deficit.[1]

Treasury's Strategy

In early 1981 the Treasury's Office of Economic Policy, which monitors social security policy for the secretary, had two major concerns: (1) to find a solution that provided a genuine correction of the system's long-term imbalance and was fair to all parties, in the sense of providing adequate warning to current workers that future benefits would have to grow more slowly than promised in existing law; and (2) to solve the short-run financing problem without jeopardizing the prospects for employment and support for the administration's supply-side tax cuts.

The long-run concerns implied a very gradual reduction in the growth of future benefits, along the lines of the Hsiao panel recommendations, and the raising of the retirement age to sixty-eight slowly over twenty to thirty years. This would give current workers time to set aside additional personal savings to offset the benefit reductions. Those closest to retirement would be largely unaffected by the cuts. Those farthest from retirement would have the largest benefit reductions, but also more time to accumulate additional savings to make up the difference.

The short-run economic concerns implied a set of benefit cuts, rather than job-destroying tax increases. Politically it was important that the corrective actions be just large enough to cover the system's needs in order not to give the appearance of paying for the tax cuts by reducing social security benefits.

In February 1981, an interagency working group was formed to develop a social security proposal for the Reagan Administration. The Department of Health and Human Services was the lead agency. The project was under the direction of Undersecretary David Swoap, assisted by the commissioner of social security, Jack Svahn, and the deputy commissioner, Robert Myers, the former

---

1. "Ford Republicans" have lambasted supply-siders for allegedly ignoring the impact of tax cuts on the long-run budget deficit. Even if the logic of their argument were correct, in view of the budgetary implications of the Ford social security decisions, it is a case of the pot calling the kettle black.

chief actuary of social security who had come out of retirement to serve in the administration. Treasury was represented by economists from the Office of Economic Policy. Other agencies, including CEA, OMB, and the Department of Labor, were part of the group.

During the last week of February and the first week of March, three meetings were held. Ideally, they should have been a forum for a fundamental review of social security, not merely a discussion of the current state of the system and how to patch it up. The long-term condition of social security, including a review of the system's basic purposes and its place in the administration's vision of a growing private-sector economy, needed to be considered.

Instead, the meetings were devoted to the study of a draft proposal already drawn up by SSA and HHS. The proposal addressed the near-term shortfall by eliminating or reducing several dozen so-called welfare elements from the system. These are miscellaneous special benefits that have been added over time, and that are available to select subgroups of the population without a commensurate increase in taxes paid to the system. Some of these benefits had the characteristics of "extra coverage," which in a private-sector insurance program would have cost an extra premium (as a family health plan does compared to an individual policy), and included such items as benefits paid to the dependent spouse or children of a retired worker. Most of the SSA-HHS proposals pared away at the periphery of the system. Most involved small savings and obscure provisions that were difficult to describe and unfamiliar to many people. Widows, orphans, and the disabled seemed to be the people affected.

This approach left the central core of the system, which was piling up trillions of dollars in unfunded liabilities, largely untouched. Treasury brought up three points. First, the need to avoid overkill and the appearance of insensitivity in the short-run proposals. Second, the need for a solution to the long-run problem for which the short-run proposals were inadequate. Third, the need to restore the original purpose of social security by changing it from an ever-growing program to a basic retirement income floor. This was essential to prevent extraordinarily high payroll taxes and their adverse impact on employment, saving, and economic growth. These ideas were well received by representatives of the Labor Depart-

ment, CEA, and OMB. Unfortunately, they were vigorously opposed by Deputy Commissioner Robert Myers.

Myers declared that the question of the role of social security had
been decided by the 1975 Advisory Council, on which he had
served. Social security was to be the nation's primary pension plan,
providing more retirement income than private saving, and that was
that. Treasury responded that the Reagan Administration in 1981
was not bound by the flawed decisions of a 1975 Advisory Council,
but Myers remained adamant. He rejected any reopening of the
choice of wage indexing over price indexing, coming down squarely
for the "dominant pension" concept of social security. He claimed
that the projected social security tax rates (of 27 to 30 percent)
would not be impossible to achieve because they would be reached
by ratcheting the rates up gradually, every few years as deficits
reappeared, so that no one would notice. If he meant that the economy would be unaffected by high employment taxes as long as they
were built up gradually, he was wrong. It was more likely, however,
that the deputy commissioner did not consider the economic effects
and simply meant that the public could be persuaded to accept enormous tax increases if they were enacted slowly over many years as
the system went through repeated crises.

Myers also declared, repeatedly, that any steps taken to resolve
the short-term financing problem would also balance the system in
the future. This statement was disturbing. In SSA jargon there is a
peculiar concept of system balance in which Myers' statement was
correct. Unfortunately, the SSA definition of balance serves to hide
a long-term imbalance.

Here is where one of the most misleading of SSA statistics comes
into play. It is called the "actuarial balance" of the OASDI system
(HI is generally excluded). SSA reports on the condition of the
OASDI trust funds over a seventy-five-year planning period. It says
the system is in actuarial balance if the average income of the system
measured as a percent of payroll equals the average cost of benefits
measured as a percent of payroll over seventy-five years. In 1982,
the OASDI system was reported to have a deficit of 1.8 percent
of payroll. In other words, the system needed a tax rate 1.8 percent of payroll higher on average over seventy-five years than scheduled in the law to match promised benefits. This "average" gives the

impression that raising tax rates or cutting benefits by 1.8 percent of payroll would make the system financially sound. This was the theory that guided the recent National Commission. But nothing could be further from the truth.

The year-by-year surpluses and deficits in the system are not uniformly spread over the seventy-five-year planning period. Nor are projected receipts in line with projected outlays decade by decade. Instead, the surplus years all fall roughly between 1990 and 2010, with widening deficits thereafter. SSA was relying on the build-up of a large trust fund between 1990 and 2010, which would be drawn down after 2010 to cover the long-term deficit until the money ran out between 2030 and 2040. What was the system to do then, when it would suddenly face annual outlays 5 or 6 percent higher than annual receipts with no trust fund to pay the difference?

In fact, the OASDI surpluses would either be spent by Congress or would have to be borrowed to finance HI deficits in the 1990s, and the whole OASDHI system would be bankrupt by about 2015. It would then face ongoing annual deficits of 12 to 15 percent of payroll under assumptions II-B in the 1982 *Trustees' Report*. (The 1983 social security legislation did not significantly alter these prospects, particularly if the Census Bureau's new lower fertility and population estimates are employed in the calculations.)

With or without HI, the seventy-five-year average is camouflage for a deteriorating system. Only if the system is brought roughly into balance on a year-to-year basis can it be permanently fixed. This means either slowing the growth rate of real benefits and raising hospital insurance premiums and deductibles for future retirees, so that benefits only rise to 15 percent of payroll (the currently scheduled 1990 tax rate), or roughly doubling the payroll tax to match the growth of benefits.

This fundamental imbalance in the system is largely hidden by the seventy-five-year summary statistic. A seventy-five-year average moves very slowly from one year to the next. Nonetheless, in each year that goes by, the summary statistic decays a bit. As the planning period shifts forward, a year of near-term surplus goes by and a year of long-term deficit is added. For example, in 1985, the planning period will run from 1985 to 2060. The year 1985 will show a surplus, 2060 a deficit. In 1986, the planning period will be 1986 to

2061. Ths surplus year 1985 will fall out of the average, and the deficit year 2061 will be rolled in. The result is a deterioration in the system's "balance."

Every year in the *Trustees' Report,* SSA gives a list of reasons for any change in the summary statistic. These reasons include changes in economic assumptions, fertility assumptions, and so on. One that appears every year is "change in valuation period." This is the admission that the seventy-five-year average is not stable. It is a moving average that was headed toward a basic deficit of 5 or 6 percent of payroll for OASDI and 12 to 15 percent of payroll for OASDHI. The summary statistic is a misleading measure of the condition of the system. The tables showing the annual deficits and the pattern that is emerging over time provide the only meaningful view of the system.

Bringing forward already scheduled payroll tax increases, as was done in the 1983 social security bill, reduces the system's long-run deficit as measured by the summary statistic. But such steps do nothing to improve the system's real balance over time. The HHS proposals of May 12, 1981, affected both short-run and long-run benefits. However, they did not affect long-run deficits nearly enough to make the system sound.

As long as the summary statistic is used as a guide to policy, there will be periodic crises in the system. Each time the trust funds start to run out, the summary statistic will be "balanced" by measures that generate short-run surpluses but leave long-run deficits. Near-term benefits will be cut very little, since it is unfair to cut benefits without adequate warning and current retirees are heavy voters. The payroll tax will rise, and with the system again in balance, why do anything to bring long-run benefit growth under control? So nothing is done until the next crisis, when it is again too late to touch benefits. The summary statistic is an ingenious device for hiding the system's long-term imbalance. It protects from scrutiny the formulas that generate the perpetual expansion of the core of social security—the old age, survivors, and disability insurance systems. It permits the occurrence of periodic crises in which Congress is stampeded into hiking payroll taxes for want of any other politically palatable option.

When it became clear that the SSA–HHS representatives were

unwilling to divert their attention from the welfare elements to the long-run problem, a private meeting was arranged between Treasury, CEA, and HHS officials. William Niskanen (CEA) and Steve Entin (Treasury) explained to Undersecretary Swoap and Commissioner Svahn the difference between wage and price indexing and the misleading nature of the seventy-five-year summary statistic. They explained that unless the system's indexes were changed, social security taxes would eventually reach 27 to 30 percent of payroll, with adverse impacts on the economy. The meeting was a failure. HHS called no meetings of the working group for more than a month. Finally, in mid-April, another meeting was held. Its purpose was to approve a set of SSA–HHS proposals to be passed forward for high-level, and ultimately presidential, review. This finished product was little changed from the earlier HHS proposals.

The SSA–HHS proposals still sought to raise more money than was needed to get social security over its immediate crisis. To cover up that fact, a very gloomy economic forecast was put forward to make the near-term shortfall appear even larger. The forecast assumed three more years of rapid inflation and falling real wages, followed by virtually no recovery for the rest of the decade—a virtual depression. This was far worse than even the subsequent reality of the 1981–82 recession, which was one of the most severe in postwar experience. At the time, the forecast was truly outlandish. The economy had just experienced a surge of real growth at a 7.9 percent annual rate, and the Federal Reserve's monetary squeeze still lay in the future.

I was concerned about the situation. The administration was about to introduce a social security proposal that did more than necessary to handle the system's short-term needs but left the long-run problem intact. In addition, the HHS forecast gave the impression that the economy was likely to undergo the worst depression since 1929–1932, despite the administration's economic program. It looked as if we had no faith in our economic program and that we wanted to pay for the tax cuts by cutting social security.

A bad situation was about to get even worse. In late April, the revised SSA–HHS proposals were presented to a group of higher-level political appointees, including the Cabinet Council for Human Resources, the White House domestic policy group, and Budget

Director Stockman. One of the proposals considered at the meeting was a reduction in early retirement benefits. Prior law provided that those retiring at age sixty-two would receive 80 percent of full retirement benefits. HHS wanted to reduce this percentage to either 70 percent or 75 percent, beginning with those retiring in January 1982.

Treasury objected. The change was to take place in only nine months. It would allow people sixty or sixty-one years of age who were planning to retire at sixty-two very little time to build up savings to replace the $500 to $800 per year in lost benefits. They would need to set aside an additional $7,000 to $12,000 in savings to earn enough taxable interest to make up for the reduced benefits. Treasury was also concerned that some people, especially the partially disabled, may have retired in 1980 or 1981 at age sixty or sixty-one on their own savings, in anticipation of a certain level of social security benefits to be received beginning in 1982 or 1983. Those who had, and those who had served notice to their employers or sold their business interests, could not suddenly change their plans or reenter the labor force. This provision gave inadequate warning to those about to retire and was retroactive for an unknown number of early retirees. It was a clear violation of one of the fairness tests—adequate warning—that Treasury was trying to apply to the proposals.

Stockman, however, was determined to increase the budget savings obtained from the package. He argued that there were few hardship cases such as Treasury described and proposed cutting the early retirement benefit even more deeply—to 55 percent of full retirement levels. Treasury asked if figures were available showing the number of people affected by this and several other provisions likely to produce a political maelstrom. Incredibly, SSA had done no impact studies. Treasury then suggested that presentation of the package be delayed until such figures were available and expressed concern that a politically insensitive approach to social security would harm the prospects for the President's economic program.

Stockman replied that there would be no chance of passing the tax cuts unless he could find additional budget cuts. He and the HHS staff argued that there was a unique "window of opportunity" available if we moved fast. Representative J. J. Pickle, chairman of the Social Security Subcommittee of the Ways and Means Committee, was supposed to be eagerly awaiting White House leadership in presenting what could become a bipartisan social security reform package. If we did not hurry, Pickle would proceed with his own plan, which would undoubtedly save less money. (Treasury's Office of Legislative Affairs was unable to corroborate this "window" theory.)

So it went through other provisions. Treasury's suggestion for solving the long-term problem by slowing the growth of initial benefits gradually over many years by price-indexing the benefit formula was rejected. Instead, Stockman urged a seven-year partial freeze by cutting the annual adjustment to the initial benefit formula in half. Stockman's proposal would save more money in the short-run if it could survive the political uproar.

The only thing Treasury took away from that meeting was an SSA pledge to do impact studies on the various provisions as quickly as possible, but they were never delivered. The $110 billion package met the satisfaction of a three-way coalition: Stockman, who wanted large outlay cuts in the near-term; the HHS political hierarchy, which wanted to squeeze the "welfare elements" out of the system; and the SSA bureaucracy, which wanted to preserve the basic core of the system as an ever-growing national pension plan that could eventually crowd out private pension plans.

The package was a political disaster in the making. When Secretary Regan and Undersecretary Ture were briefed, two problems were pointed out: first, the obvious effort to cut back social security in order to improve the short-run budget picture; and second, the presence of insensitive provisions, particularly the sharp and sudden drop in early retirement benefits. Regan decided to minimize his involvement and sent Ture as Treasury's representative when the package was presented to the President.

Ture remembers the briefing with the President as "entertaining." The two-hour briefing began with a series of charts listing certain principles, for example, welfare elements were to be cut and use of general revenues was to be avoided. Then three or four dozen options for cutting system benefits were presented, grouped together to provide small, medium, or large packages. Swoap presented the list of proposed cuts along with brief descriptions of how they operated. This was the list it had taken the working group two weeks to understand. Related items were stated technically, then glossed over to save time: for example, "This is just another technical adjustment in an overly-generous dependent's provision, Mr. President." By the time the briefing had dragged on to cutting early retirement benefits, that sensitive provision blended in with the rest. Having been overruled in the working group meetings, Treasury raised few objections during the Roosevelt Room presentation.

The next item of controversy was over inclusion of federal workers in social security. This would have brought more revenue into social security in the short term but would have enlarged the system's outlays in the long term, for a net increase in the long-run deficit. The President cut through the arguments very forcefully. He stated simply and cogently that a larger system was not desirable. Social security takes money from one group and gives to another. Nothing is saved. If you leave people their own money, they can save it and help the country grow. The President expressed the hope that private saving could somehow be encouraged as an alternative to an ever-expanding social security system.

The President also wanted to see an end to the earnings limitation. Current law restricts the amount of wage and salary income a beneficiary can earn and still receive full benefits. Every $2 in excess earnings over the limit results in a drop in benefits of $1, effectively imposing a 50 percent tax rate on wage income of the elderly in addition to ordinary income and payroll taxes.

At the end of the whirlwind briefing, the President was pressed for an immediate decision on submitting the package to Congress. HHS and OMB stressed the "window of opportunity" that would enable them to work with Representative Pickle if a speedy decision were made. In fact, they wanted to send the package to Capitol Hill the next day, May 12. The President gave no immediate assent. He replied pointedly that he guessed he had the rest of the afternoon to think it over. But by the end of the day he did agree; no other option had been presented.

The package of proposals was not sent formally to the Hill the next day. But aides anxious to get it moving quickly shared its contents with key congressional staffs, several national newspapers, and the world at large. The result was an uproar that made it unnecessary to send the package anywhere. House Speaker O'Neill let drop like a guillotine blade the window of opportunity that Representative Pickle had enticed the administration to stick its head through. The ire of the Democrats (really their great pleasure at being handed the first issue with which to stop the Reagan bandwagon) was aroused by the two features of the package that Treasury had warned against.

First, the administration was accused of trying to pay for the tax cuts at social security's expense. The House Select Committee on Aging, chaired by Claude Pepper, released a somewhat optimistic report saying that the May 12 package of $110 billion would save twice as much money as was needed to keep social security solvent for seventy-five years. Pepper said, "It would appear that the new administration is using Social Security's short-term problems for its own longer-term social and fiscal purposes, to shrink the government and balance the budget." Second, the sudden cut in early retirement benefits was sharply criticized. O'Neill said, "cutting benefits for those who retire at age 62 is a sneak attack on Social Security." Senate Minority Leader Byrd called the proposals "precipitous, harsh, and very unfair."

By May 20, the Republican majority in the Senate had joined with the Democrats to pass a "sense of Congress" resolution, introduced by Senator Dole, chairman of the Finance Committee. It declared: "Congress shall not precipitously and unfairly penalize early retirees" and "will not support reductions in benefits which exceed those necessary to achieve a financially sound system." The vote was 96–0.

The total humiliation of the 96–0 vote cost the administration's economic program all of its momentum on the Hill. It took a major effort to get things going again. Far from assisting in the battle to lower tax rates and restore growth to the economy, the May 12 package almost lost the war. It certainly lost the President much public support and contributed to the Republicans' losses in the 1982 election. By asking for too much too soon in an effort to reduce the projected deficit, the administration got nothing at all. Instead of achieving moderate savings in 1982 and 1983 which would begin to strengthen the trust funds early, helping to clear the 1984 and 1985 financing hurdle, the administration got nothing. Nearly two years were lost between the May 12 package and the 1983 social security amendments that ultimately became law. By delaying the solution until 1983, far more drastic steps had to be taken to clear the short-run hurdle.

The White House staff tried desperately to stem the damage from the May 12 debacle. The solution was to shift the problem to a bipartisan panel, as had been done in previous system crises. This helped to disperse the heavy political heat that would now accompany any attempt to deal with the social security problem. It also dispersed control over the proposals, practically ensuring that they would be more damaging to the economy than necessary and at odds with the President's goals. Thus was born the National Commission on Social Security Reform in December 1981.

The National Commission

The fifteen-member commission was selected in equal parts by the White House, the Senate, and the House of Representatives. The White House selected the chairman. With little research or consultation, Alan Greenspan was chosen. Greenspan in turn chose Robert Myers, who had recently resigned as deputy commissioner, to be executive director of the commission staff.

These personnel choices were curious. Greenspan was too troubled by the federal budget deficit to be a friend of the administration's program to lower tax rates on American labor. Furthermore, he had participated in the Ford Administration's unfortunate choice of the wrong indexing formulas in 1975, which had been recommended enthusiastically by Myers. There would obviously be no voluntary consideration of the Hsiao report by the new commission, no genuine long-term remedy, and no aversion to raising payroll taxes.

The new commission's first major decision was to limit itself to consideration of OASDI. HI was left for another panel at a later date. This was a mistake. The deficits of HI will become very large in the 1990s and enormous after the turn of the century. To bring the entire system into balance over time, it is essential that major long-run savings be achieved in OASDI so that a portion of the tax rates pledged to those two programs can be reallocated to HI. Merely bringing OASDI into line still leaves the OASDHI combined system in deep deficit. Had HI been included in the commission's purview, it would have forced a reexamination of the whole system and a major reworking of the indexes and retirement ages.

Hopes were raised at the Treasury when Martin Feldstein became chairman of the Council of Economic Advisers in the fall of 1982. Social security had been one of his areas of interest at the National Bureau of Economic Research. Feldstein was noted for his view that social security was reducing saving and would retard long-run growth. It was thought that his viewpoint would help to bring a larger perspective to the social security debate.

Soon after his arrival, Feldstein was briefed by Treasury staff on the status of the system and the commission's lack of interest in a long-run solution. Treasury suggested a shift to price indexing to slow the growth of future benefits and tax rates over time. He recognized this proposal as the Hsiao report and agreed that it deserved another look. But Feldstein's chief concerns turned out to be elsewhere. He was worried that the near-term deficits in the President's budget would crowd out private investment. He wanted to do what the Democrats had accused the administration of doing: curb the level of current social security benefits in order to reduce the overall federal budget deficit. His approach was to complete the rollback of the sharp rise in initial benefits and replacement rates following the 1972 amendments. Feldstein had been on the consultant panel of the 1975 Advisory Council formed to correct the error in the 1972 amendments. Apparently this episode made a strong impression on him because he was still trying to correct the 1972 error. He had less interest in correcting the wage-indexing mistake that was introduced by the 1975 council on the advice of its consultant panel and that became law in the 1977 amendments.

Feldstein's proposal was politically damaging not only on the social security front but also to the President's tax program. He proposed to limit social security cost-of-living increases to the rate of inflation less 3 percent. Over five years this would reduce real benefits by 15 percent. Treasury thought it unlikely that Congress would agree to such a sharp cutback in current benefits and forgo the opportunity to criticize the President for proposing it. Feldstein tried to promote his idea by proposing to balance it by cutting back on the personal income tax cuts. He proposed to limit the indexing of the income tax to the same formula of inflation minus 3 percent. This was a peculiar position for a self-styled supporter of tax indexing. At 3 or 4 percent inflation it was virtual repeal of indexing.

From the point of view of the public, this was not "balance." Social security recipients are not a distinct group from those who pay income tax. For the elderly, it meant that not only would their social security payments fall in real value, but the tax bite on their other retirement income and earnings would rise as well. They would be hit twice. Workers already facing higher payroll taxes and reduced social security benefits in the future would be hit again by bracket creep. The proposal undercut the President and reduced the administration's confidence in Feldstein's judgment in the social security area. As a result, his expertise never came to bear on the larger problem.

The exclusion of HI from consideration was a convenience to those who wanted to confine the commission's attention to the near-term shortfall of the system. SSA has always regarded HI as a threatening addition to the OASDI program. By hiding the severity of the long-term deficit, the exclusion of HI forestalled a strong challenge to the formulas that are pushing the system into becoming the nation's dominant and unaffordable pension plan. It also helped those who wanted to shift HI financing from the payroll tax to general revenues. With no reduction in the growth of long-term OASDI benefits, HI funding will have to come from general revenues.

Even with a big part of the problem swept under the rug, the commission made no progress through October, having used up most of its monthly meetings from February through October working through a blizzard of memos from Myers. In November, with its December deadline approaching, the commission finally made its second major decision. It declared that the OASDI system needed to close a deficit of between $150 billion and $200 billion over the 1982–1989 period. This estimate was based on the gloomiest of the economic scenarios, Alternative III, contained in the 1982 *Trustees' Report*. The scenario was badly out of date. It was a high inflation scenario, but inflation had fallen sharply since its publication. It was a scenario that predicted another year of slow real growth with another two years of falling real wages (which would reduce system receipts relative to outlays); yet the leading economic indicators and real wages were already turning up. It was also a scenario based on old demographic assumptions, which needed to be changed after the midsummer release by the Census Bureau of new fertility data derived from the 1980 census.

But by December both the commission chairman and the White House senior staff were panicked over the continuing deadlock in the commission. Conservatives were opposed to higher payroll tax rates, and liberals were adamantly against reducing the growth in benefits. It was clear that the commission would not have a solution by its December 31 deadline.

Alan Greenspan, Jim Baker, and his aide Richard Darman began a press campaign to bring the President and Tip O'Neill into the process. The first step was to convince the President that a compromise was possible if the commission were given an extension on its deadline. This was done. The second step was for Baker and Darman to sit down with Greenspan and the liberals on the commission to work out a deal. SSA, CEA, and Treasury were not informed. Any numerical work that was needed was done in rough and ready fashion at OMB.

The commission and the White House struck a deal. The House of Representatives passed the commission's recommendations with scarcely a change, including several technical errors of astonishing size. The final $160 billion package was 55 percent tax increases, 23 percent camouflaged transfers from general revenues, and only 22 percent benefit cuts. Once again the failure to face the real problem resulted in large tax increases. Moreover, the measure to advance the already scheduled 1990 payroll tax-rate increase to 1988 was not needed to get the system over its short-run crisis. It had two other purposes instead. One was to advance the process of ratcheting up the tax rates, which SSA was counting on for the long run. The other was to move about $14.5 billion forward into the last year of the five-year federal budget period in order to help OMB show a lower budget deficit.

The President's social security goals were defeated. He was forced to accept an enlarged system, which he had eloquently opposed two years before. Coverage was extended to new federal workers and employees of nonprofit organizations, and state and local governments were prohibited from withdrawing from the system. These steps will reduce the scope of the better-funded pension plans of state and local governments and nonprofit firms, resulting in less saving, investment, and economic growth—just as the President had warned. The increase in the payroll tax rates was partly offset out of general revenues by such measures as an income tax credit. The result is a combination of higher tax rates and general revenue transfers, neither of which the President wanted.

The taxation of half of social security benefits as provided in the 1983 amendments introduced a means test into the system for the first time. Worse yet, the method of taxing the benefits was totally inconsistent with the President's stated desire to increase incentives. The correct way to tax half of social security benefits is simply to add half of the benefits to taxable income. If politicians want to give people with lower incomes special treatment and to reduce their burden, part of benefits could be excluded from tax, with only the benefit amounts in excess of the exclusion entering taxable income. This method may push a recipient into a higher tax bracket, but the resulting disincentive would be mild compared to the way the proposal was actually implemented.

As recommended by the commission, the method of taxing half of benefits was a farce. The commission proposed that a single retiree with $20,000 ($25,000 for a married couple) in outside income from savings, private pensions, or wages be required to add half of his social security benefits to his taxable income. Single retirees earning $19,999 would pay no tax on their benefits, but anyone earning $20,000 would have to add up to $4,000 to taxable income and pay nearly $1,000 in additional tax. That is an expensive dollar of income. The marginal tax rate would have been 100,000 percent.

The House version of the bill, after loud complaints about the commission's proposal, took away part of the problem and left merely a disaster. The House phased in the taxation of half of social security benefits as other income exceeds certain thresholds. Like the commission blunder, this has the effect of raising the marginal tax rate on other income. The effect is less spectacular, however, and resulted in a 50 to 77 percent increase in the marginal tax rate on income of social security recipients. The Republican Senate could not wait to join in delivering this blow to a major Republican constituency—retired people with a median income or higher. One Republican senator (Chafee) even got an amendment passed that included tax-exempt interest in the income measure used to determine whether the taxpayer's income exceeded the threshold. The senator seemed determined that no old person who had managed to save anything for retirement would escape the net.

The result of the 1983 social security legislation was to move a retired individual with $26,000 in private retirement income from a 30 percent marginal tax rate to a 45 percent rate. A retired couple with a private retirement income of $38,000 was moved from a 28 percent to a 50 percent marginal tax rate. Social security recipients with private retirement income who are still working and have "earned income" in excess of the social security earnings limitation can face marginal tax rates in excess of 100 percent until 1990.

To understand how this happens, consider the case of the single retiree currently in the 30 percent bracket. Since his private income is above the allowable threshold, his social security income is subject to tax. For every dollar in private income above the threshold, he has to pay tax on 50 cents of social security income until he is paying tax on half his social security benefits. In other words, above the threshold, every dollar of private income results in $1.50 of additional taxable income. That raises the tax rate on his additional dollar of private income by half, from 30 cents to 45 cents ($1.00 × .30 + $0.50 × .30). The increase in the tax rate may be even higher if the added income pushes him up a bracket. This continues until half of the benefits are taxed, at which time the effective marginal tax rate drops back down.

This approach to the taxation of social security benefits makes little sense, and it is inconsistent with Reagan's desire to lower marginal tax rates and to increase saving and investment. Once people planning their retirement realize that the penalty for providing a private retirement income in excess of the threshold is to be hit with a 50–77 percent increase in marginal tax rates, their saving rate is likely to drop. The result is to make people more dependent on social security, thereby worsening the long-run problem.

The situation gets worse when you consider the interaction of the taxation of benefits with the existing limitation on earned income, which costs retirees one dollar in reduced social security benefits for every two additional dollars earned by continuing to participate in the work force. This is equivalent to an additional tax of 50 percent on additional earnings, over and above the marginal federal income tax rate. In this case, owing to the loss of benefits, many retirees will experience marginal tax rates on additional earned income in excess of 90 percent. If payroll and state income taxes on additional earned income are taken into account, the marginal tax rates can exceed 110 percent. One has to ask what happened to the administration that was going to improve incentives for people to work.

Senator Armstrong got the Senate to adopt an amendment to repeal the earnings limitation, but the Senate delayed the repeal until the 1990s. The House, though, insisted on retaining the earnings limit. The final compromise lowered the benefit loss penalty for exceeding the earnings limitation from $1 in reduced social security benefits for every $2 earned above the limit to $1 for every $3. This dropped the implicit tax on excess earnings from 50 percent to 33 percent, bringing the maximum tax rates faced by a retiree who continued to participate in the work force down from around 110 percent to 83–98 percent.

What we have here is a form of age discrimination that may not technically violate the antidiscrimination laws but nonetheless violates the spirit of the law. The entire thrust of the social security package is to deny the elderly any incentive whatsoever for being independent of the government. This kind of legislation was the result of a desperate haste to remove social security from the agenda in order to quiet the political storm that broke out in response to an incompetent approach to the social security problem.

The IMF and International Transfer Payments

Pragmatic solutions are habit-forming. Once initiated into the rites by the social security compromise, it was easy for the administration to agree to increased financing for the International Monetary Fund. Faced with a recession and an international debt crisis, principles seemed an expensive proposition.

Initially the President and the Treasury were opposed to the 50 percent increase in funding for the IMF, although some Treasury officials were determined to guide through at least a 25 percent increase. Officially this would be presented as a political compromise for diplomatic reasons. The opposition to the increase in funding did not reside in animosity toward the IMF. Rather, the President's view was that private investment is the key to economic development. For domestic political and ideological reasons, much of the Third World had made private investment unsafe or unwelcome. To compensate for the curtailed private equity, loans were being funneled to Third World and communist countries through supranational organizations, and we were aiding countries that were hostile or indifferent to our principles. Some Reaganites were also concerned about the continued buildup in debt burdens, especially since some of the money had been wasted in uneconomic projects and stolen by politicians and bureaucrats in the recipient countries. The buildup in debt can reach a point where it has to be permanently underwritten in order to avoid a crisis. The IMF had experienced rapid growth in its statutory lending obligations, and Third World demands on the United States, Western Europe, and Japan were rising. Private commercial banks felt safe in lending to sovereign countries favored by the IMF and other supranational lending agencies, and they had already gone in over their heads. Reaganites believed that piling debt upon debt was not viable and that we should resist the pressures to pass on a sinking ship to someone else's watch.

This approach was defeated when the Federal Reserve Board overreacted to what it erroneously believed was an inflationary fiscal policy. By suddenly collapsing the U.S. inflation rate, the board precipitated a domestic and international debt crisis. Loans made in the expectation of rising oil and commodity prices no longer looked good when the export earnings of debtor nations dropped. Increased funding for the IMF picked up rapid support as a necessary measure to protect the domestic banking system from the world debt bubble. According to the rhetoric, if the bubble burst, everything would go under. The domestic and international banking systems and the economic recovery would collapse, and Third World countries would fall into communist hands. In reality, unless the Federal Reserve was derelict in its responsibility to provide liquidity to banks, nothing would burst except the view that it is safe and profitable to overlend to foreign governments and governmental entities, and international finance would move in a more cautious and promising direction.

Whatever one thinks of the funding increase per se, the tactics used to sell it are a good demonstration of the kind of arguments to which haste drives policymakers in their quest for a quick solution. Our government, it was said, had no business opposing more funds for the IMF when it had a history of being the second largest user of IMF resources after Great Britain. In other words, the United States was an international loan lush itself, so what was it doing kicking up a fuss? This argument was made by numerous public officials who had to know that it was misleading (an example of safety in numbers). The United States has of course drawn on its reserve position, but not at any one time by amounts approaching the size of its quota. The statement that the United States is a large user of the IMF is correct only in terms of absolute dollars and is merely a reflection of our size. We are not a large user in any real sense. A country with a record as a large borrower would be one that has gone often to the well for an amount equal to its quota or some multiple thereof. If the United States were really a large borrower, the Third World would not want to increase the IMF's resources since it would mean they would be lending to us.

Another argument was that the U.S. economy had become more dependent on exports and, unless we provided foreigners with more money through the IMF to buy our goods, the recovery would falter. A similar argument was that the quota increase amounted to a jobs program for this country. The people making these arguments apparently forgot that countries have many trading partners and are unlikely to spend all of their new loans in one place. They forgot that money was being lent to pay interest and that the debtor countries would be under pressure to reduce imports and increase exports. They forgot that lending abroad transfers U.S. purchasing power from all domestically produced goods to exports, thereby reducing demand for the former in order to increase it for the latter. They also forgot that the IMF loan packages require increased lending by private U.S. banks. A political allocation of credit is substituted for the market place.

Money lent abroad cannot be lent to more creditworthy customers at home or used to purchase U.S. government and corporate bonds. The drain on the U.S. credit markets was a peculiar thing to go unremarked, especially when Paul Volcker, David Stockman, and Martin Feldstein were stressing that there was not enough credit to meet our own domestic needs and that taxes should be raised to reduce Treasury borrowing in an overcrowded financial market. The increased funding for the IMF not only requires the Treasury to finance it by borrowing an additional $8.4 billion. In addition, it requires some multiple of this amount in increased foreign lending by U.S. commercial banks. In testimony before Congress, Secretary Regan said that from 1977 to mid-1982 private banks lent $4.30 abroad for every dollar in IMF loans, and about this same ratio held in the case of the bailout package arranged for Brazil.

In testimony about the domestic economy before the Joint Economic Committee on January 27, 1983, Volcker warned that there was not enough credit to meet the domestic needs of the United States and that, unless federal deficits were cut, higher interest rates would work against our economic recovery. Clearly the implication was that the cost to the United States of increased funding for the IMF was either higher interest rates and a weaker recovery or higher taxes or reduced defense and social spending. But a few days later, on February 2, Volcker forgot all about these costs when he testified in support of expanded funding for the IMF before the House Banking Committee. The President might be trying to cut tax rates and restructure incentives at home, but that played second fiddle when it came to more money for the IMF and protecting the Federal Reserve from blame for an international monetary collapse that its excessively tight money had made possible.

When the claim that the banks would collapse without increased funding for the IMF made the exercise look like a banking bailout, public officials began describing the policy as a bank "bail-in," stressing that banks would be required to lend more abroad. This argument turned comedy into farce. The reason there was a crisis was that the debtor nations already had more debt than they could service and banks had already seriously overexposed their capital abroad. Yet to hear high public officials tell it, the solution was to bail the banks in deeper and pile more debt upon the debtors. This argument made it clear that the government thought that, if it could convince the public that the banks were not getting away with anything, the IMF would get its increased funding.

Behind the cover of all these arguments, a transformation was taking place in the nature and character of the IMF. Normally, an IMF loan is supposed to be a bridge loan to provide balance-of-payments financing for countries whose imports temporarily exceed their exports. More recently the IMF has taken an expanded view of balance-of-payments problems and has made investment loans to countries for "structural adjustment." These loans are supposed to allow countries to increase their exports by investing in ports and industrial projects and to reduce imports by investing in domestic energy projects. Money, of course, is fungible, and a $5.5 billion structural-adjustment loan to India in 1981 was followed by large Indian arms purchases from France.

Advocates of a new international economic order have additional ambitions for the IMF and see it as a potential agency for making wealth transfers from "North" to "South" (from the western alliance to the rest of the world.) IMF loans are not supposed to permanently underwrite a nation's debts. Conditions are imposed that force a country back into balance by reducing its imports and increasing its exports. These conditions might produce political turmoil in the countries on which they are imposed, but if only one or a few countries are in trouble at any point in time, the IMF's policies can succeed.

However, it is difficult for many countries simultaneously to adjust in the manner that the IMF requires. For example, Brazil's major trading partners include Mexico, Argentina, and Nigeria, all of whom are in a similar situation. In the aggregate they cannot all export more and import less. This implies that the IMF must soften its conditions, which implies that it must underwrite the debt in a more permanent manner, turning loans into wealth transfers. Indeed, with all of the prestige that is being poured into the bailout— the prestige of the banks, the IMF, the White House, Congress, the Federal Reserve, our major allies, the debtor countries—the bailout cannot be allowed to turn sour. If piling debt upon debt leads to a worse problem rather than to a solution, the debt is likely to be either permanently underwritten or inflated away. Either way large wealth transfers take place, and the IMF is turned into an aid-giving agency. This seems an unnecessary risk to take if, as many advocates of a bailout claim, the debtor countries are only experiencing a temporary liquidity crisis—a problem that could be handled with a grace period on debt repayment.

The alternative to the IMF-led bailouts was not default. Instead, debts can be renegotiated and stretched over a longer period in order to reduce the liquidity demands of the debt obligations. And banks can take steps to build up their reserves against their foreign loans. But instead of facing the real issues, the decision was made to pass the problem on to the future, just as was done in the case of the social security crisis.

The Flat-Rate Tax

The longer problems are evaded, the more drastic the remedies must be. This is true not only for the buildup of social security and international debt obligations, but also for the burden of taxation on incentives.

President Reagan's effort to change economic policy in order to restore the growth performance of the economy bogged down in the fight over the 1983 budget. For three decades policymakers had been taught to accept recession's deficits as "automatic stabilizers" that buttress demand and prevent the economy from worsening, but the Reagan Administration made the deficit such a political issue that it was denied the protection against budget deficits that orthodox economics had provided previous administrations. As the *Wall Street Journal* noted in an editorial during the first week of January 1983, "the President's program was undermined by the forecasts of grandiose deficits."

The direction in which the resolution of the stalemate moved— higher spending and higher taxes—eviscerated much of the change in fiscal policy that Reagan achieved in his first year in office. The original strategy of balancing the budget through higher economic growth faded from sight as policymakers focused on narrowing recession's deficits with higher taxes. Battered by pressures to compromise on the budget, Reagan accepted a business tax increase that was supposed to narrow the budget deficits by $229 billion over the 1983–1987 period. Instead, the recession worsened, and the deficits widened by $612 billion between the mid-session review (summer 1982) and OMB's budget projection in December.

The attempt to establish a policy of economic growth was stalemated by the budget deficit, leaving a serious disharmony in policy proposals. There is heavy political pressure to reduce the projected budget deficits, but no political consensus on how to do the job. Sufficient cuts in nondefense spending are difficult to achieve, and the need for a buildup in defense spending is widely recognized. Raising taxes undercuts supply-side policy, and higher taxes have so far failed to reduce the deficits. While pragmatic policymaking is failing in the unpromising effort to compromise the budgetary problem, the opportunity is going unused to make an imaginative effort to solve the problem by adopting a flat-rate tax system.

A flat-rate tax, especially if it were based on consumption, would inject far more incentives into the economy than any previous tax reductions. By curtailing or eliminating most deductions and exemptions, marginal tax rates could be dropped to a low flat rate without any loss of revenues. Better incentives mean higher economic growth. To understand the importance of growth to the budget consider that the U.S. economy grew on the average about 3.5 percent per year in real terms between 1950 and 1980. This growth performance produced a $2.6 trillion GNP in 1980 and federal tax revenues of $517 billion. In spite of this, the government was still $60 billion in the red.

If the economy had grown 1.5 percent faster each year, the 1980 GNP would have been $4 trillion. The growth of the economy would have provided privately for many of the people that the government is feeding and housing through the federal budget. Not only would the need for tax revenues be less, a smaller percent of GNP taken in taxes would produce more revenues. It takes about 20 percent of a $2.6 trillion GNP to produce $517 billion in tax revenues, but only 15 percent of a $4 trillion economy produces $600 billion in revenues. That would have balanced the 1980 budget and left a surplus with which to begin reducing the national debt, thus reducing the interest drain on revenues.

A basis for establishing a flat-rate tax was set forth in the Treasury Department's *Blueprints for Basic Tax Reform* prepared while William Simon was secretary. The transition to a flat-rate system would be difficult or easy depending upon how the gains and losses of the transition balance out. For example, homeowners could lose their mortgage interest deduction, but they would gain from lower with-holding and from a lower marginal rate on all growth in income.

Distributional gains and losses are an important consideration, but it is a mistake to concentrate too narrowly on distributional questions, especially in static terms. Economic growth is still the engine of progress for most taxpayers and particularly for those at lower-income levels. A tax system that fosters economic growth provides people with a built-in opportunity to get ahead. Those who wish to redistribute income should rely on the expenditure side of the budget. It is not the progressive income tax per se but government transfer payments that redistribute income. Efforts to achieve redistribution through the tax system discourage the rich from earning taxable income. The resulting tax burden on the middle class has become oppressive. It would be more sensible to use the tax system as an efficient instrument to raise revenue and promote economic growth. If income redistribution is necessary, it should be pursued through the expenditure side of the budget, with taxes raised proportionately redistributed only to the poor. The way we are headed now is placing a heavy overload on the tax system. Clear warning signals have arisen in the form of sluggish economic performance, a growing underground economy, and large budget deficits.

Tax reformers who want to close loopholes but maintain the progressive income tax and the high statutory tax rate on corporate income often campaign under the banner of "equity." Reform, however, does not mean simply closing loopholes. Many of the so-called tax loopholes were put into the law because certain activities were being smothered under the blanket of high tax rates. The loophole is a lifeline that lets economic activity continue to breathe under the layer of taxes. If the tax rates were lowered, as they would be under a flat-rate system, the loopholes would not be necessary. If the loopholes were closed without lowering the tax rate, the activities would be smothered, in which case no revenues would be raised.

A piecemeal attack on deductions and exclusions is likely to fail by producing a greater demand for government spending programs. For example, the taxation of fringe benefits, such as medical insurance, and the elimination of deductions for medical insurance premiums and medical expenses raise the cost to the individual of privately provided health services and increase the demand for publicly funded health services. To prevent the elimination of deductions from creating an increased demand for government programs in health and housing, a move against exclusions and deductions would have to be a part of a program to lower other taxes and increase economic growth so that people could provide for their own wants.

A flat-rate tax would treat all income the same, whereas the current tax system discriminates in favor of, and against, different sources of income. A flat-rate tax would also treat all individuals and households the same, whereas the current tax system discriminates against individuals and households on the basis of marital status and size of income. The current tax system discriminates against married income earners and against people who achieve financial success by requiring them to pay a disproportionate share of the tax burden. This is an anachronism when all other forms of personal discrimination—race, sex, and age—have been declared illegal.

Fairness is requiring a person or household with ten times as much income to pay ten times as much in taxes, which is what a flat-rate tax does. No one has ever proved, nor can it be proved, that fairness is requiring a person with ten times as much income to pay twenty times as much in taxes. The "ability to pay" argument in favor of progressivity does not claim that a progressive tax system is fair; it merely says that the rich can be treated unfairly because they are better able to afford it.

Beyond fairness, there is the issue of effectiveness. Under the current tax code, it often pays people in high brackets not to make profitable and productive investments that would increase both their taxable income and, through the higher employment that would result, the incomes of others. Instead, it pays them to purchase tax shelters that lower the taxes on existing income. There is something wrong with a tax system that lets people do better by minimizing their taxes than by maximizing their earnings. The rising rate of unemployment over the last decade is one of the costs of a tax system that encourages capital to move out of productive investments and into tax shelters.

The economic gains to be had from a flat-rate tax are substantial. In a flat-rate system the marginal income tax rate is equal to the average tax rate, and there is no penalty for earning more income. All taxpayers would be allowed to keep a much larger percentage of all future income earned, whether from a raise or promotion, overtime, or saving and investing. In addition, part of the tax burden would be shifted from currently taxed productive activities to activities that have been driven off the books into the underground economy, and part would be shifted to capital that is currently employed in tax shelters where it produces tax savings instead of taxable income. A low flat-rate tax would make shelters and off-the-books activities less profitable and would add more capital and increased economic activity to the tax base. By reducing the tax wedge between gross and net pay, a low flat-rate tax would reduce the prices of goods and services and encourage the employment of labor. By reducing the double taxation of dividends, it would encourage the substitution of equity for debt.

The fairest society is the one that provides the most opportunities for people to succeed. In this sense as well, the current tax system is unfair to everyone. A low flat-rate tax system would allow people to succeed and to attain financial independence—and not punish them for doing so.

A Gold Standard?

Even if Congress were to accept William Simon's dictum that the nation deserves to "have a tax system which looks like someone designed it on purpose" and to undertake a fundamental reform, the better incentives of a low flat-rate tax could still be overpowered by the adverse consequences of an erratic monetary policy. Indeed, the perception in some quarters that President Reagan's supply-side tax cut did not work stems from the failure of monetary policy.

If monetary policy continues to fail, supply-side fiscal policies will not be enough to carry the economy to a higher real growth path. In the conduct of monetary policy, discretionary judgments have replaced principle. The view was that the monetary authorities could do a better job if they were unencumbered with restraints and had the advantage of flexibility. However, in practice, discretionary behavior is not predictable and so uncertainty rose in the financial markets; discretion also allows the monetary authority to behave in self-protective ways. The removal of constraints on the Federal Reserve was gradual, and in today's system of fiat money and floating exchange rates, it seems to be complete. In the public mind the stability of financial markets rests on nothing more than the credibility of the Federal Reserve chairman.

Monetary uncertainty is a form of bad taxation, and disillusionment with discretionary management has produced demands to make the Federal Reserve accountable by placing restraints on its behavior. Monetarists want to impose a quantity rule on the board that would require the central bank to meet preannounced targets that provide moderate, steady, and predictable growth in the money supply. Advocates of a gold standard want to impose a price rule that would define the value of the dollar in terms of gold, thereby committing the government to the protection of that value. Unless there is a reduction in monetary uncertainty, measures may be taken to end the independence of the Federal Reserve and to make the central bank part of the Treasury. That in itself would not clear up the difficulties in the Federal Reserve's operating procedures or establish the appropriate rule, but by introducing a more direct political accountability, it might increase the political incentives to find a framework for monetary stability.

Not everyone sees the Federal Reserve as a failure. Some economists believe that Volcker dealt with inflation in the only way possible by closing down the economy. From this standpoint the problem is to continue to deal with inflation. The Federal Reserve is hearing from its academic consultants that that will require a decade of pain and suffering. For example, at a meeting on May 12, 1983, consultant Stanley Fischer, a professor at MIT, told the board of governors that "if the Fed is determined to preserve its gains in the fight against inflation, it will have to run the risk of creating another recession fairly soon after the end of the last one." Fischer told the board that the proper conduct of monetary policy means that "the prospect for the eighties is that the decade will look much like the fifties, with concern over inflation dominating monetary policy and ensuring several recessions." To keep all this tight money from raising interest rates, Fischer recommended fiscal austerity, such as higher taxes, to reduce federal budget deficits.

Fischer's advice might sound like a strategy designed to destroy the Republican Party, but the board was hearing the same words from Alan Greenspan and Martin Feldstein as soon as the economy began showing signs of a robust recovery. The idea that economic growth must be combated or it will cause inflation has serious implications for incumbent politicians. They would not only have to cope with the unemployment and output effects of such a policy (which could increase the deficit more than higher taxes could reduce it). They would also have to cope with the effects of repeated recessions on the social security system and the world debt situation. Such a policy as Fischer recommends is not viable politically or economically. A way must be found to finance economic growth without renewing fears of inflation.

Part of the problem is that, having overreacted to inflation, people now expect the Federal Reserve to overreact to unemployment and keep the roller-coaster cycle going. The weekly money numbers and movements in the federal funds rate are read like tea leaves by market participants for signs of when to dump "securities"—an old name that does not reflect the risk of holding stocks and long-term bonds in an uncertain monetary environment. (In order to break the roller-coaster pattern of expectations, the Reagan Administration had wanted to bring down the inflation rate gradually.)

Others, including both some Keynesians and some advocates of a gold standard, believe that monetary policy is a failure but do not blame the Federal Reserve. Instead, they blame the monetarists for forcing a monetarist policy on the board. As a veteran of Washington policy wars, I can only smile at this point of view which attributes such power to monetarists. Supply-siders with a supply-side President and a supply-side Treasury had trouble imposing a supply-side policy on the administration. Yet monetarists with no presence on the Federal Reserve Board or on its staff are supposed to have imposed monetarism on the board.

The Federal Reserve did not close down the economy in 1981–82 because it was following a monetarist policy or paying attention to Beryl Sprinkel at Treasury or Jerry Jordan at the CEA. It slammed on the brakes because it was hearing from Alan Greenspan, Herbert Stein, and many others that the Reagan Administration had an overly expansionary fiscal policy,[2] and that no matter what the

2. Although they were saying something else, Laffer and Wanniski were unintentionally telling the Federal Reserve the same thing by opposing lower federal spending. As assistant secretary of the Treasury I had to contend with an environment inside government and outside that could not differentiate between supply-side economics and an inflationary fiscal policy.

board did with monetary policy it would be unable to offset the inflationary fiscal policy (especially with "core inflation" so high). The board simply decided that it was not going to hold the bag for an inflationist administration and turned off the money. Later, when the board saw to its surprise that it had collapsed the economy and brought on an international liquidity crisis, it reacted to its own previous policy and began pouring out the money. A few commentators have put a good face on the Federal Reserve's self-protective behavior by claiming that the board followed monetarism until it saw that it did not work, at which time it abandoned monetarism, adopted the price rule, and began pegging the price of gold.[3]

The case for gold and the fixed exchange rate system that goes along with gold does not rest on special pleading. A gold standard puts constraints on the central bank and bases policy on principle rather than on a shifting pragmatism. In so doing it fulfills a main objective of monetarists themselves, which is to substitute rules for discretionary authority. The true enemies of the gold standard are inflationists, and the monetarists are not inflationists. Inflationists can ignore a price rule as easily as they can ignore a quantity rule, and in some cases fixed exchange rates can play into their hands. When I hear supply-side economist Robert Mundell and French socialist François Mitterrand both call for returning to a fixed exchange-rate system, I have to think that they have different goals in mind. A fixed rate system that committed the United States to the support of the French franc would allow Mitterrand more scope for his socialist policies. There can be no assurance that the real outcome of a fixed exchange rate system would not be a mechanism for milking the United States.

If monetary uncertainty persists, the case for gold is likely to advance on broader grounds: it would entail such a large policy change that people would believe that the government would stick with it for more than six months. After a certain point, only a return to firm principle can restore stability to a monetary and fiscal environment that has too long experienced the shifting winds of pragmatic policies.

3. For example, Jude Wanniski wrote in the *Wall Street Journal* on May 27, 1983, that "the chairman of the Federal Reserve, Paul Volcker, last summer broke with the deflationary monetarist policies the White House had been pressing on him."

10

Restoration and Resistance

AFTER HAVING MANEUVERED THE PRESIDENT INTO AN ISO-
lated position in which he had to accept a major tax increase in August 1982, the President's senior aides set the stage for yet another
tax increase in the January budget. In anticipation of the struggle,
the President publicly stated his point of view in a speech before the
U.S. League of Savings Associations in New Orleans on November
16, 1982. He warned that repeal or delay of the third-year tax cut or
of indexing would "show the white flag of surrender to big
spenders." Reagan made it clear where he thought the deficits were
coming from: "A propaganda campaign would have you believe
these deficits are caused by our so-called massive tax cut and defense build-up," but "there is simply no escaping the truth: current
and projected deficits result from sharp increases in non-defense
spending." Two weeks later in a speech before the National League
of Cities in Los Angeles, the President stressed that there was only
one way out of the current deficit problem: "The answer lies in stimulating the economy and increasing productivity."

But the President's aides had long stopped taking their cue from
him and moved quickly to disavow him.[1] Two days later (Decem-

1. By January 1983 the recognition that the President was being undermined by a
campaign against his economic program carried on by his senior aides had reached beyond Reaganites and the editorial page of the *Wall Street Journal.* On January 14 an
article appeared in the *Washington Post* by Mark Shields, an editorial writer for the
paper, titled "Leak, Leak, Sink, Sink." Shields described the political destruction of
the President and his program at the hands of aides who "provide us hourly with tasty
insider stuff about the President's indecisiveness or lack of comprehension." The sav-
age lampoons of the President by his staff had created an image of Reagan as a "dotty
ideologue who is intractable and not very bright." Shields wrote that "the Democrats
would love to take credit for the job done on Reagan. But they cannot. The unfavor-
able picture of Ronald Reagan has been created and developed by Ronald Reagan's
own advisors." Shields wondered what the President thinks "when he reads the latest
bulletin (co-authored by his advisors without attribution) announcing that nobody in

ber 1) an article appeared in the *Washington Post* reporting that the President's call for strong economic growth had aroused "the consternation of some administration officials." Reagan understood that an economic recovery would let him resist the pressures for higher taxes. So did his aides, and they refused to forecast a recovery that would reduce the deficits. Stockman again raised his projections of the deficits, this time to over $200 billion a year, and he buttressed them with a new argument that they were structural rather than cyclical, that is, they would not go away even if there were to be an economic recovery.

Any hopes the President might have had about forecasting a recovery in his January State of the Union address were foreclosed by Martin Feldstein, the newly appointed chairman of the Council of Economic Advisers, who pushed through over Treasury's opposition a forecast of a paltry 1.4 percent real growth for 1983. The Treasury staff could not believe Feldstein's low forecast, which was far below that of a normal recovery. But Feldstein, who had come to Washington to save the reputation of the Reagan Administration from the "wildly optimistic" forecasts of supply-siders, made it clear that the alternative to his forecast was his resignation. Faced with the inflexibility of the newly appointed CEA chairman, Secretary Regan gave in.

The President was in a box once more. His budget director handed him a forecast of a horrific string of massive budget deficits, and his CEA chairman forecast that there would be no economic recovery worthy of the name in the coming year. His staff had painted his program a failure, leaving him no alternative to their argument that he would have to raise taxes in order to lower the deficits in order to have an economic recovery.

In his State of the Union address on January 25, 1983, Reagan proposed a large standby or contingency tax increase, consisting of a surtax on corporate and personal income and an excise tax on oil, in the event that deficits did not decline. Since the President's aides

---

the country agrees with the President's economic policies." He found the continual attack on the President from within "no tribute to the President's managerial abilities" and thought that "the Reagan presidency cannot survive either without the President's vision of what he wants to accomplish or with the whispered slander of the President from his own appointees."

did not expect the deficits to decline, this was seen as the first step toward getting Reagan to accept the inevitable. Joseph Kraft observed in the *Washington Post* two days later that "the call that issued forth sounded like a retreat that might lead to a rout."

The overestimated budget deficits and the underestimated economic growth were greeted in the press as "realistic." Ken Bacon and Bob Merry declared in the *Wall Street Journal* that "the new budget represents a triumph of traditional Republican economics over the supply-side hopes reflected in Mr. Reagan's last two budgets." The President was almost trapped, but the "prudent" Feldstein forecast lacked credibility with private forecasters. There were too many signs of a stronger recovery, and the Feldstein forecast did not last a week. In his congressional testimony on February 2, Feldstein did not defend his low growth forecast, saying instead that there were stronger and stronger signs that recovery was imminent.

Then the Congressional Budget Office's February 1983 report to the budget committees appeared. Amid all the calls for higher taxes, the CBO came to terms with the supply-side revolution. The CBO stressed that "besides burdening the taxpayers, all taxes impose efficiency costs on the economy. Higher income and payroll taxes almost surely discourage work effort and saving to some extent, and excise taxes distort economic choices." The report also pointed out that it is not enough to postpone a tax increase until a recovery is underway. At any time, tax increases "could, if not carefully designed, inhibit long-term investment and economic growth. Any tax increases aimed at dealing with the long-term deficit problem should therefore be designed to minimize adverse effects on recovery and long-term growth." Significantly, one of the three goals of CBO's deficit-reduction strategy was to "minimize disincentives to work, save, and invest, and improve the allocation of investment resources."

Alice Rivlin did not join the assault on the President, and the effect of the CBO report was to pull up short those administration officials who were saying that taxes did not matter but deficits did. Suddenly they sounded less supportive of their President than the congressional appointee of the liberal Democrats. Indeed, CBO often forecasted a better outlook than the administration did. In September 1982, as Stockman stoked the fires of the deficit hysteria, CBO issued an update of the economic and budget outlook. It showed that on a high-employment basis the budget deficits projected for 1982–1985 averaged less than 1 percent of GNP, hardly a figure to justify the grave tone in which Stockman spoke.

As the recovery that the President had been told could not take place gathered steam, Reagan was confirmed in his opinion that OMB and CEA were too pessimistic about his policies. His advisers had told him that the deficits would keep inflation high, but the inflation rate had collapsed. They had told him that the deficits would keep the interest rates high, but a fantastic rally began in the financial markets. They had told him there would be no recovery, but one appeared. They had told him it would be weak and faltering, but it grew in strength.

Faced with total defeat, Stockman escalated his efforts. On April 18, 1983, he told a cabinet meeting that unless the deficit were reduced, economic recovery would be lost. Unless a budget compromise could be struck with Congress (which would require Reagan to accept higher taxes), the outlook was for a "stalemate scenario" with deficits "stuck at $200 billion per year as far as the eye can see" (certainly farther than projections can responsibly be made). Following the usual practice, the report was leaked to the press only hours after the meeting. But the tactic was wearing thin, and accomplices began falling away. Steven Weisman wrote in the *New York Times* on April 20 that "even by Mr. Stockman's standards the warning was apocalyptic." It certainly did not impress Defense Secretary Weinberger, a Reagan confidant and former OMB director. Weinberger argued that, rather than compromising away his tax and defense programs in order to reach an accommodation with Congress, the President should veto any inappropriate revenue and appropriation bills. If Congress refused to follow presidential leadership, Reagan could take the issues to the people in the 1984 election. Weinberger was backed up in his view by National Security Adviser Clark, another Reagan confidant.

Jim Baker's faction had seen this challenge coming and launched a punishing attack in the press to dissuade it. On April 9, 1983, unidentified White House officials complained in the *Washington Post* that Weinberger and Clark's "uncompromising position" angered Senate Budget Committee Chairman Domenici, causing the committee to cut the President's defense increase in half. Clark was described by White House aides as guiding the President on a "militant course."

The next week, attacks on Clark appeared in *Time* and *Newsweek*. The April 25 issue of *Time* described Clark as "the man without an agenda." An anonymous White House aide dismissed Clark as "content-free." The contempt poured out: "his ideological inclinations are visceral and seldom fine-tuned." With unintended irony, the article observed that Clark was causing problems because he "seems determined to let Reagan be Reagan."

The attack in *Newsweek* appeared on the same day for a double-barreled dose. The national security adviser has a "dismal lack of expertise in foreign affairs" and has drawn charges of "political insensitivity and intellectual shortcomings." *Newsweek* duly conveyed to Clark the intended threats: " 'There's an attitude of let him fall on his face,' explains one irate top level White House official."

These were the same tactics that had been used against the Treasury, the President's domestic policy adviser (Martin Anderson), and other Reaganites in the administration. The message never lacked clarity: get out of the way or be hacked to pieces in the press. The tactic, however, had worn out as more and more people noticed what was afoot. The Reaganite forces in Congress quickly moved to reinforce the Weinberger-Clark argument that the President did not need a budget resolution and, therefore, did not need to compromise. Letters arrived from both houses with enough signatures to guarantee a veto of any repeal of the third-year tax cut and the indexing of the personal income tax system. Thirty-four senators and 146 representatives urged the President to veto any further moves against his tax policy and pledged to sustain his action. The President no longer needed a budget compromise in order to protect the tax cuts.

As other facts came to light, the tax-increase advocates lost their grip on the "Tolkien ring of power." The President learned that the tax cut was being misrepresented by some of his own senior officials and Republicans in the Senate as so irresponsibly large that it "has eroded the tax base," resulting in $200 billion structural deficits. These claims were inconsistent with official statistics projecting tax revenues at 19.2 percent of GNP for fiscal years 1983–1986, higher than the 18.9 percent average for the 1970s and the 18.6 percent average for the 1960s. The Congressional Budget Office pointed out that the 1981 tax cut merely held revenues as a percent of GNP to approximately the levels that prevailed in the 1960s and 1970s. Others noted that the 19.2 percent figure was based on Feldstein's low economic-growth forecast and therefore was most likely an understatement.

In dollar terms, the "massive" 1981 tax cut had disappeared by early 1983. In congressional testimony Treasury Secretary Regan spelled out how the tax cut had been eaten away by the combination of the 1982 tax increase, the gasoline tax bill, continuing bracket creep, previously scheduled social security tax increases, and the social security rescue plan.

The tax increase that Stockman had pushed through in the summer of 1982 also undermined his cause. It demonstrated that higher taxes could not compensate for the falling revenues of a faltering economy. The President was told in the summer of 1982 that the Tax Equity and Fiscal Responsibility Act (TEFRA) would raise $229 billion in additional revenues and reduce the 1983–1987 deficit projections to $407 billion. Instead, by December the deficit projections had tripled to $1,248 billion (see Table 10). Moreover, Treasury brought to light the performance during the 1981–82 recession of the one sector—real nonresidential construction—where the 1981 tax reductions most escaped repeal by TEFRA. Throughout most of the recession, investment in structures remained well above its pre-recession level, instead of declining as it did in the seven previous cycles (see Chart 11). It was hard evidence that the recession would

Table 10. Deficit and Receipt Projections (billions of dollars)

	1983	1984	1985	1986	1987	Total
TEFRA receipts	22	35	43	58	71	229
Post-TEFRA deficit	115	93	74	66	59	407
Pre-TEFRA deficit	137	128	117	124	130	636
September deficit	185	187	204	226	236	1,038
December deficit	223	229	247	269	280	1,248
Rise in deficit (4–3)	48	59	87	102	106	402
Rise in deficit (5–3)	86	101	130	145	150	612
Rise in deficit (5–4)	38	42	43	43	54	220
Rise in deficit (5–2)	108	136	173	203	221	841

Real Nonresidential Construction

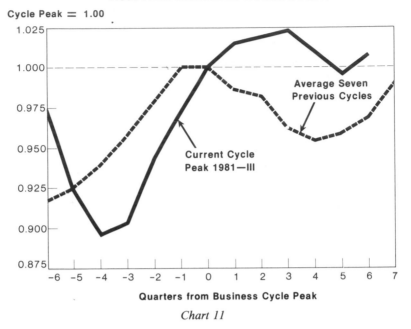

Cycle Peak = 1.00

Quarters from Business Cycle Peak

Chart 11

have been less severe if taxes had not been raised. TEFRA also indicated that spending cuts could not be bought with a tax increase.
The $3 spending cut for every $1 of tax increase promised in exchange for the 1982 tax hike never materialized.

As the tax cut dwindled, spending mushroomed. Between March
1981, when Reagan submitted his original 1981–1984 budget requests, and his budget requests of January 1983, less than two years
later, nondefense spending for the four years rose by $211.8 billion
(Table 11). Conservatives began wondering if Ronald Reagan
would run for reelection as a big spender. Margaret Thatcher's
speeches with which she launched her own reelection bid were ominous. On May 14, 1983, the *Daily Mail* (London) quoted her as refuting her critics: "They said we would cut pensions. Instead we
have raised them by two-thirds—well ahead of prices. They said we
would dismantle the National Health Service. Instead we have
nearly doubled spending on the Health Service. They said we would
cripple education. Instead expenditure per child is at an all-time
record."

The only way OMB could keep the total spending increase under the $200 billion mark was by cutting back Reagan's defense spending requests by $25.2 billion. This left the cumulative Reagan defense budget for 1981–1984 only $13.6 billion more than the amount requested by President Carter for the same four-year period (Table 12). A massive defense buildup may take place in the future, but during 1981–1984 it consists of a 1.7 percent increase in outlays over the levels in Carter's last budget—assuming Congress appropriates the amounts requested by Reagan.

As the facts came to light, the claim that massive Reagan defense spending and massive Reagan tax cuts were threatening the economic recovery in 1983–84 with massive structural deficits lost all credibility. Moreover, people began noticing that David Stockman's

Table 11. Nondefense Spending Requests and Congressional Action

	Reagan request March '81	Cong. action May '81	Reagan request Jan. '82	Cong. action June '82	Reagan request Jan. '83	Cong. action July '83
1981	493.1	498.5	—	—	497.4[a]	—
1982	506.5	506.7	537.8	546.5	541.0[a]	—
1983	506.0	509.2	536.5	555.9	590.4	598.6
1984	514.6	523.2	552.9	578.6	603.2	618.9

a. Actual.
Sources: Budget of the U.S. Government, FY 1982, 1983, 1984; FY 1982 Budget Revisions; First Congressional Budget Resolution, U.S. Congress, FY 1982 and 1983; House-Senate Conference, FY 1984.

Table 12. Defense Spending Outlays—Administration Budgets and Congressional Action

	Carter request Jan. '81	Reagan revision March '81	Cong. action May '81	Reagan request Jan. '82	Cong. action June '82	Reagan request Jan. '83	Cong. action July '83
1981	161.1	162.1	162.9	—	—	159.8[a]	—
1982	184.4	188.8	188.8	187.5	187.6	187.4[a]	—
1983	210.4	226.0	223.1	221.1	213.9	214.8	214.3
1984	237.8	255.6	250.6	253.0	243.3	245.3	240.0

a. Actual.
Sources: Budget of the U.S. Government, FY 1982, 1983, 1984; FY 1982 Budget Revisions; First Congressional Budget Resolution, U.S. Congress, FY 1982 and 1983; House-Senate Conference, FY 1984.

structural deficits had appeared out of the blue and were dwarfing the recession's cyclical deficits. According to OMB, only 31 percent of the 1983 deficit was due to cyclical factors (the recession); 69 percent was structural. The large structural element that OMB attributed to the deficit was inconsistent with OMB's own rule of thumb announced in November 1982, which says that every percentage point of unemployment adds $35 billion to the 1983 budget deficit. With the forecast of the 1983 unemployment rate near 11 percent instead of 6 percent, the 1983 deficit consisted of a $175 billion old-fashioned unemployment deficit. The administration was saying the same thing itself. The 1984 budget document states that "an average real GNP growth rate 1.33 percent higher each year over the next 6 years, compared to the prudent projections made in the 1984 budget, would result in a balanced budget by 1988. This is a high growth scenario but within the range of previous historical experience." The game was up. The massive structural deficits were based on Feldstein's forecast that did not last a week.

Doubts issued from other quarters about OMB's estimate of the structural deficit. In a study of March 9, 1983, "Structural Budget Deficits and Fiscal Policy Responses to the Recession," the Organization for Economic Cooperation and Development estimated the U.S. structural deficit to be only "half the official estimate." Moreover, OECD pointed out that "the emergence of structural budget deficits has been related to an unexpectedly slow economic growth rate in most OECD economies, following an era of rapid economic expansion. Persistent deficits have emerged because of the failure of public spending to adapt as quickly as revenues to slower long-run growth." In other words, the solution to the economic growth problem is not to raise taxes. On April 23, 1983, a forecast by the Bureau of Economic Analysis of the Department of Commerce also predicted lower deficits than OMB, placing the 1984 and 1985 structural deficits at $66.1 billion and $88.3 billion, instead of at OMB's triple-digit levels.

On May 17, 1983, the real President Reagan returned to office. At his press conference that day he spoke confidently:

It is time to draw the line and stand up for the people. I will not support a budget resolution that raises taxes while we're coming out of a recession. I will veto any tax bill that would do this ... The American people didn't send us to Washington to continue raising their taxes, spending more on wasteful programs, or weakening our defenses. They sent us here to stop that. And that's what we're going to try to do.

The President's men made it clear that he would have to do all this without their help. On May 21 a front-page story appeared in the *Washington Post* under the headline, "Reagan's Aides Said to Favor Tax Increases." The article mentioned a White House plan "yet to be revealed to the President" to increase taxes by $45 billion on January 1, 1985. The next day, the *Post* reported that the President was not interested in the plan and had said, "That may be someone's attitude in this administration, but it sure isn't mine."

During 1981–82 the supply-side approach to economic policy fell victim in part to the failure of monetary policy, in part to the ego struggle that senior aides carried on against the President, and in part to a campaign conducted against supply-side economics by elements of the media. The economic recovery and the facts lifted these constraints. But in June 1983 the President was still not home free. Many of his advisers remained locked in public displays of pessimism, despite what Commerce Secretary Baldrige said could be the strongest recovery in thirty years. By midyear it was obvious that real economic growth in 1983 would not only be higher than Feldstein had forecast in January, but also higher than the "wildly optimistic" forecast of the supply-siders. Feldstein, who had disparaged at some length the supply-siders' forecast of 5 percent real growth for 1983, announced on June 21 that he now thought that growth would be 5.5 percent for the year, 10 percent above the "rosy scenario." The same day, Secretary Baldrige said that the economy would probably grow more than 5 percent over the next two years. The numerous private forecasters who had lampooned the supply-siders rushed to raise their forecasts.[2]

2. Treasury Secretary Regan, who was vindicated by the economy's performance, was again perceived as a threat by the White House staff. To divert attention from how wrong they had been, they planted attacks on Regan in the June 20 issues of *Business Week* and *U.S. News and World Report,* with the latter reporting that "Senior Reagan administration economic officials are becoming openly contemptuous of Treasury Secretary Donald Regan's changeable economic convictions."

Nevertheless, Feldstein and Stockman moved to prevent the recovery from providing the President relief from "massive structural deficits." During the midyear revision of the forecast, they argued that the higher real economic growth rates for 1983 and 1984 should not be allowed to raise the GNP levels in future years above the levels of the January forecast. As a result, the GNP forecast for 1988 would remain at the same level *despite the recovery*. This is what the President's men mean when they say that economic recovery will not reduce the structural deficits. They wanted to forecast less growth in the future in order to offset higher growth in the present. In this approach to forecasting, the only effect of the economic recovery is to shift economic growth from future years to current years. Since the recovery disappears over the multi-year period, it cannot reduce the deficits. (The Treasury blocked this attempt to make the recovery disappear in the forecast.)

Moreover, the President had fewer supporters than before in economic policy positions, and a crisis was brewing in monetary policy. Many economists believed that the Federal Reserve, panicked by the consequences of its previously overrestrictive monetary policy, had let money growth again get out of hand. Senior administration officials were calling for Volcker to tighten policy in order to prevent an inflationary recovery. In other words, some of the President's advisers saw the strong recovery as too much of a good thing and were willing to accept higher interest rates as a way of calming down the recovery. Greenspan began paving the way when he stated on June 21 that "a modest rise in rates from current levels is unlikely to abort the current unfolding expansion" (*Wall Street Journal*, June 22, 1983).

If the President's economic program enjoyed the support of all his advisers, a unified voice could explain higher interest rates as a temporary result of a necessary monetary correction that would enable control to be regained over the money supply. However, in an administration with so many officials far out on a limb with their claim that interest rates depend on the deficit or fiscal policy, and not on monetary policy, no unified voice is present. Once interest rates move up, whether from monetary tightening or because the markets decide that rapid money growth cannot be sustained, the President's men have the opportunity to point to the deficits and declare "we told you so." They can put the President back on the defensive and pressure him to raise taxes. The experience of the first two and a half years of the Reagan Administration indicates that there is nothing to prevent the President's men from doing this. Reagan is being pushed toward a policy of raising taxes to balance the budget while federal spending grows as a percent of GNP.

Despite the evidence that Volcker was continuing to conduct monetary policy on a stop-go basis, his reappointment as chairman of the Federal Reserve Board was strongly supported by many senior administration officials. The President resisted and on June 9 stated publicly, in reference to Volcker's monetary policy during 1981–82: "If that string hadn't been pulled for so long and so hard, we might not have had the depth of recession that we've had." The President did seem to know what had happened to him but, faced with a well-orchestrated campaign for Volcker's reappointment and besieged with questions from the media, Reagan succumbed to the pressure. On June 18 he announced the reappointment of Volcker, a Democrat who gave him the recession that discredited his economic program.

By reappointing Volcker to a second term as Federal Reserve chairman, Reagan in effect absolved monetary policy from blame both for the recession and for higher interest rates. Volcker shares the view of Feldstein and Stockman that a tax increase is necessary in order for a policy of monetary ease to be continued. The higher taxes are supposed to hold down inflation, while the easy money is supposed to lower interest rates and to spur investment.

The real culprit in the struggle against the President's program is the view that investment and economic growth are better served by financing budget deficits with higher taxes rather than with Treasury borrowing. In this view the burden of borrowing falls on investment by raising interest rates, whereas the burden of taxes is on consumption.

The idea that borrowing crowds out investment while taxation crowds out consumption is a peculiar notion, with a dearth of empirical and analytical evidence in its behalf. The credibility of this point of view rests on a few weak reeds. Martin Feldstein and Otto Eckstein published an article in 1970 analyzing the evidence for the 1954–1969 period. They reported finding that a 10 percent increase in public debt held by the private sector raises the interest rate on corporate bonds (Aaa) by 15–28 basis points. In other words, a large increase in public debt results in a small increase in interest rates (one quarter of one percentage point or less).

But when the Treasury reestimated the Feldstein-Eckstein equation for the 1969–1982 period, the equation failed to produce the same results. (In fact, increases in public debt corresponded to a decline in interest rates.) The equation obviously cannot be accepted as a basis for making empirical statements about the relationship between interest rates and the deficit.[3] The Treasury is not alone in its skepticism. Numerous other studies have failed to support the Feldstein conclusion.

The argument that taxing is preferable to borrowing is also analytically defective, since it assumes that higher taxes do not impair private-sector saving or the after-tax rate of return on investment. Such taxes are hard to find, and they certainly do not include the Tax Equity and Fiscal Responsibility Act of 1982 or the proposals to repeal or cap the third year of the personal income tax-rate reductions, to repeal tax indexing, and to place a surtax on business and personal income.

TEFRA was supposed to help investment by raising revenues, thereby lowering budget deficits and interest rates. Instead, it reduced the cash flow of the business sector by the amount of the tax hike, thereby making business more dependent on borrowing to finance investment. Since firms have lower credit ratings than the U.S. Treasury, the substitution of business borrowing for Treasury borrowing has the effect of raising the interest rate.

3. In the equation, the long-term interest rate (Moody's corporate Aaa) is estimated as a function of current inflation, a distributed lag of 23 past quarters of inflation, the lagged change of the corporate Aaa rate, and the logarithms of the real per capita monetary base, real per capita private GNP, and real per capita privately held federal debt. The equation was originally estimated on the basis of data from 1954:1–1969:2. When the same variables were used to estimate the equation for 1969:4–1982:4, four of the six variables had changed signs and the regression coefficients associated with the other two variables were drastically and significantly altered. According to the equation, in the latter period when debt increases, interest rates and inflation fall—results that contradict Feldstein's argument. Treasury then reestimated the Feldstein-Eckstein equation for the original 1954–1969 period and found that the debt variable changed signs when the revised data for the period were used. Feldstein's conclusion does not hold even for the period he estimated.

In addition, TEFRA directly reduced the return on investment by raising the after-tax cost of plant and equipment. The only way TEFRA could have contributed to lower interest rates is by reducing private investment and thereby the demand for credit. Notice the irony: the government sets out to increase investment by raising revenues and lowering interest rates; instead it lowers interest rates by reducing investment.

Many people also have the mistaken idea that taxes on personal income have no adverse consequences for business other than reducing the demand for products. They believe that higher tax rates on personal income help business by reducing the federal deficit and lowering interest rates. In actual fact, higher personal tax rates reduce private-sector saving and drive up both the cost of credit and the cost of labor to firms. When the Treasury examined the effects of the Kennedy tax cuts, it was found that the personal saving rate rose. This implies that the saving rate would fall if tax rates rise, and indeed the saving rate declined as bracket creep pushed savers into higher tax brackets.

Higher income tax rates raise labor costs to the firm, thereby undermining the competitiveness of its products at home and abroad. The higher the worker's marginal tax rate, the more expensive it is to the firm to protect wages from being eroded by inflation or to give real wage increases. Since additional income is taxed at the worker's highest bracket, the higher the tax rate, the larger the gross wage necessary to correspond to any net wage.

This does not mean that deficits are good for the economy. But it does mean that the argument that higher taxes are preferable to higher borrowing is at best unproved. The way this unproven argument has been used against the President's efforts to reduce tax rates and improve economic incentives is irresponsible. The key to a successful economy is incentives. Any economic policy that forgets this—even one that reduces deficits—will fail.

Feldstein's thesis suffers from more than a lack of proof. The equation on which it rests omits the tax changes that occurred during 1954–1969—a period that encompasses the Kennedy tax cuts. These tax reductions raised the after-tax rate of return to plant and equipment, which can cause firms to bid up the interest rate in their enthusiasm to acquire funds to invest. This, and not the deficit, is the more likely explanation of higher real interest rates. They were harbingers of economic growth, not of an aborted recovery. On the other hand, the period for which the Treasury reestimated the equation encompassed a time (particularly in the late 1970s) of rising taxes on investment, falling rates of return, and slumping real interest rates—a period of economic stagnation. Higher real interest rates are not to be feared if they are signs of a higher return on capital and renewed economic growth.

When government is faced with transitional or temporary deficits, such as those incurred during recession, borrowing is a more efficient way to finance deficits than taxation. Taxation often falls on the most efficient users of resources and producers of goods and services. But in an efficient capital market, government borrowing diverts resources from the least efficient private uses. Considering the haphazard manner in which Congress raises taxes, with little or no regard for the economic effects of different taxes on employment, saving, and output, borrowing is the safest course. Tax increases, which usually become permanent, should never be used to finance temporary deficits. In the case of deficits that result from government spending growing faster than the economy, higher taxes are self-defeating. Taxation is not a substitute for the failure to control the growth of government.

Eventually economists may become sophisticated enough to differentiate between deficits that strengthen private property rights and deficits that erode them. Deficits that result from reducing the marginal tax rates on income strengthen people's claims to the income produced by their work effort and their human, financial, and physical capital. Such deficits may only be temporary because they are accompanied by an improvement in incentives, resulting in a larger tax base. On the other hand, deficits that result from a growth in transfer payments and entitlements erode people's property rights in the fruits of their labor and capital by transferring part of their income stream to others. Productive incentives decline, reducing the growth of the tax base. Government then substitutes an inflationary growth of the tax base for the missing real economic growth, and the taxation of nominal gains further erodes property rights.

Whatever the outcome of the struggle between President Reagan and his aides, unless the art and science of economics succumbs to a romanticized Marxism, escapes from reality into abstract mathematics, or is made irrelevant by instituting a planning system under the guise of an industrial policy, supply-side economics will ultimately prevail. We now have many decades of empirical evidence of the effects of disincentives on economic performance, ranging from China and the Soviet Union to the European welfare states. The effects of disincentives clearly thwart the intended results of central planning, government investment programs, and the maintenance of aggregate demand. On the other hand, there is an abundance of evidence of the positive effects of good incentives. Only free people are productive and forward-looking, but they cease to be free when their property rights are sacrificed to interest-group politics. Supply-side economics is the economics of a free society. It will prevail wherever freedom itself prevails.

Glossary

AVERAGE TAX RATE   the total tax paid as a percentage of taxable income.

BRACKET CREEP   the interaction of inflation with a progressive tax system that pushes taxpayers with unchanging real income into higher tax brackets.

CORE INFLATION   inflation that is caused by rising factor costs (such as energy) and is believed to be difficult to restrain by traditional monetary and fiscal policy.

CROWDING OUT   traditionally, the exclusion of private borrowers from financial markets by government borrowing; more generally, the exclusion of private economic activity by government taxing and borrowing.

CYCLICAL DEFICIT   the deficit in the government's budget that results from recession.

DEMAND MANAGEMENT   the policy of trying to manage the economy by manipulating the level of total spending.

ECONOMETRICS   the use of quantitative economic models to make predictions about, and simulate the behavior of, the actual economy.

FISCAL YEAR   the official year of the government used for budget calculation, beginning October 1 and ending September 30 of the next calendar year, e.g., fiscal year 1984 begins October 1, 1983, and ends September 30, 1984.

FISCAL POLICY   the use of the government's budget (taxing and spending) to affect gross national product.

FLAT-RATE TAX   a tax system that taxes all income at the same rate.

FULL-EMPLOYMENT BUDGET DEFICIT   the deficit that would remain if the economy were operating at full employment.

GROSS NATIONAL PRODUCT   the total value of goods and services produced in a year.

INCOME TAX BASE   the total of aggregate income that is subject to tax.

INDEXING   a method of preventing changes in nominal prices (inflation) from affecting the real values of incomes, government benefits, or tax burdens.

KEYNESIANISM   a school of thought that emphasizes the effect of fiscal policy on aggregate demand.

MARGINAL TAX RATE   the rate at which an additional dollar of income is taxed.

MONETARISM   a school of thought that emphasizes the effect of the money supply on gross national product.

MONETARY POLICY   the use of central bank operations to affect gross national product.

PHILLIPS CURVE   the argument that there is an inherent trade-off in the economy between inflation and unemployment (less of one means more of the other).

PROGRESSIVE TAX   one in which the share of income paid in taxes increases as income increases.

REGRESSIVE TAX   one in which the share of income paid in taxes decreases as income increases.

RELATIVE PRICES   the cost of obtaining one thing in terms of the amount sacrificed of another.

STAGFLATION   simultaneous and persistent inflation and economic stagnation.

STRUCTURAL DEFICIT   the deficit that would remain if the economy were operating at full employment.

SUPPLY-SIDE   a school of thought that emphasizes the effect of fiscal policy on incentives and relative prices.

TAX BRAKE   the rising disincentives to produce that result from rising tax rates.

TAX REBATE   a one-time reduction of taxes paid that does not permanently reduce tax rates.

TAXFLATION   the erosion of taxpayers' real incomes by the combination of inflation and a progressive income tax.

UNDERGROUND ECONOMY   the economic activity conducted off the books on which no taxes are collected.

Index